Charles A Federer

Yorkshire Chap-Books

First series: comprising Thomas Gent's tracts on legendary subjects

Charles A Federer

Yorkshire Chap-Books
First series: comprising Thomas Gent's tracts on legendary subjects

ISBN/EAN: 9783337152703

Printed in Europe, USA, Canada, Australia, Japan

Cover: Foto ©ninafisch / pixelio.de

More available books at **www.hansebooks.com**

YORKSHIRE CHAP-BOOKS.

EDITED BY

CHARLES A. FEDERER, L.C.P.

FIRST SERIES:

Comprising Thomas Gent's tracts on legendary subjects; with a memoir of the author, and a select number of facsimile reproductions of the original woodcuts.

LONDON:
ELLIOT STOCK, 62, PATERNOSTER ROW.
1889.

BRADFORD:
PRINTED BY J. S. TOOTHILL, LINGARD'S BUILDINGS, GODWIN ST.

TO

J. NORTON DICKONS, Esq.,

OF BRADFORD,

THE DILIGENT ARCHEOLOGIST, THE KIND FRIEND,

THE SINCERE CHRISTIAN,

THIS EDITION OF GENT'S TRACTS IS GRATEFULLY INSCRIBED

BY

THE EDITOR.

INTRODUCTION.

ON CHAP-BOOKS.

CHAP-BOOK literature, viz., the pamphlets, ballads, and broadsides, sold by chapmen or chafferers at fairs and markets, or hawked by them from house to house in the country, composed the only literature accessible to the mass of the people during the centuries anterior to the present. There can be no question that this literature possesses the highest interest for the student of the social, religious, and political state of our forefathers: Macaulay and Green have entirely re-written our history with the aid of a mass of political broadsides, ballads, and squibs; and it is a well-known fact that the French revolution of 1789 was prepared by the dissemination of immense multitudes of popular tracts; nor can it be denied that the social conceptions of our own peasantry were, till a recent period, mainly based upon the kind of literature which reached it through the agency of the pedlar. Chapbook literature catered for the intellectual wants of the lower and the middle classes of the people, and by it the nature of those wants, in other words, the predilections and the common bent of the popular mind can be accurately gauged.

At a time when our laws, oppressive and cruel in their nature, pressed with peculiar harshness on the labourer, who was a serf in all but the name, and on the poor toilers of every description, there naturally existed a good deal of sympathy with the bold outlaw, and a sneaking admiration even for the dashing highwayman, who professed to redress social inequalities by robbing the rich and relieving the poor. Hence the unbounded popularity of the "Lives" of Robin Hood, Dick

Turpin, Nevison, etc., a popularity such as no "Plutarch's Lives" ever attained among the cultured classes. A similarly favourable reception was given to the chapbook which described the career of some individual in the lowest rank in society, who by dint of cunning, hardihood, or sheer impudence, managed to hold his own amongst his superiors; of which class "Blind Jack of Knaresborough" may be taken as the type. It is worthy of notice that this class by no means includes the *parvenu* who, whether by good fortune or through industry and sterling qualities, had risen to a higher social position; for, regret it as we may, it cannot be denied that now, as in the past, envy not unmixed with aversion follows the individual who quits the fellowship of those who were once his equals. Nor has the record of simple "goodness" any place in chapbook literature: the "Pamela, or Virtue Rewarded" style of composition catered for the maudlin sentimentality of a portion of the upper middle classes, but possessed no relish for the rude appetite of the vulgar.

It will naturally be imagined, however, that the class of chapbooks before alluded to, appealed chiefly to the male portion of the toiling multitude, old or young; yet the cottager's wife and daughters were not forgotten. Though the hardships and injustices of life weighed on them perhaps even more heavily than on their male companions, their minds, cast in gentler mould, longed not for the present redress by deeds of violence, but more or less patiently looked for a state of compensating bliss after the close of their earthly existence. Entirely unscriptural as the conception is, every one who is accustomed to visit among the poor and the outcasts of society, is aware how deeply ingrained in their minds is the belief that present suffering entitles to commensurate recompense in the life to come. To this moiety of the common people, the "Lives" of various classes of Saints, whether canonized or not, and particularly the biographies of holy women, brought solace and congenial entertainment. It does not, however, need a very close examination to find the same idea of redress of social inequalities, which underlies the conventional character of the outlaw, reappearing

clothed in the monkish garb of the saint who on the one hand
resists and punishes the wicked in high places, and on the other
ministers to the wants of the poor, heals their diseases, and
assures them of divine favour. This will account for the striking and yet natural circumstance, that in a post-reformation
period, such chapbooks as the "Life of Saint Winefred," or
the "Life of Saint Robert of Knaresborough," written by such
a staunch anti-papist as Thomas Gent, saw the light in the
strait-laced city of York.

York was the sole centre where, during last century, the pedlar
fraternity of Yorkshire obtained their supplies of books and
pamphlets, and ballad singers their *patter*; for it is only within
the present century that similar manufactures of chapmen's
literature were established at Stokesley, Easingwold, and Otley,
and latterly at Leeds. Thomas Gent bears the undisputed preeminence among the purveyors of this kind of literature, having
been both author and printer; and the presses of his successors
in York, James Kendrew and Charles Croshaw, were almost exclusively engaged in the production of chapbooks and patter.

The present work gives, for the first time in a collected form,
the various chapbooks, pamphlets, and broadsides, which have
appeared in the county of York up to the close of last century,
with such commentaries and notes as are needed to elucidate
the text. The first series contains ten chapbooks on legendary
subjects, written and printed by Thomas Gent, and comprises
the Lives of St. Winefred, Our Saviour and the Apostles, Judas
Iscariot, Afflicted Job, and St. Robert of Knaresborough; with
a memoir of Thomas Gent. Subsequent series, in active preparation, will comprise Gent's Pastoral Dialogue: the Life of
J. Metcalf, commonly called Blind Jack of Knaresborough;
George-a-Green, the Pinder of Wakefield; William Nevison,
the Highwayman; Robin Hood's Garland, &c., &c.

The footnotes in this volume, unless otherwise stated, are
Thomas Gent's own. The original spelling and punctuation
have been preserved, except in the case of obvious misprints,
which have been corrected.

Thomas Gent.

IN compiling a sketch of the life of this enterprising York printer, we are saved the trouble and uncertainty of collecting scattered materials from various sources, by Gent's own care and foresight, in himself recording in copious detail the principal events of his life. This autobiography, the original manuscript of which is now in the possession of E. Hailstone, Esq., of Walton Hall, was published in a somewhat curtailed form in 1832 by the Rev. Joseph Hunter, under the title, "The Life of Mr. Thomas Gent, printer, of York, written by himself." Shorter notices of Gent have since been written by Mr. Charles Knight, in his "Shadows of the old Booksellers," (London, 1865); by Mr. Robert Davis, in his "Memoirs of the York Press," (London, 1868); and by Mr. Abraham Holroyd, in the "Yorkshire Magazine," (Bradford, 1872).

Thomas Gent was born in Ireland, of English parentage, in 1693. At the age of thirteen or fourteen, he was apprenticed by his father to Mr. Powell, a letter-press printer in Dublin; but the lad did not take kindly to his employment. Long hours of work and strictness of supervision rendered him dissatisfied with his situation; it appears also that, young as he was, he became entangled in a love intrigue with one of his master's servants. Gent's autobiography is discreetly silent on the circumstances of this intrigue; but that it was more than a mere boyish escapade, is shown by what transpired several years subsequently at York, when a gossiping report of it sufficed to wreck his prospects there.

In order to break off the connection alluded to, and to free himself from irksome restraint, young Gent resolved to escape to England, and managed to carry out his resolve with some forethought and determination. With all his portable property, consisting of a spare suit of clothes and seventeen pence in cash, and stores in the shape of two or three penny loaves, he got secretly on board of a vessel bound for England, and stowed himself away in the hold. Gent gives us a vivid description of the stormy passage, during which the ship had to put back into Dublin Bay; but he landed at last safely at Parkgate, near Holyhead, where the tender-hearted captain, instead of taking the little money in the lad's possession to pay for his passage, gave him a sixpence and some sound parting advice. It is doubtless to the circumstances of this first landing in England that Gent alludes in the latter portion of the footnote on page 152 of the present volume.

After suffering many hardships on the way, the lad reached London in August, 1710; and it is characteristic of his observant mind, that even under the distressing circumstances of his journey, he had taken careful note of the interesting antiquities of Chester, and jotted down the historical reminiscences connected with them. Gent soon obtained employment in the printing office of a Mr. Midwinter, of Pie Corner, Smithfield, who was principally engaged in printing chapbooks and broadsides for hawkers: a profitable business at that period, which determined the nature of the lad's future career. His occupation here was not merely the printing, but also the composition, of chapmen's literature; and on the title-page of "Judas Iscariot," we find it stated that he originally composed that work in 1711 (see page 201 of the present volume). He also did a good stroke of business for his master, in noting down the sermon which Dr. Sacheverel preached on the occasion of his suspension, by the impression and sale of which Mr. Midwinter cleared thirty pounds in one week.

Gent worked at Mr. Midwinter's office for three years, during which period he not only gained steadiness of purpose and valuable experience, but was also enabled to save a little money. When his engagement with Mr. Midwinter had terminated, he continued to do jobbing or "smouting" work, both for him and for other master printers. The following interesting extract from his autobiography very graphically describes the kind of life he led during this somewhat unsettled period:—

"I went directly to seek a place of business, when, luckily, I happened to engage with Mrs. Bradford, a quaker, and widow, in Fetter Lane, who ordered me to come the next morning. With great spirit and elasticity I flew, as it were, homewards, to the great satisfaction of my kind master and mistress, who asked me why I had not come to dinner; if I was not almost starved; or if I lit of the merchant, and dined with him? I told them the whole truth; and, going to work the next day, I continued so briskly that by Saturday night I had earned about seventeen shillings: so that, having near three pounds in bank, and a new suit of clothes of about three pounds price, which Mr. Midwinter had given me, exclusive of my other apparel, I thought that I might do pretty well in the world; in order to which, I furnished myself with a new composing iron, called a stick; a pair of scissors to cut scaleboards; a sharp bodkin, to correct the letters; and a pretty sliding box to contain them and preserve all from rustiness. I bought also a galley, for the pages I was to compose, with other appurtenances that might be of service to me when occasion should require."

"As inconsiderate youth is, too soon, over fond of novelty, being invited to another place under Mr. Mears, in Blackfriars, I very indiscreetly parted with my mistress, which entirely lost me the favour of that knowing gentlewoman. On my entrance amongst a number of men, besides paying what is called 'Ben-money,' I found soon after, I was, as it were, to be dubbed as great a cuz as the famous Don Quixote seemed to be when he thought himself a knight, and that the innkeeper was lord of the castle, in the yard of which he judged the honour was conferred; through the insipid folly thereof, agreeably to their strange harangues in praise of the protecting charms of cuzship, which, like the power of Don Waltho Clatherbank's infallible medicines, would heal all evils whether curable or not, was not very agreeable to my hearing; yet, when the master himself insisted it must be done, I was obliged to submit to that immemorial custom, the origin of which they could not then explain to me. It commenced by walking round the chapel (printing rooms being called such, because first begun to be practised in one at Westminster Abbey), singing an alphabetical anthem, tuned literally to the vowels. Striking me, kneeling, with a broadsword, and pouring ale upon my head, my titles were exhibited much to this effect:—'Thomas Gent, Baron of College Green, Earl of Fingall, with power to the limits of Dublin Bar, Captain-General of the Teagues, near the Lake of Allen, and Lord High Admiral over all the Bogs in Ireland.' To confirm which, and that I might not pay over again for the same ceremony, through forgetfulness, they allowed me godfathers, the first I ever had before, because the Presbyterian minister at my christening allowed none at his office; and these, my new pious fathers, were the un-reverend Mr. Holt and Mr. Palmer. Nay, there were witnesses also—such as Mr. Fleming, Mr. Gibbins and Mr. Cocket, staunch journeymen printers. But after all this work I began to see the vanity of all human grandeur; for, as I was not yet a freeman, I was discharged as a foreigner in about a fortnight or three weeks' time."

Mr. Midwinter at this time received a communication from one of his customers, Mr. John White, master printer, of York, who desired him to procure for him a likely person as journeyman printer. Mr. Midwinter mentioned the matter to Gent, who, however, felt disinclined to leave London just then. Some time afterwards, a chapman named Isaac, whose business took him occasionally into Yorkshire, spoke to Mr. White in such high terms of the capabilities and qualities of Gent, that Mr. White decided to make the latter the exceedingly liberal offer of £18 per annum, with board, lodging, and washing. Gent closed with the tempting offer, and removed to York.

Mr. White had agreed to allow one guinea for travelling expenses; but Gent could not come to terms with Crofts, the York carrier, who did not choose to abate anything from his regular fare of twenty-six shillings; so he resolved to perform the journey on foot, starting on Tuesday, 20 April, 1714. He passed through Caxton, Stamford, Newark, Bawtry, Sherburn, Tadcaster, and reached York on Sunday. His arrival is thus described by himself:—

"The first house I entered to enquire for my new master was a printer's at Petergate, the very dwelling that is now (at the time of writing) my own by purchase; but not finding Mr. White therein, a child brought me to his door, which was opened by the head maiden, that is now my dear spouse. She ushered me into the chamber, where Mrs. White lay something ill in bed, but the old gentleman was at his dinner, by the fireside, sitting in a noble arm chair, with a good large pie before him, of which he made me heartily partake with him. I had a guinea in my shoe lining, which I pulled out to ease my foot, at which the old gentleman smiled and pleasantly said, 'It was more than he ever had seen a journeyman save before.' I lived as happily as I could wish in this family, for Mr. White had plenty of business to employ several persons, there being few printers in England, except London, at that time: none then, I am sure, at Chester, Liverpool, Whitehaven, Preston, Manchester, Kendal and Leeds, as for the most part now abounds."

Whilst residing in Mr. White's family, Gent became first acquainted with Alice or Adeliza Guy, Mrs. White's maid: an acquaintance which soon ripened into love in spite of a considerable disparity in their ages, she being in her thirty-second year, whilst he was barely twenty-two years old. But the horizon of future happiness which had begun to unfold itself to the imagination of Thomas Gent, became suddenly overcast. Through the means of some travelling journeyman printer, who had formerly worked in Ireland, the circumstances of Gent's running away from his apprenticeship in Dublin became known in York, and seriously injured his prospects, both with Mr. White and with Miss Alice, who could scarcely hear with equanimity of her suitor's former love passages. At the twelvemonth's end, therefore, although a renewal of the engagement was proposed to him, Gent resolved to leave York and to revisit his native country.

He left York on the 15th May, 1715, and travelled through Leeds, Brighouse, Elland, Blackstone Edge, Rochdale, Bury, Bolton, Ashton, and Prescot, to Liverpool. There being no vessel ready to start for Ireland from that port, and the sole printer which Liverpool could at that period boast, not having any work for him, Gent walked through Cheshire to Parkgate where he embarked for Dublin. The passage proved even more protracted and unpropitious than his former one; for it was only after being tossed about by violent storms for several days, that the vessel was able to make Douglas harbour in the Isle of Man, where she was compelled to lie for several weeks to repair damages. This episode is also alluded to in the before-mentioned footnote on page 152 of the present volume.

His stay in Dublin was but short. His former master, Mr. Powell, threatened legal proceedings, and Gent found it advisable to recross the Irish Sea, and make his way to London. On his way thither, he spent a short time at York, and appears to have regained the good graces of Miss Alice Guy, with whom he afterwards kept up a correspondence, though no distinct matrimonial engagement was entered into. In London, Gent first worked for his former master, Mr. Midwinter, and in 1717 he was made a member of the Company of Stationers, and shortly afterwards admitted to the freedom of the city of London. Yet he did not seem to prosper greatly from a financial point of view, for we find him working both at press and at case for various printers in succession—Wilkins, Watts, Clifton, Dodds,—and occasionally undertake jobs, which in those times of political fermentation, were very risky. The following incident, related by Davis, exemplifies the nature of the risk then incurred by clandestine printers:—

"Both Gent and his employer Midwinter had incurred the suspicion of the Government. One night Gent had gone to rest suffering from a severe attack of illness. Soon after midnight, whilst he was asleep, his bedroom door was violently burst open by a King's messenger, who dragged him out of bed, helped him to dress himself, searched his pockets for papers, hurried him down stairs into the street, which was filled with constables and watchmen, and thrust him into a coach, which was ordered to drive towards Newgate. On their way the coach was stopped near St. Sepulchre's Church, and Gent was placed in a room of a public-house, and there closely watched and guarded. Presently he was amazed to see his master, Mr. Midwinter, brought in as a prisoner, and left in the room with him. From thence they were taken to Manchester Court,[o] a house at Westminster, on the banks of the Thames, which appears to have been at that time used for the temporary confinement of State prisoners. Here Gent was placed in an apartment alone, and 'debarred from friends to see him, or the use of pen, ink, and paper, to write to them.' Within a few days afterwards the rigour of his confinement was relaxed, and at the end of three days more, 'as nothing could be proved against him, he was honourably discharged.' Gent had reason to rejoice at his narrow escape. Not many months had passed since he stood near St. Sepulchre's Church in Newgate Street, and

---

* Now Manchester Buildings, on the site of Derby House formerly belonging to the Earls of Lincoln, and another large house belonging to the Earls of Manchester, very pleasant towards the Thames. *Cunningham's Handbook*, vol. ii. p. 515.

beheld a young brother printer drawn on a sledge to be executed at Tyburn for the Offence of printing a seditious libel, which was adjudged to be high treason."*

About 1721, Gent was at last able to set up a press of his own in Fleet Lane, and occasionally to employ assistants; and for about three years a succession of ballads and pamphlets, chiefly composed by himself, issued from his office. He was in a position now to commence housekeeping; but any lingering hope that he might have entertained of ultimately inducing Alice Guy to become his wife, were destroyed by the intelligence that she had married Mr. Charles Bourne, Mr. White's grandson and heir. To console himself for this disappointment, he undertook to console the bereaved widow of Mr. Dodd, in whose office he had lately been working, and he managed to ingratiate himself with her. What occurred to nip this new dream of love in the bud, is best related in Gent's own words:—

"It was one Sunday morning that Mr. Philip Wood, a partner at Mr. Midwinter's, entering my chambers, where I sometimes used to employ him too, when slack of business in other places, 'Tommy,' said he, 'all these fine materials of yours must be moved to York.' At which, wondering,

---

* His brother printer was John Matthews, a youth of eighteen, who was tried and condemned at the Old Bailey. He was charged with printing and publishing a seditious and traitorous libel, entitled *Vox populi Vox Dei*, which asserted that the Pretender had an hereditary right to the Crown, and that all rights concur in him, and endeavouring to stir up the people to shake off the present arbitrary government. The persons on whose evidence he was convicted were two of his fellow-workmen who had been concerned in printing similar libels. On the 6th November, 1719, the unfortunate youth was drawn on a sledge from Newgate to Tyburn, where he was executed pursuant to his sentence, except that the quartering of his body was dispensed with by favour of the Government. The fate of Matthews excited much public sympathy. Six months afterwards one of the printers who were witnesses against him died, and was to be buried at Islington. A mob arose and obstructed the funeral, causing so great a tumult that the next night a detachment of the Foot Guards was sent from Whitehall to see the corpse buried and to preserve the peace.

'What mean you?' said I. 'Aye,' said he, 'and you must go too, 'without it's your own fault; for your first sweetheart is now at liberty, and left in good circumstances by her good spouse, who deceased but of late.' 'I pray Heaven,' answered I, 'that his precious soul may be happy; and, for aught I know, it may be as you say, for indeed I may not trifle with a widow as I have formerly done with a maid.' I made an excuse to my mistress that I had business in Ireland, but that I hoped to be at my own lodgings in about a month's time; if not, everything was in order, so that anyone could carry on the business. But she said she would not have anyone beside me; so respectfully taking leave, I never beheld her after. I had taken care that my goods should be ready packed up to be ready when sent for. I pitched upon Mr. Campbell as my confidant in this affair, desiring my cousins to assist him, all of whom I took leave of at the Black Swan, in Holborn, where I paid my passage in the stage-coach, which brought me to York in four days' time. Here I found my dearest once more, though much altered to what she was ten years before that I had not seen her. There was no need for a new courtship, but decency suspended the marriage for some time. So, on considering the delay in her business, as well as the former ties of love that passed innocently between us, by word of writing, she gave full consent to have the nuptials celebrated, which were performed the 10th of December, 1722, in the stately cathedral dedicated to St. Peter."

Gent's marriage produced at once a great alteration in his outward circumstances. He was now a comparatively wealthy man, at the head of a first-class printing business, which was practically a monopoly; for no other printer was to be found at that period in the whole of Yorkshire and Durham. Various projects soon engaged his energies and resources, chief amongst which was the establishment of an influential newspaper for the north of England. Already, in 1719, the first number of a weekly newspaper, entitled " *York Mercury: or a General View of the Affairs of Europe,*" had been published by Grace White, widow of Thomas Gent's late master, in partnership with Mr. Thomas Hammond; but the novel experiment had not proved very successful. Gent resolved to make a fresh start under more favourable auspices. He issued the first number of the new paper under his own name some two or three weeks before his marriage with Mrs. Bourne; the title being, "*The Original York Journal, or Weekly Courant, containing the most remarkable passages and transactions at home and abroad. From Monday, November* 16, *to Monday, November* 23, 1724. *Printed by Thomas Gent, and are to be sold at the printing office in Coffee-House Yard, York; where advertisements are taken in.*"

The prosperous circumstances of Mr. Thomas Gent had in so far an unfavourable influence on his character, as they rendered him somewhat overbearing and intractable. From some expressions in his diary we can gather, too, that he did not enjoy that unalloyed domestic bliss which he had anticipated from his marriage; nor will it excite much surprise if a widow who marries again in her forty-second year, develops strong idiosyncrasies respecting the equipoise of power in a family. Gent took up a very uncompromising attitude towards Mr. John White, of Newcastle, son of his old master, and uncle to Mr. Charles Bourne, who was naturally grieved at seeing his father's property pass out of the family through Mrs. Bourne's second marriage. Mr. White, who had a printing business at Newcastle, transferred it in 1725 to York, and opened a bookseller's shop in Stonegate; much to the chagrin of Gent, who was not sparing in his allusions to his "barbarous uncle" in various of his elucubrations. In August of the same year, Mr. White issued the first number of "*The York Courant*," which eventually secured the favour of the public, and is the direct ancestor of a paper still published at York; whilst Gent's venture in journalism came to an end in 1728, after a short existence of three years and eight months.

Gent appears to have been constantly at loggerheads with his neighbours and townsmen; and he certainly never was at any pains to conciliate an opponent, but was always very ready to shower opprobrious epithets on whoever crossed his path. Competition in the printing trade was becoming more keen; several presses were set up within a short time in the city of York; and a new-comer, Mr. Cæsar Ward, who had purchased Mr. White's business, was successful in securing for himself nearly all the better class work, which formerly went to Gent's office. Another circumstance which tended to sour Gent's naturally irritable temper, was the " gross injustice " done to him by the unexpecting falling in of the lease of his house in Stonegate, which had been bequeathed by Mr. Charles Bourne to his widow. Mr. Davis thus relates the circumstance:

"Charles Bourne, not long before his death, purchased the house in question, which was held under a lease, granted by a former prebendary of North-Newbald in the cathedral church of York, for three lives, of whom two were then in being. But Bourne was not informed when he made the purchase that, some time previously, a succeeding prebendary had granted a reversionary lease to another person, the effect of which was to deprive Bourne and his successors of the right, which they would otherwise have been entitled to exercise, of renewing the existing lease. Bourne did not discover this fact until after he had paid his money. His widow abstained from imparting it to Gent until after they were married. When Gent ascertained that the house would pass irrecoverably from him and his wife, upon the death of " a weak old gentlewoman," the surviving life in their lease, he was beside himself with rage and disappointment. He fancied that the loss of his property would plunge him into irretrievable ruin. 'With heavy sighs and bitter anguish,' he exclaims, "did I bemoan our tottering condition." Poverty and its gloomy attendants constantly stared him in the face.

He first attempted to prevail upon Mr. Alderman Read,* the lessee in reversion, to afford him some redress, and upon that gentleman's refusal, he poured out upon him all the vials of his wrath. He then applied to the Rev. Mr. Hitch, who had been appointed to the stall of North-Newbald, upon the death of the prebendary by whom the reversionary lease was granted. Mr. Hitch treated Gent with courtesy, but was unable to assist him. At length the dreaded event happened. In January, 1740, 'a heavy stroke of adverse fortune' befel him. The old lady died whose life was the last in the lease, and Gent and his wife had to relinquish possession of the house in Stonegate, which they once hoped would have been a refuge for them when they should have to quit Coffee-Yard, where he was only tenant from year to year."†

Gent could not forbear venting his resentment on every occasion, likely or unlikely; notice, for instance, the suggestive lines—

> Worse than absorbing Brutes, who swallow Lands,
> Or hinder good Men to renew their Rights

in the "Life of St. Winefred (p. 152 of the present volume); or the highly suggestive and original definition of oppressors in the index to the same work (see "Oppressors" on p. 168 of the present volume).

Of Gent's literary activity it is difficult to speak without admiration: true, some modern literati, Mr. Robert Collyer, of New York, among the number, affect to sneer at Gent's attainments, and have nothing but contempt for the rude woodcuts and vile typography of his later productions. But

---

* John Read esquire, of Sandhutton near York, Lord Mayor 1719 and 1746.

† During the severe winter of 1739-40 the river Ouse was frozen over, and Gent was glad to gather a few pence by setting up on the ice a *quasi* press, and printing for sale on small broadsides some of his own woodcuts and doggrel verses, to which he added the name of the purchaser. Mr. Hailstone possesses one specimen, and another was in the collection of the late Mr. Summer, of Woodmansey, near Beverley.

Mr. Hunter, whose authority as an historian and antiquary is unquestioned, and who is no mere amateur critic, declares that "Gent's performances were not, like too many modern books of topography, mere bundles of pillage from the works of ingenious and painstaking authors, but contained matter honestly collected, and not, before his time, made public by the press." The extent of his miscellaneous and general information, the result of an indefatigable course of reading and research, was enormous; and his data are correct to an astonishing degree. The editor of the present volume has verified some hundreds of Gent's references to works of the most varied description, and found every one of them strictly accurate.

To draw up a complete bibliography of the works issued from Gent's press, or composed by him, has, at the present day, become impossible; most of his London productions are irrevocably lost. An excellent list of the publications which issued from his York press, is found in Davis' *Memoirs of the York Press*, though the sixty-nine items which it comprises could, without much difficulty, be augmented to near a hundred. The most important of them are: "The Antient and Modern History of the Loyal Town of Rippon;" "The History of the Royal and Beautiful Town of Kingston-upon-Hull," both of which works have been reprinted; a History of York: a History of England, together with a History of Rome; a number of classical works for Mr. Clark, master of the Grammar School at Hull; the Life of St. Winefred; and the History of the Great Eastern Window in York Cathedral. The Life of Afflicted Job (page 231 in the present collection) is the only extant production of Gent's Scarborough Press.

In his History of Hull[*] he thus speaks of having embarked in a printing establishment at that attractive and already then fashionable watering-place: "I beg leave to mention as a memorial, that a printing-office was first set up

---

[*] P. 185, *note*.

by me in Scarborough about June 16th, 1734, in a house in Mr. Bland's lane, formerly called his cliff; a most pleasant situation, leading to the beautiful sands; and I hope, God willing, some time or other to print the antiquities of that delightful town and castle." In his autobiography, under the date of 1733, he says, "My nephew, Arthur Clark, was sent with materials to furnish a printing-office in Scarborough; from which we had a prospect of the ocean. The gentry from the Spa used to visit us, to have their names, and see the playhouse bills and other work printed."

In 1761, Gent lost his wife (see his elegy on p. 227 of the present volume); after which event his circumstances became gradually more and more embarrassed, so much so that he was at last no longer able to procure the needful supplies of new type and office furniture; the result being seen in the wretchedly poor paper and typography of his later works. His last production, *Judas Iscariot*, had to be printed for him by a brother printer, probably Thomas Mitchelson. Through the influence of some kind friends, among them Mr. Drake, the historian, Gent was elected a pensioner of Allen's Charity, which served to keep him from absolute want. His death took place in his own house in Petergate, on the 19th May, 1778, in the 87th year of his age. He was buried in the parish church of St. Michael-le-Belfry, "where more than fifty years before, he and his wife had wept together over the grave of their infant and only child Charles" (see p. 227).

THE
HOLY LIFE and DEATH of
ST. WINEFRED;
AND OTHER
RELIGIOUS PERSONS.

In FIVE Parts.

Wherein is set forth the Glory of *North-Wales*, thro' the powerful Vertue of *Holy-Well*, in *Flintshire;* and a just ACCOUNT of *some* of the *many* wonderful CURES that have been perform'd, thro' the Blessing of Heaven, by the salutary Streams of that most sacred Fountain.

With pious ANNOTATIONS *from the* Holy Scriptures, *and* Early Writers of the Church, *concerning the Judgments and Mercies of Almighty GOD: Who punisheth wicked Oppressors, but preserves the Souls and Bodies of the truly Faithful: Such, of every Denomination, who, following the Prescriptions of most learned Doctors, shall humbly rely on* HIS Divine Providence.

Also proper CUTS to distinguish particular Passages relating to the cruel Sufferings of our Blessed *SAVIOUR*, who died for *Our* Sake; and those precious bleeding Victims of both Sexes sacrificed for their *Love to HIM:* with other mournful and instructive Remarks never published by any writer of the *LIFE* of this noble and celebrated Virgin.

Done into Verse: *With an* EPITOME *in* Prose, *and a compleat* INDEX *for the greater Delight and Ease of the Reader.*

Qui honorat Martyres, honorat CHRISTUM. S. AUG. de Sanctis.

Dedicated to a DIVINE of the *Establish'd CHURCH.*

Written by THOMAS GENT.

YORK: Printed by the Author in his new-built Office in *PETER-Gate:* And sold by JOHN HOPKINS, in *Preston, Lancashire;* and other Booksellers in the Country. MDCCXLIII.

To the Reverend

MR. JOHN STANDISH.

SIR,

  SEVERAL Years have elapsed since I have had the Happiness of enjoying your Company; and since Providence has for a long Time removed me from the *First* CITY in *England*, to THIS, which learned Writers agree to be the *Second;* wherein, passing thro' several afflicting Vicissitudes, notwithstanding my sedulous Endeavours, I am at present placed a considerable Distance from you; and likewise approaching towards the Decline of Life; or, what very much resembles it, a State of Sorrow, thro' a sudden Infelicity, common to the best Persons, which I forbear *now* to mention; GOD knows whether I shall ever behold you again. Think it not strange, dear Sir, in me, who was, like You, brought up in the orthodox Faith of the establish'd Church, that I have thus endeavour'd to treat of a Virgin Martyr, renown'd from Antiquity for being esteem'd the *Patroness of* WALES; when I tell you, That, in my Journeys twice thro' that Country, to visit the sincerest and dearest of Friends that ever I had to confide in, I met with such courteous Usage from the kind Inhabitants, heard so many wonderful Things credibly reported of that once most charming LADY, and the surprizing salutary Effects that flow with the Streams of her celebrated Spring; I was resolv'd to shew my Gratitude and Fidelity, as well as my

humble

humble Genius or Pen would permit me, whenever Providence allow'd me Time and Opportunity. It has done both very effectually within the Space of about fix Months paft; but how far profperoufly, in relation to ferve me and mine, in fupplying us with common Neceffaries for our Prefervation, I humbly fubmit to the Courtefy of my ingenious Readers; amongft whom I cannot fay I have ever been unhappy. You will, I hope, pardon me, that I now reckon You in the Number: For, if I may judge by that innate Sweetnefs of Temper that crown'd your flourifhing Youth, both in the School, and Univerfity; and, as I have lately heard from a Relation, by your moft affectionate Enquiries after my Station, as tho' (like another Gentleman, now with GOD, whofe Life much refembled Your's, and no way unlike You for comely ‡ Perfonage) nothing could be more agreeable than to fave me from falling under the *Frowns* of an inconftant World, made worfe by *wicked Artifice*, as You have glorioufly eftablifh'd Others from the Dread of the *former*, and Venom of the *latter;* I may more eafily imagine, that the following Sheets, which I now dedicate to You, will not prove in the leaft manner unacceptable.

No doubt I may meet with as kind Ufage from Many, what I don't doubt from You, as thofe pious Authors, who have pleafingly fhaded the too great Luftre of their moft divine Sentiments behind the beautiful Veil of Parables and Similitudes; thro' which, by the Eye of Faith, the Truth is but partly feen. Thus when I mention the Concourfe of Pilgrims that frequently vifit the flowing Streams of fair *Holy-Well*, like the Ancients who travell'd to the famous Rivers of the *Eaft:* or as many devout Chriftians in our Time journey to *Paleftine*, to view the Remains of the once famous *Jerufalem* on Earth, in order to be more enamour'd with the happy Expectations of *That* above! Methinks all thefe infpiring Actions may fet us pondering, how we only act like Pilgrims

and

---

‡ A late Prebendary, and Chaplain to the Prince of *Wales*.

and Strangers on the troublesome Stage of this transitory Life, languishing and thirsting after heavenly Fountains. If these pious Conclusions are allow'd, I think the Offence, that may be given to many curious Persons in this Age, as to the Miracle of a wonderful Conjunction after a cruel Decollation, will, I trust, meet with kind Pardon. None need question that in past Ages there have been artful Tyrants wrapt in Ermin, as well as simple Knaves in Furr: So that, if we believe Mr. *Camden*, we may be fully ascertain'd, that the Lady was as villanously robb'd of her Chastity, as a good Person might be of an Estate. Her Grief might occasion her to wish for Death to ease the bitter Anguish of her Soul! The good Priest might comfort her, by telling her, That GOD, to Whom belonged Vengeance, would never lay any Guilt to her Charge; and that, being re-consecrated, she might proceed, as she had begun, in the Way towards eternal Glory. Such an Interpretation, with proper Additions, I imagine, might be made to soften the severest Censure: But since I design not in the least to disprove the Miracle, or assume a Power over the Judgment of any Person whatever, I humbly leave the Whole to the favourable Determination of my most courteous Readers. 'Tis very probable they may kindly say, That the lovely Subject of my Pen is nothing but what is agreeable to several of my innocent Flights; that something of the *miranda* is necessary to render a Book acceptable; and courteously agree, with a learned [*] Gentleman, that, "endeavouring to "get a Livelyhood for *my* Family, *I* deserve Commendation "for *my* Industry:" Yet when they come seriously to *READ*— a Villain's brutal Actions, and *THINK*—how much I have justly exposed that unprince-like *griping* Wretch in the most horrid dragonical Form, by representing injur'd Innocency in the deepest Distress; when they behold those tender Sentiments of Humanity, Virtue and Piety, which correspond with the most material Parts of the Christian Religion, and

many

---

[*] *Mr. D. in the Preface to his Vol. in Folio.*

many excellent Precepts of the moſt experienc'd Philoſophers; when they confider what clear Proofs I bring of the Almighty's wond'rous Power from the pureſt Fountains of Holy Scriptures, and Eccleſiaſtical Writings of the moſt early Times; when they find I endeavour ſorrowfully to diſplay the cruel Sufferings of the ever-bleſſed Son of GOD, and tell of the bleeding Martyrs who triumph'd with amazing Heroiſm amidſt the moſt horrid Cruelties that the fierceſt of crimſon Tyrants, or a Conclave of incarnate Dæmons could invent: I ſay, when my Readers find theſe Animadverſions faithfully exhibited; no doubt but, through divine Aſſiſtance, their Kindneſs and Reſpect may, at length, be more apparent to *me*, who ſtrives to do my utmoſt to pleaſe Them; at leaſt to *mine*, much dearer than any Enjoyment this ſublunary World can afford me.

Whilſt I was expatiating on the Beauty of the lovely St. *Winefred*, the ſweet Remembrance of your once moſt amiable Siſter ⁰ Mrs. ANNE STANDISH, now with GOD, often came into my Thoughts; eſpecially when I conſider'd her dutiful Affection to her tender Parents, that charming Symmetry with which Nature had adorn'd her, join'd with a moſt angelical Diſpoſition of Mind, that, had ſhe flouriſhed in an Age, when Saints were held in greateſt Eſteem, I believe, for intrinſick Piety, and every beloved Accompliſhment, ſhe might juſtly have found a Place in the Kalendar. Nothing appeared more innocently endearing, than the tender Regard ſhe conſtantly had for me, whom ſhe uſed to ſtyle her *dear Uncle;* except the Addition of her pleaſant and pious Converſation, whilſt walking many Summer's Evening in the Garden, which partly her ſoft white Hands had planted: Nothing more grievous than when I heard of her conſuming Illneſs, which by ſlow Degrees had waſted the fair Virgin almoſt to a Shadow,

---

* Remember'd by me, Pag. viii. of the Index, in my laſt Vol. publiſh'd *A.D.* 1741, amongſt the Names of devout Ladies and Gentlewomen, who died in the laſt and preſent Century, and are recorded for illuſtrious Examples in an excellent Work lately ſet forth by Mr. *J. Wilford.*

Shadow, and prevented her Acceptance of an Invitation into *Wales;* except when I was told of that remarkable Inſtance of her Love, who on her Death-Bed deſired to be ſupported 'till ſhe had peruſed my Anſwer to her laſt Letter; and, with Tears, expreſſing her Satisfaction I had not forgot her, ſhe appear'd reſigned to the Will of Heaven, and died ſoon after!—— I cannot but commend the Sincerity of that good Gentleman for his elegiac Performance in her deſerved Praiſe; which was printed at the earneſt Deſire of your tender Parents Mr. *James* and Mrs. *Rebekah Standiſh:* Yet I cannot help thinking otherwiſe, but that her Merits deſerved little leſs than an angelick Quill to ſet them forth in brighter Luſtre.—Death, I hear, has lately removed another of your lovely Siſters; † for which ſad Loſs, in my Spirit, I ſincerely condole with You, and All who reſpected Her.

You will, I hope, pardon this long Dedication. 'Tis the firſt; and, perhaps, the laſt Inſtance I may ſend You this Way, as it were an humble Offering from a ſincere Heart. Think not, dear Sir! that the Remembrance of my Friends can ever ceaſe to revolve in my Soul, whilſt the leaſt Spark of Memory ſhall continue to illuminate my Underſtanding. With almoſt infinite Pleaſure do I hear, that your Dignity and Ability have but increaſed your Humility and Beneficence. I need not add much more; ſince, with thoſe two ſhining Excellencies, none of the graceful inhærent Virtues can ever be wanting; and that I truly know your innate Modeſty is as far reluctant to hear any Adulation, as my ingenuous Temper appears diſtant from the Uſe of it. However, nothing ſhall anticipate this juſt Prayer, That Heaven, for your munificent Actions, may accumulate Bleſſings upon you here; as IT will, I can reſt aſſured, eternally be your happy Place of Reſidence hereafter.

Be pleaſed, Sir, to conſider, alſo, this Work as the Effects of ſolitary Hours, I might almoſt ſay, in a recluſe Life, agreeing
with

---

† Mrs. REBEKAH, late Spouſe to the Rev. Mr. PAIN.

with that more thoughtful Difpofition of Mind, to which for fome Time the Winds of an adverfe Fortune have driven me. And tho' my Station and Circumftances neceffarily require my Invention to labour almoft inceffantly, in order to fupport thofe whom I am obliged in Honour and Confcience, under GOD, to preferve and defend to my utmoft Power; yet, I believe this Piece had never thus appear'd in View, but for the unexpected Kindness of an ingenious Gentleman, adorned with excellent Qualifications, who encouraged me to publifh it, and proved a generous Subfcriber. I have obey'd his Requeft in the moft graceful Manner that my humble Talents would permit me: Which, I hope, will not only oblige *Him;* but Thofe who are worthy of *His Friendfhip.* And, I truft, Sir, when You have paffed by, in Candour, fome wandering Thoughts, which in Love you may think fit to pardon; you will be pleafed to accept this Dedication as the only Token of the tender Refpect that I ever had, and ever fhall continue to have for You, whilft

YORK, *I am,*

PETER-Gate, REVEREND SIR,

1743. *Your affectionate Uncle,*

and humble Servant,

THOMAS GENT.

CONTENTS.

CHAP. I. OF the Birth and Education of St. WINEFRED; and of her early Piety. Part I. pag. 41.

CHAP. II. How BUENO, a most religious Priest, took particular Care to direct the innocent Virgin in the Ways of Holiness, and Knowledge of Faith. Ibid. pag. 44.

CHAP. III. Some excellent Instructions that he gave on her Enterance into a Life of Sanctity. Ibid. pag. 48.

CHAP. IV. How CARADOC, an Heathen Prince, sued for unlawful Love; with the most melting and religious Speeches she used, in order to divert him from his sinful Purposes to deflour her. Ibid. pag. 52.

CHAP. V. Her Method to escape his Lust; with the prophetick Arguments she used, 'till at last he took away her precious Life. Ib. p. 57 to 60.

CHAP. VI. How her tragical Fate came to be known, and what suddenly happened thereon. Part II. p. 63.

CHAP. VII. The heavy Judgment that befel the cruel Prince; with the Miracle of the flowing Spring that issued from the Place she was beheaded. Ibid. pag. 65.

CHAP.

CHAP. VIII. *How, being restor'd to Life, on the Prayers of St.* BUENO, *she lived in such an holy Manner, that at length she became a celebrated Abbess.* Ibid. pag. 67.

CHAP. IX. *Her Exhortations to the Virgins under her most religious Care.* Part III. pag. 96 to 102.

CHAP. X. *The Continuation of the Life of St.* BUENO. Ibid. pag. 103, &c. *and* Part IV., pag. 111, &c., *where his pious Foundations are further mentioned, with the Manner of his Death and Burial.*

CHAP. XI. *The Death of St.* WINEFRED, *with the Translation of her Body from her Nunnery to* Shrewsbury, *where she was enshrin'd.* Part IV. pag. 114, 121, 123.

CHAP. XII. *The Nature of St.* WINEFRED'S *Well. The Opinions of the Learned concerning its sovereign healing Vertues, which indeed are* (†) *wonderful; and, by several Instances of Cures contain'd in this Book, may be justly attributed to the Divine Power in Heaven, that has highly glorify'd the Saints and Martyrs, by whose amazing Providence the Faithful are comforted in their Afflictions of Mind, Body, or Estate.* Ibid. pag. 131 and Part V.

What follows is a compendious Account of S. *Winefred's* LIFE in Profe; with an Index to the Poem, directing where the moſt material Points are exhibited, for the greater Eaſe and Delight of every courteous READER.

(†) *It may well be said of sacred Springs, as what is mention'd in regard to other Fountains.* " Nam ſive quantitatem conſideres, illa eſt ſtupenda; " ſive qualitates, illæ ſunt utiliſſimæ; ſive motum, ille eſt admi- " randus; quæ omnia nos manu ducent ad Dei Opt. Max. admira- " tionem & adorationem, cui ſoli fit laus in ſolidum."

British PIETY Display'd

In the GLORIOUS

LIFE, Suffering, and DEATH

Of the Blessed

St. WINEFRED:

A Noble VIRGIN, martyr'd for her renowned Chastity, in *Wales:* Where, at Her Celebrated FOUNTAIN, called HOLY-WELL, many afflicted Persons have been happily freed from their most dangerous Distempers in past Centuries: The salutiferous Quality of which Water, continuing in the present Age, occasions its FAME to be spread in far-distant Kingdoms.

Ecclesia nunquam florentior, quam cum afflictior inter cruces & gladios suorum martyrum pugnas & victorias spectavit.— Natura rerum ad Deum nos erigit. Quam magnifica sunt Opera Tua, D O M I N E !

"*DEUS ter Optimus Maximus in aquis summas excellentissimas recondivit vires salutares, quarum tanta est præstantia ut longè multumque omnibus aliis remediorum generibus sint superiores.*"

PART *the First.*

YORK: Printed by THOMAS GENT.

How amiable are Thy Tabernacles, O Lord of Hosts! My Soul longeth, yea, even fainteth for the Courts of the Lord: My Heart and my Flesh cryeth out for the Living GOD. PSAL. LXXXIV. 1, 2.

The PREFACE.

      Who have treated of a City fair,
I   *With great Delight that equaliz'd my Pains;*
      Spread her Cathedral's Glories far and near,
  'Tis hop'd, to laſt whilſt Time on Earth remains:
Now do each Muſe invoke, whilſt I ſhall ſing
A Virgin's Fame, thro' an amazing Spring.

Who ſhall peruſe, altho' their Faith to believe
  The Miracle be not the ſame of mine;
Yet Virtue's Charms can ne'er our Thoughts deceive,
  But under pleaſing Veils will e'er combine,
To make us (a) fly thoſe Things we ought to ſhun;
And do what Heav'n commandeth to be done.

This happy Iſle, which ſtill in Glory ſhines,
  Has been adorned by Virgin-Martyrs dear;
Long fam'd for Goodneſs, bleſs'd by great Divines,
  With Kings, who now bright Crowns of Glory wear:
EDMUND, *for one; high-prais'd by God-like (b)* KENN,
The moſt ſeraphic of all mortal Men.

Similitudes and Parables are ſweet:
  At once they wound our Souls, as quick they heal:
Lord (c) Verulam St. Alban *thought 'em meet*
  Before his Work, which Learning doth reveal:
And other Writers, to their laſting Fame,
Yield ſuch Delights beyond my Pen to name.

                                  JUAN,

   (*a*) I. PET. ii. 11. *Dearly Beloved, I beseech you, &c.*

   (*b*) Biſhop of *Bath* and *Wells*, in his Epic or Heroick Poem on that truly pious Prince, who was murder'd by the *Danes*.

   (*c*) In his *Atalantis*, preceding the natural HISTORY, and that excellent Treatiſe, intitul'd, *Historia vitæ & mortis*.

(d) JUAN, *of* Ofma, *moſt tranſcendent writ*
　His Philothea, *as on Pilgrimage:*
Thro' thorny Ways he leads us by his Wit,
　And with his Saint helps us to mount the Stage:
That pleaſing Summit of true Happineſs,
In Lines ſo ſoft, as Words can well expreſs.

And (e) Hugo, *in his emblematick Strains,*
　To Souls afflicted mighty Comfort yields;
Religion breaths to heav'n-lov'd Nymphs and Swains,
　Whether he treats of Rivers, Groves, or Fields.
No Place, no Thought, nor Action lies conceal'd,
But has GOD'S Will, or Part of it, reveal'd.

If, with the Honour which I yield the Saint,
　The World ſhould prove indulgent to my Pains;
'Twou'd ſtop my mournful Pen from ſad Complaint,
　Since 'tis their Love that proves the Poet's Gains:
My Harp, which on the Willow's lain too long, (f)
In Gratitude, ſhould anſwer to my Song.

The SPRING, *I treat of, thro' the World is fam'd;*
　The LADY *once was held in high Renown;*
Cures have been done, too num'rous to be nam'd;
　And ſhe was honour'd with a Martyr's Crown.
Let Scruples ceaſe, that this poor Work may take,
If not for mine, yet for fair Anglia's *ſake.*

(*d*) A Prelate in *Caſtile*, under the Archbiſhop of *Toledo*.

(*e*) HERMANNIUS HUGO, who wrote a Book, intituled,

Pia Desideria: Viz.	1. Gemitus 2. Vota 3. Suſpiria	Animæ	Pænitentis, Sanctæ, Amantis:

So much eſteem'd, as to become of uſe in *England;* and, being tranſlated by *Edmund Arwaker*, M.A., with ſome Alterations, was dedicated by that Gentleman to Queen *ANNE*.

(*f*) Alluding to ſome Misfortunes the Author has lain under.

The Holy LIFE *and* DEATH *of*

S. WINEFRED:

A beautiful Lady in North-Wales; *who, for defending her Chastity, was beheaded by an* Heathen *Prince, named* CARADOC, *Son to King* ALAN.

CHAP. I.

The Argument of this Chapter.

Of WINEFRED, *whose Birth and Station Were honour'd thro' her Education.*

LONG after (1) *Merlin* had strange Things foretold,
  And VORTIGERN, with his beloved Queen,
Were burnt to Ashes in their tow'ry (2) Hold,
  A Sight the most lamented to be seen!
When great (3) AMBROSIUS nobly won the Field,
And made some of the proudest *Saxons* yield:

Fair (4) *Cambria* was rever'd, thro' British Kings,
  Who bravely did their cruel Foes withstand;
The Themes of Bards; the purest, clearest Springs
  Of Blood, which ever flow'd within the Land:
From whence CADWALLIN, who the Sceptre sway'd,
And, with his Valour, Piety displayed.

'Twas

---

(1) A Welsh Prophet, who lived in the 5th Century.

(2) A Castle in Herefordshire, mention'd by CAMDEN.

(3) See my compendious History, concerning this King.

(4) Wales, an unconquer'd Country, where the ancient Britons resorted to, on the coming of the Saxons into England; who for a long time kept their Language and People pure without Mixture. 'Twas anciently divided into several Kingdoms; but now a Principality belonging to our King's eldest Son.

'Twas in his (5) Reign a Worthy did appear,
  THEWITH, a (6) Lord, enrich'd by Fortune's Hand;
Who, ſtill made happier in a Spouſe moſt dear,
  Had ev'ry earthly Pleaſure at Command;
When Heav'n was pleas'd to bleſs them with a Child,
By Nature graceful, lovely, pleaſant, mild!

Like to *Aurora*, in the Month of *May;*
  Or blooming Spring, ſo were her tender Years!
None view'd, but lov'd; nor lov'd, but what did pray,
  That Heav'n might guard this Object of their Cares!
And that thoſe native Charms, ſo fair begun,
Might ſpread their Luſtre like the glorious Sun.

The candid Robe of Baptiſm which ſhe wore,
  So far from ſoiling with one ſable Stain;
Her Innocence did cauſe its Whiteneſs more
  To ſeem like Skies ſerene, or ſilver Main;
Such as the moſt Inſenſate ſtrong might charm;
Deſires of Heav'n to raiſe, of Earth diſarm.

Nurs'd by her Lady-Mother, whoſe fair Truſt
  She'd not commit to any Stranger's Care;
True Virtues were imbred, ſo fix'd at firſt
  In her chaſte Heart, no Vice could harbour there:
But when of Years to know the Ways of Youth,
Bright her (7) Example prov'd to tender Youth!

The

---

  (5) Which laſted fifty Years.

  (6) Trebwith, or TENITHE, mention'd in *Aurea Legenda* to have been Son of Glynbus the Senator; who flouriſh'd about the Middle of the ſeventh Century.

  (7) Longum iter eſt per præcepta, breve & efficax per exempla.

The Glitt'ring of bright Jewels feem'd as dim,
  When e'er by Faith fhe view'd her bleffed Lord:
No Sight on Earth appear'd fo fair as HIM;
  Or (8) Thofe, who preach'd to Her His heav'nly Word.
Divinely meek, fhe'd wafh poor Pilgrims' Feet;
And mingle Tears with melting Accents fweet.

When e'er fhe fee poor Strangers pafs the Road,
  If partly naked, fhe would Garments give;
Or, looking hungry, quickly fend them Food;
  And comfort thofe, who in Diftrefs did grieve.
None to her Gates did come in woful Tears,
But for her Kindnefs fent to Heav'n their Pray'rs.

Angelick-like, fhe to GOD'S Altar came;
  There, rev'rently, whilft Myft'ries were reveal'd,
Her Soul was fo infpir'd with holy Flame,
  Her Ardency could never be conceal'd:
All faw her Zeal, which did to Heav'n impart
The fweet Defires of her love-fick Heart.

Lov'd by her Saviour, and the heav'nly Hoft,
  What Wonder was it Earth fhould fpread her Fame?
Or that her Thoughts fhould center in what moft
  Infpir'd her Soul with evangelick Flame?
He, who in Heav'n fhines with eternal Bloom,
Could only in this Virgin's Heart find Room.

                                                CHAP.

---

(8) Quàm decentes funt fuper iftos montes pedes evangelizantis, pronunciantis pacem, evangelizantis bonum, pronunciantis falutem, dicentis Tzijoni: regnat Deus tuus! IsA. liL 7.

CHAP. II.

The Argument.

How B'uno, sprung from princely Train,
The holy Priesthood did obtain;
When to his pious Care was giv'n
The Virgin, to bring up for Heav'n.

THERE dwelt a (9) Lord in Western Part of *Wales*,
   Who wed a Lady virtuous, rich and fair;
And GOD, who never yet true Virtue fails,
   Gave them a Son they hop'd might prove their Heir:
Yet neither Lands or Houses were his Aim;
But Heav'n, from whence his blessed Spirit came.

For from the Time that he could learn to read,
   And say devoutly Night and Day his Pray'rs;
Virtues did Virtues constantly succeed;
   Whilst Learning rais'd him for the Church's Cares.
So zealous prov'd, he left his native home;
Became a Priest, and then abroad did roam.

As distant Altars now he did attend,
   From far and near he was encompass'd round:
So when he preach'd upon our latter End,
   No Eye was dry, no Heart but felt the Wound.
Weeping he spoke, which shew'd for Souls he wept;
And like a Shepherd dear his Flocks he kept.

Tho'

---

(9) Named Aprwst AP Glinliw, who owned a Territory called Glewisig: He was related to CADOC and KENTIGERN, Bishops of Beneventum in Italy, and Glascow in Scotland, canoniz'd Saints; as also to LANDATUS, Abbot of Bardsey (or Bardeney) in Lincolnshire.

Tho' poor, the Nobles did Affiftance lend,
  To build thofe Churches which he pleas'd to found;
There placing Priefts GOD'S Worfhip to attend,
  He ftill improv'd; and follow'd in this Round
Of Glory, 'till infpir'd to find a Place,
Where he with Joy might end his pious Race.

Whilft to Lord THEWITH he did once repair;
  "My Lord, *faid he*, I'm come to beg a Boon.
"For *JESUS'* Sake, do, grant a little Share
  "Of your fair Land to build a Church upon;
"That I, devoutly, may yield Heav'n its due;
"And daily pray, my Lord, for your's, and you.

"This Life is fhort, my Lord; and what you have
  "Can only blefs you whilft this Side the Urn:
"Now if you grant a Place our Souls to fave,
  "Heav'n more than Int'reft will your Soul return.
"Cæleftial Guardians 'till your Death will wait;
"And Life eternal make your Joys compleat.

O good BUENO, *ftraight that Lord reply'd*,
  Take what you pleafe, as to your Will feems good,
I joy to think that near me you'll refide,
  To feed our Souls with facramental Food, (10)
My Daughter dear, (11) BRUENA call'd by Name,
Will much rejoice, when fhe fhall hear the fame.

Forth-

---

(10) "Quia Tu, ô æterna Veritas, id nobis revelafti, & facratiffimo "Tuo ore dixifti, HOC EST CORPUS MEUM."

(11) How her Name was changed, will be hereafter fhown.

Forthwith the blooming Damsel did he call,
  Who quickly stood before her Father's Sight!
Such Innocence, and Modesty withall,
  Did charm the Priest with spirit'al Delight;
For Nature ne'er produced One more fair,
Like to an Angel did she bright appear!

Smooth was her Forehead, more than Iv'ry white;
  The Brows, two lovely Arches, seem'd divine:
Her Eyes like sparkling Di'monds cast a Light;
  Vermilion Blushes in her Cheeks did shine:
Lips, red as Coral, added still a Grace
To the enchanting Features of her Face.

Most artless was display'd her flowing Hair,
  With graceful Ringlets nat'rally to deck;
That, spreading, made her like a Nymph appear,
  With waving Lustres to her milk-white Neck.
Her Shape throughout was Symetry refin'd;
But, Oh! what Beauties graced her heavenly Mind!

For whilst to them she did her Words apply,
  Nervous, yet sweet, her Answers did appear:
The Priest, stirr'd up with holy Rhapsody,
  Did her a Saint most fit for Heav'n declare:
Inspir'd to pray, "Indulgent Heav'n, *said he*,
"Preserve this Mirror of Virginity!"

Then, frequently, as he GOD'S Word did teach,
  She at his Feet with due Attention heard.
Whate'er he of our blessed Lord did preach,
  No Admonition, but she did regard.
Whole Nights, whilst others slept, she'd pray and weep;
And in the Church her pious Vigils keep.

                                                One

One Time she to the holy Priest did say,
  "Dear Sir, beseech my Parents to comply
  "With my Desire; which is, I earnest pray,
  "To live a Maiden, and a Virgin die:
  "That with no earthly Spouse I may combine;
  "But join with CHRIST, all lovely, all divine!"

This World you tell me, and my self well knows,
  Is but a Place of Tryal, and of Sin:
To shun the latter, I've the former chose;
  And, as I'm young, fain would my Course begin;
To consecrate my Life to GOD above,
Since Heav'n I'm sure inspires my Soul to love.

To hear her speak in such pathetick wise,
  Her Tears, like Fountains, springing from the Hills;
Streams also fell from good *Bueno's* Eyes,
  As trickling Waters from descending Rills.
O Child for Heav'n! *he said*, I'll haste straightway;
For sure they will so just a Call obey.

He found them in an Arbour close retir'd,
  Conversing of the unseen Joys above;
And told them what, spontaneous, she desir'd;
  Surpriz'd, they wept, and shew'd parental Love.
Consent obtain'd, now was her chiefest Care
To please her Lord with Reverence and Fear.

No more rich sparkling Gems, or gilded Zone,
  The graceful Scarf, or costly Robes, attire:
And yet beneath an humble Veil is shown,
  Such heav'nly Beauties Angels might admire:
Within her Parent's House she chose to dwell,
Because as yet was unprepar'd her Cell.

CHAP.

CHAP. III.

The Argument.

What good instructions Bu'no gave,
To guide her to the silent Grave;
And, in exhibiting Advice,
Foretold the Way to Paradice.

THE rev'rend Priest then taught her to prepare
    For sacramental Strength her tender Heart;
To 'void Offence; no Envy to appear;
    But Hope, and (12) Charity most sweet, impart:
With lowly Reverence to kneel before
GOD'S Altar, where with Faith she should adore.

Seek that high (13) Kingdom, which will never end;
    That Prince eternal, 'mongst His shining Train;
Whom (14) Youth unfading decks, whom Joys attend
    And in whose Strength our hopes are not in vain!
Pleas'd, He looks down, whilst we to Him aspire;
Nor fails to grant each pious Soul's Desire.

PRAYER, when we rightly wish that Heav'n would grant
    Not what (15) we please, but what our LORD thinks fit;
No doubt may find Relief in each Complaint,
    When we our Wills to That of His submit:
Like *Jacob's* Ladder, up it mounts. to Heav'n;
To CHRIST it seeks, who asks what will be giv'n. (16).

                                        Think,

---

    (12) I. Cor. xiii. 4. Charity suffereth long, and is kind, &c.
    (13) Tu regnum quære, cujus regni non erit finis. Rex illius æternus est, æterni incolæ. DREXEL.
    (14) Heb. i. 11, &c.—Psal. civ. 31.—Exod. xv. 18.
    (15) Tho. à Kemp. De Imitatione CHRISTI.
    (16) Mat. vii. 7, &c.—James i. 5 and 17 Ver., &c.

Think, think, *he faid*, how little, Child! you be;
  And what you owe to Him, who did create
Thy Frame from *nothing !* Great His Majefty,
  Who quick can raife, as foon annihilate.
Since he infpires thy Soul for Grace to pray,
Bear then thy Crofs, and feek to Heav'n the Way. (17).

Two Perfons more with this Great GOD admire;
  The Son, fweet JESU! fuffered cruel Death:
And HOLY GHOST, which teaches to defire;
  Yielding that Comfort no where found on Earth.
Unbounded Love in all the Heav'nly THREE,
To eafe our Yoke from *Adam's* Mifery.

Conform to GOD entirely your Will:
  The (18) Burden's light what you for Heav'n endure.
No Suff'rings fear; but dread all doing ill;
  For *Confcience wounded*, hard is found a Cure.
(19) *Redeem the Time.* (20) Life's Hour-Glafs doth run:
And ev'ry Caufe of Sin be fure to fhun.

If Anger chance to rife within Thy Breaft,
  For ftern, vile Ufage, which thou may'ft receive: (21)
Humility will calm that Vice to reft,
  So fhall it ne'er abfurd Dominion have.
This will, like (22) Coals of Fire, thy Foes ev'n warm;
Give Peace within, and all without muft charm.

And

---

(17) *Isaiah* xxx. 21.—*Jer.* vi. 16.—*Hebr.* x. 20.
(18) *Jugum meum suave est, & onus meum leve.* MAT. xi. 30.
(19) *Vitum brevem esse, artem longam.* HYP. Icit. Aphor.
(20) *Vita est*
Somnus, bulla, vitrum, glacies, flos, fabula, fanum;
Umbra, cinis, punctum, vox, sonus, aura, nihil.
(21) *See Psal.* lv. 12, 13. *For Relief, read the* 22d *Verse.*
(22) Rom. xii. 20. *If thine enemy hunger, feed him, &c.*

And should you (23) lose your All by Wretches vile,
   In Patience still you shall possess your Soul:
(24) Base impious Slanders, only at them smile;
   Thy Innocence shall conquer all Controul.
Desire not Death, that Sorrows may be ended;
Nor pant for Life so much, as b'ing amended.

In harmless Labours take you some delight:
   And whilst embroider'd Work thou shalt prepare,
With intermingled Gold, and Silver bright,
   In languish'd Thoughts send up a mental Pray'r.
Children instruct; for them thy Love must be,
To learn the Truth, as is my Care for thee.

Thus let thy Eye by Faith be fix'd thereon,
   That no one Blemish may be seen, or wrought:
Think as if GOD was constant looking down;
   Who knows, as sure He does, thy ev'ry Thought.
Think ev'ry Day of Life you draw more nigh
To the vast Ocean of Eternity.

Since die we must, like (25) *Water spill on Earth*,
   And in our Habitation (26) *known* no *more!*
Let us now strive to shun a second Death:
   For what avails all Pomp and wordly Store
To any one, who shall in Pleasures roul,
And lose the precious, dear, immortal Soul? (27)

                                     Let

---

(23) *Multæ sunt afflictiones justi; sed ex omnibus illis eripit eum JEHOVA.* P s a l. xxxiv. 19.
  (24) *See Psal.* xxxi. 11. *Ver.* 14 *and* 18.
  (25) II. Sam. xiv. 14. *For we must needs die, &c.*
  (26) Job vii. 9, 10.——*Psal.* ciii. 16.
  (27) *Mat. xvi.* 26. *For what is man profited, &c.*

Let the Laſt Judgement ever be in Mind,
  Since 'tis on that ETERNITY depends.
O dreadful! pleaſing Word! no Years can bind,
  That on the Wicked, on the Juſt attends!
(28) Pleaſures, ne'er-ceaſing, ſhall the Bleſs'd obtain;
The Curs'd, eternal Flames, and endleſs Pain!

Soon we may (29) chance to bid this World adieu,
  All human Splendor for Heavn's Sake defpiſe:
But let the Poor (30) be ever dear to you,
  Becauſe that ſuch are precious in its Eyes:
And as thou haſt a Virgin State profeſs'd,
O let thy Love for JESUS be exprefs'd.

This, and much more, the holy Prieſt did ſay,
  The Parents heark'ning whilſt he taught their Child;
Deep ſunk the Doctrine which he did diſplay,
  With Pow'r divine, and yet ſo ſoft and mild,
That WINEFRED refolv'd to (31) ſeek her Love,
Both on the Earth, and in the Realms above.

O ſweet Defire! that her Soul, when flown,
  By lovely Queens, and *Sion's* Daughter, bleſs'd,
Might be compar'd unto the ſhining Moon,
  Or as the riſing Morn, by them confeſs'd:
Haſt'ning to meet her deareſt Lord at laſt,
In ſpringing Joys, when all her Winter's paſt. (32).

CHAP.

---

(28) *Aut gaudendum in cœlo æternum, aut æternum in tartaro ardendum.*
DREX. de Eter.
  (29) *Nescit homo finem suum,* ECCL. ix. 12.
    Ut tibi mors felix contingat, vivere disce:
    Ut felix possis vivere, disce mori.
  (30) II. *Cor.* ix. 7.—*Mat.* vi. 4, and xiii. 12.—*Luk.* xi.
  (31) *Cantic.* iii. 1, 2, 3, 4.—(32) Med. AUG. *Cap.* 55.

CHAP. IV.

The Argument.

How CARADOC, *to his great Shame,*
Did strive the Virgin to defame;
Who bravely that bad Prince withstood,
With virtuous Speeches, wise and good.

ONCE, so it happen'd, on a Sabbath Day,
   Sickness confin'd this lovely Maid at home;
And whilst her Parents in the Church did pray,
   An Heathen Prince into their House did come.
Struck with Surprize, the Damsel quickly rose;
And like a Lady decent Manners shows.

My Lord, *she said*, pray what's your noble Will?
   That I may let my tender Parents know:
They're now at Pray'rs; and, tho' I'm weak and ill,
   For them with nimble-winged Speed I'll go;
Or, that I may not your good Patience wrong,
Please, take a Seat; their Stay may not be long.

Sit down, *he said*. It is not them I want:
   My bus'ness, Virgin! only is with thee.
With me! *reply'd she*, in a Voice most faint:
   What can I do, or wou'd you have with me?
Much you can do, he said, *since from the Grave*
You can your Prince and dying Lover save.

'Tis you have rais'd a Fever in my Mind:
   Thy Beauty, Charmer, is, like *Pallas,* fair!
Fit for a King, who is to Love inclin'd;
   Such is thy Mein, thy Sweetness, and thy Air!
I pain for you, intended Spouse! whose Dart,
'Twas, gave the Wound; and you must cure the Smart.

With that her lovely Colour went and came:
  Now pale her Cheeks, which quickly turn'd to red;
Whilſt he, whom Thoughts of Virtue could not tame,
  Reſolv'd to wound her Soul, with Fear o'erſpread:
And leſt that noiſeleſs Time ſhould him prolong,
He gave more Vent to his deceitful Tongue.

Lady, *ſaid he*, you know my royal Blood;
  But can't conceive how much I you adore;
Nor can my Words find Utt'rance as they ſhou'd,
  So much your Sweetneſs wounds me more and more.
Let not Diſdain cauſe my warm Heart to change;
Or turn my Love to Madneſs wild and ſtrange.

My Lord, *ſhe ſaid*, I'm far beneath your (32) Grace;
  Too young for Wedlock; and, indeed, unfit
For me to take an higher L A D Y's Place,
  By Birth renown'd, and worthy more of it:
Therefore, great Prince! your Honour do not ſtain;
But let true Glory mitigate your Pain.

Beſides, you ſee, my Spirits are but faint;
  My Health is waſted, and fair Beauty fled!
Add not, I pray, to this, my ſad Complaint;
  And when I tell my Lord, that I am wed.
Yes, yes, O Prince! I'm join'd to Heav'n above;
My Soul! my All! for J E S U is my Love!

Talk not of Sickneſs, nor of nuptial Toys,
  Said C A R A D O C; you ſet me all a-flame.
My Heart is fir'd with Love's fermenting Joys;
  Too hot to bear, too raviſhing to name.
But what has Heav'n to do with Beauties here?
Let Gods take Goddeſſes; Men, Ladies fair.

How

---

(32) *Ubi humilitas, ibi majestas.*

How can you think the Pow'rs did e'er create
  So fair a Virgin, but to be enjoy'd?
Or was I born to this my mighty State;
  That my Defires fhould ufelefs prove, or void?
I muft enjoy you.——At which Words he fwore,
And ftrove by Force to throw her on the Floor.

With weeping Eyes, *fhe faid*, (33) Do not begin
  To ftrain a Conqueft you may blufh to own.
Be rather Victor over carnal Sin,
  And with chafte Thoughts befeech the Heav'nly Throne,
That Satan's fiery Darts you may repell,
Who ftrives to fink your precious Soul to Hell.

Talk not of Devil, nor his flaming Dart,
  The Wretch did fay; for neither do I care.
You, more than Hell's black Pow'rs has fcorch'd my Heart,
  That from your Lips I nothing pleas'd can hear,
Unlefs it be to yield unto my Arms,
To roul in Luft, and rifle all your Charms.

I thought, *faid fhe*, dear Prince! in holy Bands
  You had defign'd me for your lawful Wife.
So made, I own, that Grandeur, (†) Riches, Lands,
  Might make me happy all the days of Life:
But fhould my Virgin-Treafure firft be gone,
Then I may be abandon'd, and undone!

O think, my Lord! that to be rich and great,
  Without true Virtue, there's no Happinefs.
That will our Souls from Earth to Heav'n tranflate;
  Than beft of Friends 'tis better to poffefs.
'Twill banifh Dæmons; Angels good invite;
Prove Guide by Day, and fure Defence at Night.

Alas,

---

    (33) *Virtus adversus agitata crescit: vulnere virescit; inter injurias erigitur; inter miserias floret.* DREX.

    (†) *Divitiæ non malæ, sed earum abusus.*

Alas, my Lord! in Death, thy gilded Tow'rs,
  And fpacious Lands, no more can pleafe the Sight.
No Entertainments, Gold or Jewels your's,
  When call'd to take from this vain World your Flight.
Think now, O Prince! upon your better Part,
And let R E L I G I O N center in your Heart.

Renowned Sir! do, let me You befeech,
  By thefe my Tears, all Vice to fet afide:
Regard a fimple Maiden's virtuous Speech;
  Nor be offended, or my Woes deride.
Simple, indeed, the haughty Wretch did cry,
Thus to reject fo great a Prince as I!

With that fhe pray'd: O pity, Heav'n! my Cries!
  Thou, who did'ft fkreen the young Men from the Fire,
Defend my Virtue from thofe Hands and Eyes,
  Howe'er it be thy Pleafure I expire.
O let my Soul, devoted unto Thee,
Be without Spot, and from all Blemifh free!

She tho't fhe heard: (34) Do thou his Might withftand;
  And if he fmites thee, patient bear the Wound:
Thy precious Blood full Judgment fhall demand,
  And as clofe Cement to the Church be found.
He can but (35) *kill the Body*, do his worft:
(36) Fear not, you'll live, when he fhall fall accurft.

Again

---

(34) *Invoca Me in die tribulationis eruam te & honorificabis me,* PSAL. l. 15. Alfo PSAL. xci. 15. PSAL. cvii. 6, with other Parts of Scripture.

(35) MATT. x. 28. *And fear not them which, &c.*

(36) *Etiam, quum ambularem per vallem lethalis umbræ, non timerem malum quia tu mecum es, &c.,* PSAL. xxiii. 4.—You will find fuch heavenly Support in other Writings of King DAVID, in JOB, the Epiftle of St. Paul to the *Romans,* and St. *James.*

Again the Prince did urge: Do but comply,
  And make me not submissive thus to stand:
But if you will my earnest Suit deny,
  Force shall constrain; and even, out of hand,
Destroy thy Beauty when I've cropt the Flower:
For nothing can, or shall, withstand my Power.

The modest Virgin, much destress'd in Mind,
  Silent, sought Heav'n his Wishes to elude.
O Prince! *then said*, your Pow'r seems unconfin'd;
  Nor durst I on your Patience far intrude:
Yet pray you stay my Parents dear Return;
That you, nor I, or them, have Cause to mourn.

I will not wait, *he cry'd;* nor lose my Time.
  But, ah! my Lord! *she answer'd*, I'm undress'd:
I'll to my Closet, where, like Beauty's Prime,
  I shall array my self to be possess'd:
Like *Persia's* (37) Queen, who in bright Robes did shine,
And with (38) *Cytherea's* Airs may make you mine.

Well, take your Will, *said he;* but don't be long.
  She went.—Enjoy her now, *he swore*, I must.
Deceit, I see, must be proclaim'd with Tongue;
  Or where's the Prince that can fulfil his Lust?
That, like a Deluge, human Force pervades,
And makes a prey of Widows, Wives, and Maids.

Thus, gentle READER, here the Contrast's giv'n;
  Virtue and Vice; each striving to excell.
How fair is One, in Grief imploring Heav'n!
  How foul the other, like the Fiend of Hell?
But, Oh! the diff'rent State that is between,
By what hereafter follows, may be seen.

---

(37) ESTHER v. 1.   (38) *Venus*, so call'd.

CHAP. V.

The Argument.

How WINEFRED *strove to escape*
The Prince's base designed Rape.
The Arguments with which a while
She did her cruel Fate beguile;
'Till, at the length, he gave the Wound,
Which laid her bleeding on the Ground.

HER Closet enter'd, fast she lock'd the Door,
   And thro' a private Passage took her Flight:
But his sharp Eyes so sudden did explore
   Her Motion, that she cou'd not 'scape his Sight.
Quick he pursu'd with dreadful sword in Hand,
And did the Reason of her Flight demand?

Great Prince, *said she*, I could not do no less
   Than shew my Care both for my self, and you.
'Twas Virtue made me fly in this Distress.
   O wou'd it had conceal'd me from your View:
But since this bitter Conflict makes me speak,
Hear yet a while; 'tis chiefly for your Sake.

Shou'd you compel, your Pleasures soon decay;
   But (39) Punishment, without Repentance, never!
Who for a (40) transient Hour, or a Day,
   Would risk their Souls for (41) ever, and for ever?
Besides, you know, to GOD I'm consecrate;
Which must more horrid make your wretched State.

I told

---

   (39) "*Pœnæ gehennales torquent, non extorquent; puniunt non finiunt corpora.*" PROS.
      (40) I. JOH. ii. 17. *And the World passeth, &c.*
      (41) JUDE 7. Ver.—*Suffering the Vengeance of* ETERNAL *Fire!*

I told you once, you might a Princefs find
  More fair than I to blefs you with her Love:
And fuch Enjoyment, of *Hymenœal* Kind,
  Your Gods, if fuch there be, muft high approve:
But if you break Heav'n's Laws, the Pow'rs divine
Will dire revenge this woful Caufe of mine.

Thou ftubborn Girl, *faid he*, And doft thou fcorn?
  So taunt my Fury with your Hopes of Heav'n?
Do'ft think that him, who wore a Crown of Thorn,
  Did'ft mean that I of you fhould be bereav'n?
What Prieft has preach'd to thee this Virgin Pride?
And would have others, not himfelf, deny'd?

O fay not fo, thou wicked Prince! *faid fhe:*
  Thy Wrongs repent, and lay your Sword afide.
Affure thy tyrant Heart, I'll ne'er agree
  To thy Embrace, whatever me betide:
So both your Smiles and Frowns I now difclaim.
Slay me you may, but not my Perfon fhame.

Bafe Wretch, *faid he*, thou might'ft have been my Wife,
  But fince I'm treated with fuch bitter Scorn,
Soon fhalt Thou yield, or quickly lofe thy Life;
  For fuch Contempt is never to be borne.
So faid, with grafping Hand, he feiz'd her Hair;
Yet fpoke, as tho' he had a Mind to fpare.

And will you not, *he faid*, with me comply,
  But force this Arm thy treach'rous Blood to fpill?
Yes, Prince! *faid fhe*, than lofe my Virtue die;
  Of two Extreams it is the leffer ill.
Nay, greater Good: A (42) Martyr I fhall reign,
But, by my Fate, pray what muft you obtain?

For

---

(42) *O quàm multas & graves tribulationes paſſi ſunt Apoſtoli, Martyres, Confeſſores, Virgines, & reliqui omnes, qui Chriſti veſtigia voluerunt ſequi!* Tho. à Kemp. lib. i. cap. 28.

For if you plunge your Blade within my Breaſt,
  And turn my livid Veins to Springs of Blood;
When by Death's Seal my dying Eyes are preſt,
  Your Wiſhes too muſt periſh in the Flood!
But, what's far worſe, no more Content you'll find;
For (42a) NEMESIS will e'er torment your Mind.

Ev'n gentle Zephirs, in their *Weſtern* Breeze,
  Shall prove like (43) *Zenith* in moſt direful Storms!
The trembling Sprays, with various Sorts of Trees,
  Will ſeem as Ghoſts in all their dreary Forms!
And believe GOD'S (44) Prophet, who doth plainly tell,
No Peace will be, where Wickedneſs ſhall dwell.

However, if by Murder I muſt fall,
  (45) *Faithful* I'll prove until my lateſt Breath:
For to conſent, I neither will; nor ſhall
  Be forc'd to Luſt by any Prince on Earth.
And, now you know my Mind; I wiſh, thro' Heav'n,
You may abſtain, repent, and be forgiv'n.

The juv'nile Tyrant then with Rage did foam;
  Yet loath to ſtrike, ſuppoſing ſhe would yield,
He urg'd in vain; nor did ſhe fear her Doom,
  But as Chriſt's Championeſs ſhe kept the Field.
Mercy, ſweet JESU! was the Virgin's Cry:
Pity me, JESU! for your Sake I die.

Die

(42a) *The Goddess of Punishment, as acknowledg'd by the* Heathens; *whose Arguments she applied.*

(43) *The Firmament exactly over head, made terrible by strange* Phænomena, *Thunder, Lightning, &c.*

(44) ISAIAH xlviii. Ver. 22 *and* lvii. 21.

(45) Agreeable to *Rev.* cap. ii. v. 10. and cap. iii. 11. *Esto fidelis usque ad mortem, & dabitur tibi corona vitæ. Tene quod habes, ut nemo accipiat coronam tuam.*

See also MARK xiii. 13. *Whoſoever shall endure to the End, the same* virtuous Soul *shall be saved.*

Die then, *quoth he*, thou moft obdurate Maid!
Then, as to Heaven moft piteoufly fhe cry'd, (46)
With fuch a Force he ftruck his glitt'ring Blade,
That quickly did her milk-white Neck divide.
Low fell the Body! down he threw the Head!
Whilft fanguine Streams like trickling Rills did fpread.

As by CHRIST'S Suff'rings, tho' fupernal Call,
We learn to bear Affliction's bitter Stings;
So Her EXAMPLE, truly virginal,
Should make us flight all temporary Things:
For if to Heav'n we ftedfaft prove in Love,
We fhall be blefs'd on Earth, and crown'd Above. (47)

---

(46) As tho' fhe had faid, "*Si vis ut moriar, dulcis* JESU! *suscipe spiritum meum!*"

(47) *Beati qui persecutionem patiuntur propter justitiam, quoniam ipsorum est regnum cælorum.* MAT. V. 10.

The END of the Firft PART.

British PIETY Display'd

In the GLORIOUS

LIFE, Suffering, and DEATH

Of the Blessed

St. WINEFRED:

A Noble VIRGIN, martyr'd for her renowned Chastity, in *Wales:* Where, at Her Celebrated FOUNTAIN, called HOLY-WELL, many afflicted Persons have been happily freed from their most dangerous Distempers in past Centuries: The salutiferous Quality of which Water, continuing in the present Age, occasions its FAME to be spread in far-distant Kingdoms.

Ecclesia nunquam florentior, quam cum afflictior inter cruces & gladios suorum martyrum pugnas & victorias spectavit.— Natura rerum ad Deum nos erigit. Quam magnifica sunt Opera Tua, DOMINE!

"*DEUS ter Optimus Maximus in aquis summas excel-*
"*lentissimas recondivit vires salutares, quarum tanta est*
"*præstantia ut longè multumque omnibus aliis remediorum*
"*generibus sint superiores.*"

PART *the Second.*

YORK: Printed by THOMAS GENT.

Quis ascendet in Montem DOMINI, aut quis stabit in loco Sancto EJUS? Psal. xxiv. 3.

"Ibi sanctæ MULIERES, quæ voluptates sæculi & sexus "infirmitatem vicerunt." *Meditat.* AUGUST. *Cap.* xxv.

" *Fœlix cæli quæ præsentem Regem cernit anima.*
" *Et sub sede spectat alta orbis volvi machinam.*
" *Solem, Lunam, & globosa cum planetis sydera.*

Thrice happy Souls, in seeing CHRIST how bless'd!
And underneath your Feet this World express'd:
The Sun and Moon, with Stars that bright appear,
Revolving each within their proper Sphere;
And you secur'd from any Kind of Fear!

Quia ibi nulla erit persecutio, nulla tribulatio, nullus penitentiæ labor, nullus gemitus, nullus dolor, nulla tristitia.

Levavi oculos meos in montes, unde veniet auxilium mihi.
De ætern. felicitat. Sanct. & PSAL. cxxi. 1.

The Second PART of
The Holy LIFE and DEATH of
S. WINEFRED.

CHAP. VI.
The Argument.

How soon her Death came to be known,
And what did happen thereupon.

READER, suppose that, on bright Angel's Wings,
   The Virgin's Spirit soar'd to Heav'n's high Gate;
But do not think she reach'd the King of Kings
   In Throne (48) empyreal, where the Patriarchs wait.
And yet imagine in a glorious Place, (49)
Where nothing dwelt but Harmony and Peace.

Thrice happy Virgin! *said her Guardian dear,*
   What now you see, pays for a World of Pain;
Yet CHRIST to serve, must not be thought severe,
   That you once more return to Earth again;
And, after long Example bright, to sever;
Then live amongst Heav'n's inward Courts for ever.

                                                            See,

---

    (48) *Where the Beatifick Vision is beheld; the very Place of GOD'S immediate Presence.*

    (49) *Where the Saints shall be as resplendant as the brightest Sun, when, after their earthly Conflicts, they shall mutually triumph in recounting their past Victorys, is thus expressed in the Works of S.* AUSTIN.

              Nam & sancti quique velut Sol præclarus rutilant.
              Post triumphum coronati mutuo conjubilant.
              Et prostrati pugnas hostis jam securi numerant.

See, see yon diftant Angle how it fhines;
  From thence your Bridegroom cafts his piercing Eyes.
He knows your Soul how inwardly it pines;
  As he does ev'ry Martyr dear that dies.
Thofe radiant Gleams Affurance is to thee,
You'll live with HIM to all Eternity.

Join'd with Attendants, in their bright Array,
  Unto her Lord all tun'd their melting Voice;
And as her Tears by Heav'n were wafh'd away,
  In blifsful Smiles the VIRGIN did rejoice.
No Tongue can tell the Joys when ANGELS meet;
Raptures divine! and Melody moft fweet!

Leave we a while to their feraphick State,
  And now defcend unto the fanguine Earth.
The dear Remains let us commemorate,
  That gave to this moft ftrange Relation birth;
From whence a Church was raifed to this Day;
Where painted Glafs her Hift'ry doth difplay.

The precious (49a) Body bleeding did remain;
  The Hill was colour'd with a crimfon Red;
And whilft the Murd'rer look'd like curfed *Cain*,
  Rowl'd gently to'ards the Church the lovely Head:
Pafs'd thro' the Porch, reach'd to the fontal Ifle;
Which fhew'd the Prince did her of Life beguile.

Lord

(49a) *Happy we, in the sharpest Tryals, by imitating those who were made strong; when Women received their Dead raised to Life again; and others were tortured, not accepting Deliverance, that they might obtain a better Resurrection: Whose Faith follow, considering the End of their Conversation.* HEB. ix. 35. and xiii. 7.

Lord! what a Sight was this! nor ghaſtly made,
  Tho' pale, and thus depriv'd of vital Breath:
For Heav'n preſerv'd her Charms, which did not fade,
  But prov'd their Vict'ry over cruel Death.
The Prieſt and People wept to ſee the Sight!
But moſt her Parents mourn'd their Hearts Delight.

CHAP. VII.

The Argument.

The Prince, who could not well repent,
Meets ſudden Death! A ſad Event!
The Miracle, that is diſplay'd,
By ancient Writers, of this MAID.

BU'NO did then his (50) Eloquence diſtill,
  To eaſe ſad Grief with which they did abound;
And with them, mourning, did aſcend the Hill,
  Where they the bleeding Virgin's Body found.
The Tyrant CARADOC was ſtanding by,
As tho' he ſcorn'd, or had not Pow'r, to fly.

The holy Prieſt, who bore the Virgin's Head,
  Told the Spectators all her ſpir'tual Charms:
How no Enticements could her Mind miſlead
  From the dear Circle of her Saviour's Arms:
A Martyr true ſhe well eſteem'd might be,
Who had by Death (51) ſav'd her Virginity.

But

---

(50) *So well did he prove a sympathetick Love to be that* flos deliciarum *to the Afflicted, that it well might be said of him as of* ORIGEN, Cujus ex ore non tam verba quam mella profluere videbantur.

(51) CAMBDEN *says, that she was actually ravish'd, as hereafter will be shewn; tho' it is contrary to the Opinion of most Writers, that mention the Saint.*

But, oh! thou impious Wretch, that here doth ſtand,
  A Statue like, tho' far from briny Salt,
As *Lot's* frail Wife, who diſobey'd Command,
  Yet ne'er committed ſuch a bloody Fault:
Does not thy Heart relent, condemn the Deed,
That thus has made an Heav'n-loved Virgin bleed?

Thou haſt prophan'd the ſacred Day of Reſt;
  Thy Birth obſcur'd; and, by the blackeſt Crime
Of Murder, made both Heav'n and Men deteſt
  Thy Memory until the lateſt Time:
Better to kneel, beg Mercy of the Lord,
Than on the Graſs to wipe your ſtained Sword.

To whom the Prince: Thou doating Fool, give o'er.
  'Twas you that cauſ'd this ſimple Wretch's Fate;
Who would have yielded to blind *Cupid's* Pow'r,
  Had you not preach'd her in Religion's State.
Long might ſhe liv'd, did ſhe not me controul;
But ſince ſhe's dead, *Jove* reſt her ſilly Soul.

Bu'no reply'd, O thou unprince-like Youth,
  Since no Compunction from thy Soul proceeds
Quick ſhalt thou find confirm'd a woful Truth,
  Juſt Puniſhment for thy accurſed Deeds.
Soon as he ſpoke, the Body like black Clay, (52)
Fell to the Ground, which Dæmons bore away.

Behold,

---

(52) *Some write, He fell to the Earth, and immediately expired; tho' they could not otherwise perceive the vindictive Hand of the Almighty in so quick and tremendous an Execution. Others suppose, that Body and Soul instantaneously sunk into the Regions of Darkness, and were received by* terrible Devils; *who, as a very learned* Author *writes, are styled* seirim, *derived from a Word which signifies* horrere, *because usually tendring themselves to View in the most glaring, frightful and horrible Forms.*

Behold, *said* Bu'no, what a fearful Shame
Has him befall'n, who GOD'S (52a) Laws withstood:
See from astringent Earth a crystal Stream,
As intermingles with the Virgin's Blood! (53)
Which, trickling to the (54) *Vale* will prove a Well,
The Fame of which shall distant Ages tell.

CHAP. VIII.

The Argument.

How Winefred, *to Life restor'd,*
Again on earth did praise the Lord:
Became an Abbess much rever'd,
And as a Saint most bright appear'd.

BUT tho' the Tyrant cut her Thread of Life,
And stopt the Progress of that Vow she made;
Heav'n can't be mock'd by vain contending Strife
Of Tyrant's Rage. For her, lamented Shade!
We'll try, *said* Bu'no, what our God will do.
Come, join with me; I'll pray for her and you.

What

(52a) *Non patitur lusum fides,* says a great Divine.

(53) *An ingenious Author writes, That* GOD, (*who in the Beginning moved on the Waters,* Gen. i. 2) *sometimes deliver'd or shew'd to the ancient Priests and Prophets a certain Matter* per beata spectacula, *and communicated for the Use of His Worshippers. At other seasons the Streams were guarded by a presiding Angel, as mention'd in* Rev. cap. xvi. ver. 5. *Which is more generally affirm'd in* Joh. cap. v. ver. 4. *that after the divine Messenger had stirred the Pool of* Bethesda, *whatever diseased Person had Power by a strong Faith, to wash therein, without being thrust away by an invisible Arm, was certainly cured of all Diseases.*

(54) *Some write, That, for want of a Spring or Rivulet before this Miracle, the Place was called* DRY-Vale.—*King* David, (Psal. cvii. 35.) *in praising the Lord, tells us, That* He *turneth the dry Ground into Water-Springs; which agrees with* Isaiah xli. 18. I will open Rivers in high Places, and Fountains in the Midst of Vallies: I will make the Wilderness a Pool of Water, and the dry Land Springs, *&c. See also* Ps. civ. 10.

What Wonders have not GOD's true Prophets done?
Which none can doubt whoe'er the Scriptures read.
(55) Judgments difplay'd, and welcome Favours fhown
To the (56) Difeas'd; nay, even rais'd the Dead!
And fure Heav'n's Powers, (57) from all Ages paft,
Do ftill exift, and will unto the laft.

Did

---

(55) "*Talis fuit* Dathani, & Abironis *exitus, quos* MOSEN *perduelli* "*animo obfirmatos hiatu discendens miserabiliter absorpsit. Talis mors* Abfalonis, "*quem majestatis pertinacem reum feralis hasta confixit. Tale quinquaginta* "*satellitum, quos in* ELIAM *parvæ reverentes cœlum flammarum globis armatum* "*devoravit. Tale fuit* Hebræi *hominis exitium, quem cum infami* Madianitide "*vindex trajecit gladius, & lectulum genialem miscuit cum funebri.*" WHICH WORDS OF *DREXELIUS*, in his Preparation for Death, &c., I thus endeavour to render: Such was the dreadful End of *Dathan* and *Abiron*, for whom (for departing, thro' their obftinate Temper, from MOSES, who proved GOD in his Creation by Tranfmutation of his Rod into a Serpent, plaguing *Egypt*, turning the Rivers into Blood, and dividing the Sea, &c.) the Earth open'd, and fwallow'd them up, NUMB. xvi. 32. As fuch appeared the Fate of *Abfalon*, who, for rebelling againft his royal Father, was pierced through the Heart with a deadly Spear, II. SAM. viii. 14, 15. The Companies of 50 armed Guards, who, with too little Reverence, had fummon'd the Prophet ELIJAH before their Prince, Heaven deftroy'd them with Globes of Fire, II. KINGS, i. 10, &c. (as tho' they were the Arrows mention'd by *David*, Pfal. cxliv. 6.) And fuch was the Cataftrophe of the unfortunate *Hebrew*, with the infamous *Midianitess*, *Num*. xxv. 8. ftabb'd together in their very Crime, by the Avenger of Wickednefs, whofe Sword mingled the genial Bed with all the mournful Signs of a fpeedy approaching Mortality.

(56) Refembling what GOD was pleas'd to fhew to afflicted *Job*: For when he had humbled himfelf, as mention'd in *Chap*. xi. 4, 5, we are told, from a Tradition of the Eaftern Inhabitants, that, upon the Almighty's purpofing to make no farther Tryal of that illuftrious Sufferer, he fent the Angel *Gabriel* from Heaven; who, taking him by the Hand, rais'd him on his Feet: And ftriking the Earth with his Foot, immediately fprung up a clear Fountain; in which Water *Job* having bath'd himfelf, as alfo taken fome internally, he became as healthful as ever he had been in his juvenile Years.

(57) If we look but in the Writings of the Prophet *Jeremiah*, *Isaiah*, *Habakkuk*, &c., we fhall foon be convinc'd of the Almighty Power and Majefty from and to all Eternity.

Did not (58) *Elisha* Iron cause to swim,
  Without the (59) Load-Stone, passing Nature's Laws;
And other Wonders are ascrib'd to HIM,
  Thro' GOD, who made the World, the supreme Cause.
CHRIST from the Cave caus'd *Lazarus* to come;
And after Death rose from the silent Tomb.

So said, with Tears, he plac'd the Virgin's Head
  Close to the Wound by which the Sword did sever;
And then with Decency his Mantle spread
  O'er the fair Corpse, that now was join'd together.
JESU! *said he*, whose Love did chiefly move
This Virgin's Heart to honour Thee above!

Hear now our Pray'rs, which ardently we make;
  Your holy Martyr to new Life restore:
Still, still to praise Thee for Thy People's Sake,
  That so her Virtues may shine more and more.
She lov'd you dear; for you her Soul did melt;
And for your Sake the Pains of Death she felt.

Let now your Pow'r to the World appear,
  Tho' far unworthy to be blest again
With such a Saint, that from an heav'nly Sphere
  We should call back to cause her future Pain:
But as poor Souls are precious in Thy Sight;
Let Her, thro' Thee, prove to the Earth a Light.

Think

---

(58) II. KINGS vi. 6. *And the Man of God said, Where fell it? And he shew'd him the place. And he cut down a stick, and cast it in thither, and the IRON did swim.*

(59) Or Magnet, *the Verticity of which was discover'd about* 400 *Years ago, by the learned* ROGER BACON. *It has two Poles, N. and S. diversely inclin'd towards the Center of the Earth, yet mutual in their Attraction to Iron or Steel. But I refer the Reader to* HARRIS'S Lexicon Technicum *for a further Account.*

Think of Thy Church, and promifed Defence,
  (60) 'Gainſt Waters Rage, and horrid Flames of Fire;
And let us know thy great Omnipotence,
  That this thy fallen Servant my refpire.
Pity her Fate, commiferate our Fears;
Regard our State, and mitigate our Cares.

May facred Virgins e'er admire her Charms,
  Who conſtant fought Thee as her chiefeſt Good;
And ſtrive to be encircled in thine Arms,
  Altho' vile Mortals feek to fhed their Blood:
And when more perfect made, late may the Urn
Receive her Mold, her Spirit to Thee return.

Being divine! O grant us our Defire!
  Re-animate this dear, this lifelefs Clay!
(61) Son! with the Father! Holy Ghoſt! infpire!
  Thou Source of Light! of Truth! the Life! the Way! (62)
More did he pray, than can recite my Pen:
To which the People, weeping, cry'd, *Amen.*

Then did the Virgin raife their Hopes forlorn:
  Moving the Veil that cover'd her fair Face:
And as the Sun-Beams gild the rifing Morn,
  Gently fhe rofe from humid Earth's Embrace;
Saluted all that humbly kneeling were,
And with them offered up due Thanks in Pray'r.

'Tis

---

(60) ISAIAH xliii. 2. *When thou paſſest thro' the Waters I will be with thee; and thro' the Rivers they shall not overflow thee; when thou walkest thro' the Fire, thou shalt not be burnt; neither shall the Flame kindle upon thee.*

(61) *The bright Morning Star.* REV. xxii. 16.

(62) JOH. xiv. ISA. xxx. 21. And in many other Places are exhibited the divine Influences of the bleſſed Trinity.

'Tis hard to fay what inward Raptures mov'd,
  When they this wond'rous Miracle beheld!
Such furely were by gracious Heav'n approv'd,
  Which view'd the Tears in ev'ry Eye that well'd:
For round her neck did feem a Thread of Silk,
Whiter than Skin, which was as white as Milk. (63)

Some Legends fay, the Circle was of Red;
  Of Scarlet Dye, like Blood which from her flow'd;
But, to pafs by Reports which might be fpread,
  Let us remark how well fhe ferv'd her GOD.
No Heart inflam'd could fhow more Love than fhe;
A perfect PATTERN of true PIETY!

For once more BU'NO made her take the Veil
  Of Sanctimony, facredly to dwell;
And then to *Ireland* that Saint did fail,
  Leaving the humble Virgin to her Cell.
(64) Near to the Church feven Years fhe liv'd profefs'd,
And as a darling SAINT by all confefs'd.

She had Confeffors: (65) SENAN one by Name;
  A Prieft, whofe facred Knowledge made him fhine;
The other, (66) DEIFER, of equal Fame,
  That, like the former, led a Life divine,
Thefe told her how fhe might the Church obey,
And yet her Virtues to the World difplay.

Nor

---

(63) *The first Syllable of her Name* WIN, &c., *in the* Saxon *Tongue, being to* win, get, *or* obtain ; *and the latter,* FRED, *or* FRID, *denoting* Peace: *But the Britons are said to call it* GUINFRID, *which is interpreted* WHITE, *fair, and of a beautiful Aspect, answering to the lovely Character I have given. Tradition has it, That after her Death, when her Spirit appeared to any of her Votaries, either to comfort them in Sickness, or warn them of their approaching Dissolution, they presently knew her by the aforesaid Circle. The Miracle is said to have been perform'd about the Year of Salvation* 644.

(64) *Her House I have seen delineated, as tho' the Building, or Part thereof, was yet remaining.*

(65) *He deceased in the Year of Incarnation* 660.

(66) *He died A.D.* 664, *much about the Time of S.* WINEFRED'S *Death. Both were so remarkable in discharging the Duties of their Christian Profession,*
that

Nor failed to come a (67) noble beauteous Train
  Of DAMSELS, who lived round in Piety:
The Duties learnt, fhe taught to them again,
  To love the LORD in pure Virginity;
And, warn'd by Heav'n near (68) *Denbigh* did refide,
In which fair Convent VIRGINS did abide.

For in the Middle of the filent Night,
  Good DEIFER was order'd, in a Dream,
To warn St. WINEFRED to take her Flight,
  And go to Holy SATURN, call'd by Name:
Whofe Head was cover'd o'er with Silver Hairs;
And crown'd by Learning, as he was by Years.

Scarce filver-fhining *Cynthia* ceas'd to fhed
  Her lunar Glory, and the rifing Sun
Had fipp'd the pearly Dews, as from his Bed
  He rofe his conftant circling Courfe to run:
Who with parental Love, and genial Heat,
Enliven'd where he fhone with Joys compleat.

He had but juft peep'd o'er the dusky Hills,
  When the fair Saint was at her Morning Pray'rs;
Whofe weeping Eyes did flow like cryftal Rills,
  And as bright Pearls appear'd her falling Tears.
She took her leave, and haften'd to that Cell,
Where Him fhe fought with Sanctity did dwell.

He

---

that whilst St. BUENO *was enabled by the* Britifh *Nobility to erect several Churches, he did not forget to have them dedicated to their immortal Honour.*

(67) *It is recorded, They were Ladies and Gentlewomen of very great Families, according to the plain Manners and Customs of that Age.*

(68) *By the* Britons *called* KLED-VRYN, *signifying the craggy Hill; formerly the old Town, where the present Church stands. The new one is at the Bottom of the Mount, more conveniently situated.*

He, like (69) ANTONIUS, took moſt ſweet Delight
In Contemplation of GOD'S Works ſo fair;
The (70) Elemental Change of Day and Night,
With various Seaſons of the rolling Year:
Each Equinox of (71) Spring and (72) Fall he knew;
The Summer's (73) Solſtice, and the (74) Winter's too.

He knew each Seed contain'd a Plant in kind;
And in that Plant a Seed of Species new;
In which another Plant did lurk behind,
And there a Seed of diff'rent Nature grew.
So without End from what they firſt aroſe;
And all by Moiſture, which from *Terra* flows.

This, preſs'd by Air, found Paſſage to the Roots,
He knew, was pregnant with Salts, Sulphur, Oyls;
That ſubtle Sap, in Sun-ſhine upward ſhoots,
Which Night condenſes, ripens as it cools:
How (75) Infects Eggs in Water, Air or Earth,
By *Sol's* bright Rays receive their favour'd Birth.

How

---

(69) *A noble Ægyptian Monk and Hermit, that liv'd One Hundred and Five Years, the most part in great Sanctity.*

(70) *Elementa, cælum, ortus & occasus siderum, diurnæ nocturnæque vicissitudines, quadripartita anni varietas, quæ duo aquinoctia vere, & autumno: ac totidem solstitia æstate & hieme complectitur, quorum decursu herbæ exolescunt & deficiunt, suoque tempore emergunt ac reviviscunt, quum multa indicent ac commonstrent, tum à morte ad vitam reversionem ac reditum, quo suo tempore corpora per resurrectionem restituenda sunt in integrum, documenta præbent.* LEM. de occult. Nat.

O LORD, how manifold are thy Works! in wiſdom haſt thou made them all: the earth is full of thy riches. So is this great and wide ſea, &c. PSAL. civ. 24, &c.

(71) March 10. (72) Sept. 11. *When equal Day and Night.*

(73) Circ. JUN. 11. (74) DEC. 11. *Longest and Shortest.*

(75) *Nihil in natura rerum tam minutum, tamque vile, aut abjectum, quod non aliquid admirationis hominibus adferat,*

How unfeen Fluid, which the Globe furrounds,
  Helpful to Plants, or animalian Life,
And ev'ry Ufe; as well in forming Sounds,
  That charm the Ear, and footh a World of Strife:
How agitated, heated, cool'd, congeal'd,
Comprefs'd, by hidden Caufes, or reveal'd.

Such the (76) Sun's Rays, or fubterraneous Fire;
  Sulphurs and Salts which here and there do float;
Nitres that fix, and Clouds approaching nigher,
  All which the various Winds we hear promote:
Hard Storms that hurtful Vapours far dilate;
And Breezes foft to cool the fultry Heat.

How Exhalations from the Mines below
  Caufe Lightning blaze, and Thunder to refound;
Why Dews, with Showers of Rain, and Hail, or Snow,
  Too heavy grown, alternate fpread the Ground:
How Ocean's daily Steams, forc'd by the Wind,
Sink into Mountains 'till a Vent they find.

Thefe Sources form, whence Rivulets proceed,
  Which leffer Rivers caufe, as great Ones do;
Whofe flowing Streams encircle as they fpeed,
  As which fhould foremoft yield the Sea its due:
Whofe Waters, balanc'd in GOD'S pow'rful Hand,
Seem but a Drop, the Earth a Grain of Sand.

SATURN did ftudy what pertain'd to Fate,
  Much like our Bodies to Sepulchres led;
Reviv'd in vernal Blooms, which fhews that State,
  When Lands and Oceans fhall yield up their Dead:
Why Darknefs to reviving Light gives Way,
And *Phofphor* ufhers in the coming Day.

Or

---

(76) This was the Doctrine of *Zoroaster*, a Philofopher near the *Persian* Gulph, mention'd in the Travels of *Cyrus*.

Or why *Aurora*, with her darting Gleams,
  Unfolds æthereal Gates that Sol might ſhine;
Or ſtreak the Eaſt with his refulgent Beams,
  Like Harbingers ſent with a Pow'r divine:
Why twinkling Stars do ſeem to quit their Spheres,
When *Phœbus* with his glorious Face appears.

Why Earthquakes happen, whence the reſtleſs Tide,
  That in ſome Kingdoms drown adjacent Lands;
In other Places, failing to preſide,
  Appear arenal and delightful Strands;
'Till changing, like ſucceſſive Wind and Rain,
All peaceful ſeem their former State to gain.

Thro' Nature's Womb he'd ſee moſt hidden Things,
  Why Waters petrify, or Land gives Way;
Why flaming Mountains, or ſtrange boiling Springs,
  Whence various Diſports on the Land or Sea:
Each Min'rals Force in ſubterraneous Streams;
And Comet's Power, which the Sky inflames.

Why fruitful Earth, when bleſs'd with timely Show'rs:
  Gives Juice and Verdure both to Herbs and Trees;
Beauty to Gardens, grac'd with various Flow'rs,
  And grateful Odours, that our Smelling pleaſe:
Why genial Heats cauſe Birds and Beaſts to love,
And piercing Cold our nervous Senſes move.

The Sun's Propenſion to'ards the diſtant (77) Poles,
  His Declination from æſtival Height;
Why that revolving Luminary rolls,
  'Till *Hyem's* Signs he doth in Order greet:
How the bright Moon doth thro' the (78) *Zodiack* ſteer
Within one Month what takes him up a Year.

                                                 What

What Springs the human Body do compofe;
  How interweaving Art'ries, Nerves and Veins,
Form Bafons, Pumps, Canals; what Liquid flows
  Throughout the whole; how moving Solid reigns:
Why Cartilages, Bones, and Mufcles fine,
Form Cords and Levers for this nice Machine.

Since Heav'nly Pow'rs created all thefe Things,
  Blefs'd, *he would fay*, thofe who adore GOD'S Name,
For WHOM great Bifhops, Nobles, Princes, Kings,
  Have Structures rais'd, to their moft pious Fame;
Where faithful Souls cœleftial Doctrines hear,
With filial Love and reverential Fear.

Tho' well he knew, as learn'd St. PAUL did tell, (79)
  GOD did not *dwell in Temples made with Hands;*
His Omniprefence he would yet reveal,
  Beyond Circumference of Seas or Lands:
For as fam'd (80) *Lucan* owns, look where you will,
Th' Almighty Being will be prefent ftill.

In HIM was All, beyond all Nature's Laws;
  The primal Caufe; THIS, SATURN had allur'd;
Made him flight Riches, covet no Applaufe;
  Altho' not like an Anchoret immur'd:
But to all Comers open was his Cell,
That all might witnefs how the Saint did dwell.

'Twas

---

(77) The Points, from North to South, on which the Axis of the World is by the Learned faid to turn round.

(78) A Circle of greateft Magnitude on the material Sphere, which equally feparates the Æquinoctial, or Equator. In the Middle is the Ecliptic, beneath which the Sun moveth.

(79) *Acts* xvii. 24. *GOD made the World, &c.*

(80) JUPITER *est quodcunque vides, quocunque moveris.*

'Twas fituated on a fair Afcent,
  Within a Rock, whence he the Ocean view'd:
Here, with much Labour, gaining fweet Content,
  He added Rooms to what old Hermits hew'd;
Incrufted round with Shells like fhining Ore,
Which had been gather'd from the neighb'ring Shore

More inward was a Chapel, fmall, but neat;
  Where, by removal of a Stone, the Light
From the bright Eaft, an Altar moft compleat,
  Cut in the Rock, charm'd the Spe&ators Sight!
For whom he pray'd in Tears, fince well he knew
Thofe melting Signs would fet them weeping too. (81)

Before the outward Door, there was a Green,
  By Flowers enamel'd, where a Spring did run:
On either Side embow'ring Trees were feen,
  To skreen from Wind, or fhade from Heat of Sun.
Here warbling Birds, which often hither came,
Did join with SATURN, and the purling Stream.

Tall was his Perfon, of majeftick Air;
  His Beard to Girdle reach'd, his Robe to Feet;
Sanguine his Cheeks, his Forehead high and bare,
  With Eyes quick-piercing, and a Voice moft fweet.
Humble and courteous, as the Scriptures tell,
Like Bleffed J E S U S, at *Samaria's* Well. (82)

This was the Man, fo much by Heav'n belov'd,
  Fit to make known what G O D would not conceal;
An Angel's Theme unto a Prieft approv'd,
  That fhould, like (83) ANANIAS, Truth reveal;
Tell to the lovely VIRGIN how to trace
Her weary Steps, and find a refting Place.

None

---

(81) ———————————*Si vis me flere, dolendum est*
  Primùm ipsi tibi; tunc tua me infortunia lædent,
  TELEPHE! — HOR.   (82) JOH. iv.
(83) *Acts* ix. 17. *And* Ananias *went his way, &c.*

None but an Angel let him underſtand,
　That She, whom CHRIST did love, was on the Road.
This caus'd the holy Hermit, out of hand,
　Place All in order in His ſweet Abode :
Which ſhows, that Cleanlineſs, how poor we be,
Agrees with true religious Piety.

And as deſcending to'ards the flow'ry Plain,
　He ſaw how nimbly ſhe her Steps did trace
More fleet and fair than Nymphs, whom Poets feign,
　Becauſe adorn'd with Angel's Mein and Grace :
Faſt as his Feet could move, he ſtrove to meet;
And then, as Words could flow, with Kindneſs greet.

The Cell attain'd, both on their bended Knees,
　Moſt humble Thanks did offer up to Heav'n ;
Which done, what Food he had wherewith to pleaſe,
　With Pleaſure to the holy Maid was giv'n :
Her Drink was Water, clear as Cryſtal fine ;
More ſweet to her, than any ſparkling Wine.

Refreſhment o'er, the Hill on t'other Side,
　With the fair VIRGIN, he did ſlow deſcend ;
As tho' that Time too faſt away did ſlide
　To part him from ſo dear a heav'n-lov'd Friend :
And, as he went, the Ways he eaſier made,
Removing Brakes that ſhe might ſofter tread.

Where ends my Travel ? *cry'd the Virgin chaſte.*
　Daughter, *ſaid he,* thou well-belov'd of Heav'n,
To fair (84) *Clutina's* Vale, I pray you, haſte ;
　Where further Knowledge will to thee be giv'n.
You ſoon will meet a dear and heav'nly Friend,
Who knows your coming, and can tell your End.

　　　　　　　　　　　　　　　　　　See

---

(84) So called from the pleaſant River *Cluyd,* which ſeparates the Province of *Flint* from that of *Denbigh.*

See yonder Rocks and Precipices dire,
  That feem conjoin'd, and as (85) embattel'd rife;
Proceed that Way, in Thoughts to Heav'n afpire,
  The more you view thofe Mountains touch the Skies.
Admire the Hand of GOD in all his Ways;
For Nature's Works declare her Maker's Praife.

But left Night fhadows e'er you reach the Vale,
  As 'twill, I believe, before I can my Cell;
Keep the right Hand towards the flow'ry Dale,
  And by Sun-fet you'll find an Houfe to dwell:
For o'er the Door is written: PILGRIMS, *dear !*
Enter, you'll find kind Entertainment here.

And when To-morrow near thofe Hills you come,
  You'll fee they part, and foon will greet your Eyes
The lovely (86) Valley in its fpangling Bloom,
  With Sweets and Odours, to your pleas'd Surprize.
Fair Groves and Meadows charm on ev'ry Side,
And in the Middle cryftal Streams do glide.

Daughter, if I may call you fo, farewell!
  Happy, fince CHRIST enjoys your tender Heart:
My Pray'rs fhall be for you within my Cell,
  Heav'n to receive you, when from Earth you part.
Thank you, Good Father; but I pray beftow
Your Benediction on me e'er I go.

His

---

(85) *Mira enim naturæ folertia montium horum juga mænium pinnas mentiuntur.* THAT IS, For fuch is the admirable Workmanfhip of Nature that the Tops of the *Eaftern* Mountains refemble the Battlements of *ftrong* Walls, &c.

(86) CAMDEN, alfo writing of *Denbighfhire*, fays, The Vale (which is about 17 Miles long from N. to S. and 5 broad towards the Sea) is adorn'd with green Meadows, yellow Corn-Fields, many fair Houfes, and beautiful Churches. The Eye muft needs be charm'd with fuch a fair and lovely Profpect.

His Bleſſing giv'n, quick ſhe trod the Ground,
   And by Sun-ſet approach'd a lovely Field;
When a (87) White-Houſe near to a Church ſhe found,
   With Gates and Doors that did a Splendor yield:
The ſame wherein ſhe was to lodge that Night;
Where Peace did dwell, and Virtue ſhined bright.

The Damſels, who this Hoſpital did keep,
   With Emulation ſtrove moſt to attend,
Until their lovely Gueſt inclin'd to ſleep;
   Then to GOD'S Safety her they recommend.
All early roſe, and ſetting forward ſoon,
Sweetly they journey'd 'till it was high Noon.

When, having reſted, to take ſome Repaſt,
   Which they had brought, beneath an Oaken Tree;
With Love endearing they did part at laſt,
   In mutual Kindneſs and Sincerity:
Some Steps they trod, look'd back, and bid farewell!
Then ſhook their Hands, with Sighs no Words can tell.

And now ſhe haſtens, then a while ſhe reſts;
   Her Eyes, to Heav'n up-lifted, flow in Tears;
Her lilly Hands, near to her riſing Breaſts
   Infolded, ſhow her Zeal in fervent Pray'rs.
The Pow'r unſeen, who every Action knows,
Protects the charming Virgin as ſhe goes.

Or elſe, kind Reader, think how Angels bright
   Hover'd around her with their ſhielding Wings:
For when a Sinner turns, with great Delight
   'Tis known in Heav'n; the Tyding quickly rings:
And as great Joy doth fill the higher Sphere, (88)
Saints do not want their kind Protection here.

                                                    The

---

(87) *Called* Tyguyn *by the ancient* BRITONS.
(88) LUKE xv. 7. *I say unto you that likewise joy, &c.*

The Virgin pafs'd thro' fev'ral pleafant Vills;
  Beheld the Beauties of the charming Vale;
View'd Churches, Houfes, Fountains, Brooks and Rills;
  Whatever Art or Nature did reveal:
Fair Nymphs and Swains, for Charms and Strength renown'd;
Fine Flocks and Herds, with which they did abound.

But while thefe Things revolved in her Mind,
  What Bleffings Heav'n did to the Earth impart;
Soon fhe perceiv'd how glitt'ring Turrets fhin'd,
  Which rais'd Ejaculations from her Heart.
She wept for Joy to find a Place on Earth,
To live to die; and die an happy Death.

The Convent met her in their Habits meet;
  Tears in their Eyes, they bid her welcome home;
Each Virgin kifs'd her; fome did wafh her Feet;
  And All were pleas'd the Saint to them was come.
Thrice happy fhall we be, each Lady faid;
Blefs'd is the Place, where lives fo dear a Maid.

Wytheriacus was the Building call'd; (89)
  Part govern'd by THEONYE, Abbefs fam'd;
And where, contiguous, very ftrongly wall'd,
  Were Monks, taught by her Son, (90) *Elerius* nam'd;
Soon after which in CHRIST fhe did expire,
Whilft he was Prieft to all the Virgin Choir. (91)

Soon

---

(89) *Commonly called* Guitherine, *in* North-Wales, *within the Province of* Denbigh; *which is a most healthful Country.*

(90) It was this Gentleman that erected the Monaftery; who, by conjoining the Exercifes of eremitical and monaftical Converfation, had fundry Difciples of religious Gentlemen and Ladies under one Roof, tho' in different Apartments.

(91) *However, 'tis said, that he was Confessor to S.* Winefred; *and is very much commended for his Piety and Learning.*

Soon to the lovely Saint, as One divine,
   He urg'd the Office, as moſt fit to rule;
And make the Houſe ſtill more and more to ſhine,
   Thro' her Improvements in Religion's School.
For who more fit than ſhe to be obey'd,
That had ſuch glorious Chaſtity diſplay'd?

Humility now lovely did appear
   In her, whoſe Charity was unconſtrain'd:
To various Wants ſhe did her Bounties ſhare,
   With Words ſo ſoft that due Attention gain'd.
Labour enjoin'd, when ſhe thought fit and meet,
Were to the Virgins eaſy, pleaſant, ſweet.

Some ſpun raw Wool; nor others did diſdain
   To twirl the Spindle with their Fingers ſmall.
To 'tend the Sick, and keep the Chambers clean,
   Seem'd no Diſhonour to the Beſt of All:
Alternately ſuch Offices they ſhar'd;
And who prov'd humbleſt was the moſt rever'd.

The pretty Birds that thro' the Air do ſkim;
   Beaſts of all Kinds which on the Earth abide;
The ſhining Fiſhes, that in Oceans ſwim,
   Or what in cryſtal Rivers ſwiftly glide:
Theſe pious Ladies clearly did impart,
Thro' Strength of Thought, with curious Needle's Art.

The SPRING, as riſing in its Infant-State,
   With *Flora's* fair Diverſity of Blooms;
Not ſcorch'd as yet by too fermenting Heat;
   But, like fair *Tempe's* Airs, ſheds ſweet Perfumes:
And SUMMER too, with all its Charms o'er-ſpread,
In lovely Manner were by Them diſplay'd.

                                        Summits,

Summits, like *Ida's* Pines, which reach the Clouds;
  Around subsiding Fountains, Groves and Fields;
Plains, grac'd with Avenues, like bless'd Abodes;
  And ev'ry counter Walk that Pleasure yields:
With ev'ry Plant King Solomon could tell,
Those Ladies Fingers wrought exceeding well.

Cities they wrought near undulating Streams,
  Which by Reflection two-fold did appear;
Like Mirror Lakes, when Nature downward seems,
  With Earths conjoin'd, and separated Air:
As tho' by Shades of Swans, or Ships, or Trees,
So near we view'd far-off *Antipodes*.

Autumn resembled much our Lives Decay,
  By falling Leaves, when Melancholly reigns;
And Death-like Winter, short'ning more the Day,
  Transform'd the Waters into gelid Plains.
Thus did the Virgins trace the Seasons round,
And shew'd the Works of Heav'n to be profound.

At Meals Instructions most divine were giv'n;
  Or Lives of Saints read of fair *Anglia's* Line:
Such who were judg'd for Virtue bless'd in Heav'n,
  And who on Earth would never cease to shine.
Whilst thus to active Piety inclin'd,
A sure Defence was placed o'er the Mind.

In Painting some would draw the Martyrs dear,
  How rack'd, and scourg'd, suspended, burnt to death:
Yet in their Torments shew'd no Signs of Fear,
  But rather Courage, 'till their latest Breath:
Whom Tyrants Threats nor Promises could move
To save their Lives, such was to Christ their Love!

Others

Others again defcrib'd immortal Joys,
   Like *Nectar's* Streams diftill'd o'er pearly Sand:
How blifsful Torrents, with harmonious Noife,
   Adorn the Meadows of that heav'nly Land;
Where fmiling Banks are crown'd with fadelefs Flow'rs,
And martyr'd Virgin's blefs'd in facred Bow'rs.

The END of the Second PART.

British PIETY Display'd

In the GLORIOUS

LIFE, Suffering, and DEATH

Of the Blessed

St. WINEFRED:

A Noble VIRGIN, martyr'd for her renowned Chastity, in *Wales:* Where, at Her Celebrated FOUNTAIN, called HOLY-WELL, many afflicted Persons have been happily freed from their most dangerous Distempers in past Centuries: The salutiferous Quality of which Water, continuing in the present Age, occasions its FAME to be spread in far-distant Kingdoms.

Ecclesia nunquam florentior, quam cum afflictior inter cruces & gladios suorum martyrum pugnas & victorias spectavit.— Natura rerum ad Deum nos erigit. Quam magnifica sunt Opera Tua, DOMINE!

"*DEUS ter Optimus Maximus in aquis summas excellentissimas recondivit vires salutares, quarum tanta est præstantia ut longè multumque omnibus aliis remediorum generibus sint superiores.*" That is, *The Most Glorious and Omnipotent* GOD *has conceal'd the greatest and most excellent salubrious Efficacy in the Waters; which have so prevalent a Power, that they are far superior to all other Kinds of Remedies.*

PART the Third.

YORK: Printed and Sold by the Author THO. GENT, in *Petergate, Anno Dom.* MDCCXLII.

I was glad when they faid unto me, Let us go into the Houfe of the LORD.

Pray for the Peace of Jerufalem: they fhall profper that love thee. *Pfal.* cxxii.

Venerationis locus in templo eft.

By Faith Abraham *when he was tried offered up his Son* Ifaac, Heb. xi. 17. —— *GOD fo loved the World, that he gave his only begotten Son, that whofoever believeth in him fhould not perifh, but have everlafting life.* Joh. iii.

Many are my perfecutors, and mine enemies: yet I do not decline from thy teftimonies. *Pfal.* cxix. 157.

I will wafh mine Hands in Innocency: fo will I compafs Thine Altar, O LORD! Psal. xxvi. 6.

The Third PART of
The Holy LIFE and DEATH of
S. WINEFRED.

Continuation of the Eighth CHAPTER.

SOME Virgins, in embroider'd Work employ'd,
  With Silk and Silver curioufly inlaid,
Adorn'd the Rooms, in which appear'd no Void,
  But Art induftrious feem'd moft fair array'd.
But whilft fome Scarlet fpun; which Ladies wore;
Others made Garments for the needy Poor.

The Chapel was adorn'd with Di'monds bright;
  The Hyacinth, the (92) Em'rald, and (93) Saphire:
Deep Sardins black, and Golden Chryfolite;
  Opal and Iris; Rubies feem'd like Fire.
Fine precious Stones, and Pearls for Diadems,
With Life of CHRIST inlaid amidft the Gems.

The (94) Parent-Colours here were plainly feen;
  The tawney Orange, and the flaming Red;
The fainting Vi'let, and refrefhing Green,
  And diff'rent Blues that in the Skies are fpread:
With Lilly white, that Nature feem'd to glow,
Exhibiting both Scenes of Joy and Woe.

As

---

(92) Its Vertue is faid to expel the fatal Effects of Poyfon.
(93) *Pliny* writes, that it's of a fine blue, or azure Colour.
(94) "*Perfecta pulchritudo sita est in suavitate coloris, & harmonia* "*membrorum.* PLATO.

As of CHRIST'S wond'rous Birth, and Senfe divine;
  The (95) Miracles which he ftupendous wrought;
Endearing Meeknefs, that fo bright did fhine,
  Surpaffing ev'ry human Act or Thought:
And as he nearer to his Paffion drew,
Attracting Sights did offer to his View.

For as amidft the Twelve he feem'd to fit,
  Shewing his Fate, in breaking of the Bread;
JUDAS did feem to be in fullen Fit,
  And PETER tho' of Fear he had no Dread.
Alas! their Weaknefs our Redeemer knew,
And prophefy'd what foon became too true.

Ent'ring the (96) Garden, there he was difplay'd,
  With Sadnefs fill'd, by his Apoftles feen:
And, whilft they flept, moft fervently he pray'd,
  Kneeling in Sorrow on the verdant Green:
Whilft Drops of Sweat increafed like a Flood
Of intermingled Water with his Blood.

Next Scene difcover'd CHRIST as Captive led
  To CAIPHAS, and of his own deny'd; (97)
Accus'd, as having much Diftraction bred,
  To PILATE; and to HEROD fent in Pride.
Scoff'd at, brought back, and ftript unto to the Skin,
To wound his precious Body for our Sin.

O cruel

---

(95) I refer the Reader for a fhort Account of them to a little Book in Verfe, fet forth by me; which I carefully extracted from the Evangelical and Ecclefiaftical Writers, in an eafy, chronological Manner, for my better underftanding.

(96) *In the 26th Chapter of St.* Matthew, *Ver.* 30, *&c.*

(97) *But he deny'd before them all saying, &c. Ver.* 70.

O cruel Lictors! worſe than Heathen *Rome!*
To bind our dear Redeemer's ſacred Hands!
His Body ſcourge, 'till precious Blood did come!
  Where but from Hell had you ſuch dire Commands?
Pilate did waſh his Hands; but, gracelefs, you
Compell'd the Judge to what he would not do.

Nor this enough, you thought: A ſcarlet Robe
  Cloſe to His wounded Body girt with Zone;
A Crown of Thorns, as tho' his Head you'd probe,
  With num'rous Wounds; theſe you with Scorn put on:
You pull'd the Garment off to cauſe more Pain; (98)
And let the tort'ring Diadem remain.

Women beholding ſeem'd for to deplore;
  Bearing his Croſs, which ſcarcely could be borne;
And as he fell, with Clubs they bruis'd moſt ſore
  That ſacred Fleſh their Rods and Whips had torne.
Well might he ſay Words melting and divine,
Were ever Sorrows like to theſe of mine!

Thus did the Virgins paint the (99) Lamb of God,
  Fair without (100) Blemiſh, brighter far than Gold;
That Lamb, which is the (101) Light of Heav'n's Abode,
  Of Whom the (102) noble Prophet had foretold;
The Croſs, the Altar, with the Sacrifice;
And mournful Angels hov'ring in the Skies.

What

---

(98) *It is astonishing to think of their unheard-of Cruelty; that, whilst they mock'd our Blessed* LORD, *they should invent Torments answerable to their malicious Contempt. The Robe, which they had fixed close to his Body, became cemented with his precious Blood; so that when they tore it off by Violence, it no doubt caused great Misery. The Thorns occasion'd 72 Wounds, saith* Oroſius.

(99) *Joh.* i. 29.——(100) I. *Pet.* i. 19.——(101) *Rev.* xxi. 23.
(102) *Isa.* liii. 7.

What Sorrow did the Virgin MARY feel,
  An Evangelick Quill doth plain impart; (103)
Such as more piercing prov'd than deadly Steel,
  A Sword of Grief to wound her tender Heart!
Well may ſhe be in future Ages blefs'd,
As by her Son's dear Church ſhe is confefs'd.

Thus having ſhewn him in the Pains of Death,
  And lifelefs like an harmlefs Lamb that's ſlain;
His Brightnefs quickly pierc'd the folid Earth,
  And caus'd the Gates of Hell to burſt in twain:
A joyful Time to Thofe who were detain'd,
When they at length their bleſſed Freedom gain'd.

For when that NICODEMUS, Ruler bright,
  With pious JOSEPH, did the Corpfe obtain;
Embalm'd with Spices, wrapt in Linnen white,
  Had laid it in a Monument moſt clean:
The Pow'rs of Hell and Earth became afraid,
When Strength divine had rais'd him from the Dead.

But his Difciples beſt of all could tell,
  When to their wond'rous Sight he did appear;
What Sweetnefs to their Souls he did reveal,
  As likewife to his tender Mother dear;
'Till forty Days b'ing paſt, he did afcend
To Heav'n's high Kingdom, which will never end.

From thence he fent to them the HOLY GHOST,
  Which his Difciples did fo high infpire,
That thofe who heard them feem'd in Raptures loſt,
  Whilſt o'er their Heads appeared Tongues like Fire.
And as an Emblem of cœleſtial ⁰ Love,
There hover'd in the Midſt an heav'nly Dove.

Then

---

(103) *Luk.* ii. 35. * *Acts* ii.

Then all the Saints, in proper Order plac'd,
  Seem'd to difplay the high fupernal Court;
Each Nitch was with a comely Image grac'd,
  And all the Pillars of majeftic Sort.
The Windows glorious, lofty ev'ry Spire,
That charm'd the Sight, and did the Mind infpire.

St. CHRISTOPHER, who bore the heav'nly Child,
  Seem'd to wade deeper in the fwelling River;
Whilft on his Shoulders the fweet Infant fmil'd,
  Pleas'd that his Weight had made the ftrong Man quiver.
Thrice happy Thofe, to whom our Lord appears,
And ftrikes their Souls with holy Joys or Fears!

The Pulpit moft ftupendous did appear,
  With glitt'ring Angels; Figures of pure Gold;
Seraphs and Cherubs; all the Orders were,
  As tho' alive, fo nat'ral to behold:
The TABERNACLE in exalted Place,
And every Thing that could GOD'S Altar grace.

The Tombs of Paftors, Lords, or Hero's great,
  Were here and there in decent Manner rais'd;
Fair Ladies who had rais'd the Church's State,
  Here found Sepulchres, and were folemn prais'd:
And thus next Heav'n their Oratory feem'd;
Or *Noah's* Ark, a Place of Safety deem'd.

For here the Sick were cured by her Prayers;
  Deep Wounded Spirits met Soul-faving Health:
Whilft the Opprefs'd were eafed of their Cares,
  And Poor fupply'd with beft of well-fpar'd Wealth.
None to the Gates that came to beg or pray,
For JESU'S Sake, were empty fent away.

                              O what

O what a lovely SANCTUARY this!
   Blefs'd *Afylum* to thofe who were oppreft!
Inftead of Sorrow, here to meet with Blifs!
   Or yokeful Labours, find refrefhing Reft!
Such as make eafy Life's hard Pilgrimage,
And help them over this terreftrial Stage.

For when the Sick were on their Death-Beds laid,
   There wanted not with them who did condole;
But, what was more, due Preparation made,
   Whereby to fave each dear immortal Soul;
And, when the fleeting Ghofts this Earth did leave,
Took Care to lay their Bodies in the Grave.

CHAP.

CHAP. IX.

The Argument.

Virgins S. WINEFRED furround,
Whilft fhe declares her Thoughts profound;
From Reafon and from Scripture tells
What's Happinefs, and where it dwells.

YE facred Virgins, innocent and fair,
　　Who now are (104) veil'd, to ferve the Lord of Heav'n,
O let the Words, which I fhall here declare,
　　Deep in your tender Hearts be fo engrav'n;
That, leaving Parents, *People,* All, thro' Duty,
The King may have great Pleafure in your Beauty. (105)

Think of (106) *Obedience,* which you have profefs'd,
　　Let Chaftity and Patience ftill be found;
Free from the World, now fet your Souls to reft,
　　That Perfeverance may at length be crown'd.
Look on this Place, as 'tis, Religion's School;
Where, tho' I govern, thro' kind Heav'n I rule.

'Twas for your Sake I did Submiffion learn,
　　As you, no doubt, will do the fame for mine:
And then the Pow'rs, which all our Acts difcern,
　　Will knit the Union, make us fo combine,
As to find Favour in their bleffed Sight,
Since to (107) fear GOD in Wifdom we unite.

　　　　　　　　　　　　　　　　RELIGION

---

(104) About 25 Years old was the ufual time; but now they are accepted much younger, according to Judgment.

(105) *Psal.* xlv. 10, 11. *Hearken, O Daughter, &c.*

(106) I. *Pet.* v. 5. *Likewise ye younger, submit yourselves, &c.* *Multò tutius est, stare in subjectione, quam in prælatura.* KEM.

(107) *Initium enim sapientiæ timor* DOMINI.

RELIGION, truly, makes us all to find
  What 'tis we are, and lefs our felves elate;
The Body's Illnefs oft brings Health of Mind, (108)
  And That renews us to a better State.
It makes us think, and caſt (109) on God our Care,
Who is our (110) Shepherd, and whofe Voice we hear. (111)

Whilſt fome for Gain explore the raging Flood,
  And others Towns and Cities fet on Fire;
Whilſt vile Oppreffors do enfnare the Good,
  'Till in deſtructive Luſts themfelves expire: (112)
Whilſt griping (113) Mifers, glutting in their Store,
Exult, thro' Joy, in feeing others poor.

Whilſt fome in Waters perifh, fome in Flame,
  Or thro' the Force of fharp avenging Steel;
Or in damp Prifons, fill'd with Care and Shame,
  The greateſt Pains and Cruelties do feel:
Perhaps are fallen from an high Eſtate,
Which make their Lives of Miferies replete.

Whilſt Reafon feems extinct, and Paſſions glow;
  When Anger roars more fierce than ſtormy Winds:
Whilſt Envy's pointed Stings no Limits know,
  'Till (114) Death at length its filly Owner binds;
Happy are we fecur'd from all thofe Thralls,
No Harms will come within our peaceful Walls.

For

---

(108) *Corporis morbus animi salus.*   DREXEL.

(109) *See for Comfort in Psalm* lxxiii. *Verse* 23, &c. *And in the fifth Chapter of the First of St.* Peter, *Ver.* 6, 7.

(110) I. *Pet.* ii. 25. *Psal.* xxv. 1.   (111) *Joh.* x. 3.

(112) I. *Tim.* vi. 9. 10.   (113) *Non qui parum habet, sed qui plus cupit pauper est.—Quam difficulter qui pecunias habent, introibunt in regnum DEI.* Luke xviii. 24.   (114) *Job* v. ii.

For here no Thoughts impure can wound the Heart;
  Nor yet deluding, or deluded Man,
Thro' Sin's Propenfion, work our bitter Smart,
  Tho' they attempt to do the worſt they can.
No, never ſhall vain Youth attain their Ends,
To make us loſe GOD'S Favour, and our Friends.

'Tis true, we do the nuptial State decline,
  But not condemn what is approv'd by Heav'n.
Where Love connubial reigns, 'tis ſure divine;
  And as a fruitful Bleſſing THAT is giv'n.
If virtuous Spouſes righteous Laws purſue,
They may love CHRIST, and one another too.

But when that true Affection is not found,
  Expos'd they float as on a boiſt'rous Sea;
'Till almoſt loſt in Cares, in Troubles drown'd,
  Each drives to Ruin in a diff'rent Way:
And what a gloomy dreadful State is this,
To fly thoſe Paths that lead to Bow'rs of Bliſs!

Love comes from Heav'n: 'Tis there they ſing and love.
  When Virtue ſhines in Youth and harmleſs Maids,
Deſcending Joys will ſhade them from above,
  Whilſt nothing here their Happineſs invades.
May mutual Comforts bleſs them whilſt on Earth,
And Love eternal crown them after Death!

Nor let our State, we voluntary choſe,
  Be leſs eſteem'd, becauſe more ſet apart
To *follow the bright Lamb where-e'er he goes,* (115)
  For which he yields to us his precious Heart:
Dearer than Children doth his Love proclaim;
As promis'd to us, with a better Name. (116)
                                              Then,

---

(115) *Rev.* xiv. 4. (116) *Even unto them will I give a better place in mine house, and within my walls, a place and a name better than sons and*
                                                              daughters,

Then, happy Virgins! if, with pure Defire,
You long to imitate your Saviour dear;
Faith's (117) Author, unto Whom we fhould afpire,
Who fends us (118) Comforts to difpel our Fear;
Which, like (119) foft Showers, lovingly defcends;
And proves Him kindeft, deareft, beft of Friends.

With Food and Raiment let us be content; (120)
For what we have our grateful Love exprefs.
Expect not always Bleffings to be fent,
As tho' no Sorrows grac'd our dear Recefs.
We muft be (121) try'd, as Gold is purg'd by Fire.
No Place on Earth from Grief is quite entire. (122)

Alas! the Defert did not wholly fhield
The bleffed JESUS in his Solitude;
For Satan, like a Champion of the Field,
Attack'd his Lord whilft fafting in the Wood.
But tho' the Tempter rages near at hand,
He none can hurt without divine Command.

The Prophets, perfecuted, Heav'n rever'd;
So did K. *David*, by his Son brought low: (123)
And *Hezekiah's* Plaints were kindly heard
By Him, who did his deep Affliction know:
Who bids us call, will hear us when we cry;
And, whilft we truft in Him, will raife us high. (124)

Whoe'er's

---

daughters. Ifa. lvi. 5., *i.e.* Nomen conjugis dabo eis. *Non enim falso canit Ecclesia de sanctis virginibus, Venis ponsa Christi, accipe coronam quam tibi Dominus præparavit in æternum.* BELLAR. de ætern. felicit. fanctorum.

(117) HEB. xii. 2. (118) See Pfal. iv. xxvii. xxxviii. cxxi. &c. (119) *Deut.* xxxii. 2. (120) I. *Tim.* vi. 8. *Phil.* iv 6. (121) II. *Tim.* iii. 12. *Job* vii. 18. (122) *Ubi namque tribulatio, ibi & consolatio; ubi consolatio ibi & gratia est.* Drexel. (123) *Psal.* cxix. 71. (124) *Isa.* xl. 31.

Whoe'er's (125) unlearnt fad Sufferings to bear,
  Impatient proves beneath the heav'nly Rod;
Difpleafing Him, we know, who (126) *loves us dear*,
  And is no lefs than our Almighty GOD!
To be rejected, we fhould always fear;
Not any Pains that can attend us here. (127)

Now what will make us lov'd in *JESU'S* Sight,
  Is CHARITY, (128) fair *Virtue's* comely Queen;
Sweet Union's Stamp, clear as cœleftial Light;
  That Love, which loves what's holy to be feen:
Entire (129) Submiffion to the Will of Heav'n,
In whatfoe'er State we fhall be driv'n.

Let (130) Contemplation reftlefs Paffions calm;
  And wing'd with Love to full Perfection gain:
'Twill prove as unto painful Wounds a Balm;
  When we, by Labour, that high Mount attain:
Where, like (131) *Olympus'* Top, is conftant Reft,
And Heav'n's bright Profpect plainer is expreft.

S. *Paul*, who well thofe endlefs Manfions knew, (132)
  Recounts the Acts by which we may afpire. (133)
Like David's Sounds, from which the Dæmon flew, (134)
  Elfe Meditation's like a filent Lyre; (135)
Whereby Temptations might fo bear us down,
As to make void our glorious promis'd Crown. (136)

Avoid

---

(125) *Tanto quisque minus est doctus, quanto minus castigationis patiens.*

(126) *Quem enim diligit Dominus, castigat, &c.* Heb. xii. 6. *Psal.* xciv. 12.

(127) *Ne timeas flagellari, sed timeas exhæredari.*

(128) *Radix omnium bonorum est charitas. Quid suave fecit jugum paupertatis, & continentiæ, & obedientiæ tot milibus religiosorum & sanctimonialum, nisi oleum charitatis ?* Bellar.

(129) *Divinæ voluntatis regula sine omni exceptione est. Bonum est tibi humiliari sub potenti manu Dei.* Drexel.

(130) *Contemplationis pluma nos sublevat, atque inde divinâ dulcedine ad cœlum erigimur.* BONAVENT. (131) *Olympi cacumen semper quietum.*

(132) II. *Cor.* xii. 2, &c.

(133) *Rom.* xii. &c. (134) I. *Sam.* xvi. 23. (135) *Meditatio sine exertio similis est lyræ taciturnæ.* (136) *Jam.* i. 12.

Avoid Prefumption, equal as Defpair; (137)
   Two dang'rous Rocks, on which fo many fplit:
Without GOD'S Help, alas! moft weak we are;
   But (138) ftrong to act, if He fhall think us fit.
In awful Silence, ancient ev'n as time, (139)
Think moft of Him in Thoughts the moft fublime.

But if to fpeak at any Time requir'd,
   Let your Difcourfe be fhort and reverent.
Speech is the Gift of Heav'n, fo much admir'd,
   The Mind's fair Index, Nature's Ornament!
How melts the Heart, whilft it perfuafive reigns;
And, like fweet Mufick, trickleth thro' the Veins.

True in your Words, like Hours to the Sun;
   Juft in your Actions; all exact agree:
No Inj'ries do, but rather bear what's done,
   In Imitation of DIVINITY:
Pray for your Foes; for Vengeance doth belong
To GOD, who knows when to revenge our Wrong.

Thrice happy They, altho' on Earth opprefs'd,
   Whom Heav'n to vifit kindly condefcends!
Unknown to Men, by Angels are carefs'd,
   Whofe Love exceeds That of the proudeft Friends.
Blefs'd Comforters, whom GOD is pleas'd to fend;
And dear Conductors when all Sorrows end! (140)

Nor think like *Bab'lon's* Streams this Life appears,
   Where (†) Floods do threaten, and high Billows foam; (‡)
Nor ftrive to add to thefe our ftreaming Tears,
   Too apt to fhow'r as Sicknefs calls us home!

Since

---

(137) *Rarissimè vicit, qui victoriam ante pugnam desperavit.*
(138) *Psal.* cvi. 2. *and* cviii. 13.   *Isa.* xl. 29, 31.   *Phil.* iv. 13. *Joh.* viii. 12.   *Rom.* viii. 31.   *Si Deus pro nobis, quid contra nos?*
(139) Thought coæval with Eternity, before Nature began.
(140) *Job.* iii. 17.   *Psal.* xci. 11.   *Luke* xvi. 22.
(†) *Psal.* lxix. 2.   (‡) Or like troubled fea, *saith* ISAIAH lvii. 20.

Since Heav'n's Phyſician then can beſt avail, (141)
When ſkilful Doctors round our Beds do fail.

Then, whilſt amidſt the gloomy Shades of Death,
  With Conſcience pure, we need not be afraid; (142)
But in the Lord (143) moſt precious yield our Breath,
  When Angels bright our hov'ring Souls ſhall lead,
With heav'nly Muſick, borne upon their Wings, (144)
To meet our lovely Spouſe, the King of Kings.

Holy of Holies! Oh! that wond'rous Place! (145)
  There dwells the Prince of Angels we revere!
With Saints ſurrounded in his Throne of Grace,
  Refulgent Brightneſs fills the glorious Sphere!
Whilſt Joys expreſsleſs thro' Heav'n's Choir abounds,
And Harmony in ev'ry (146) Manſion founds.

Tho' diff'rent Glories moſt reſplendent ſhine,
  Yet equal Pleaſures charm the Ever-Bleſt: (147)
For there the Love of (148) GOD in All combine,
  That tends to mutual Charity and Reſt:
Where Saints inceſſant praiſe, and never tire;
But fill'd with Raptures ever do aſpire. (149)

This, I pray GOD, we may at laſt obtain,
  For which let one another Heav'n beſeech.
So ſaid, ſhe bleſs'd her lovely Virgin Train,
  Who wept in Love to hear her melting Speech.
With ſtedfaſt Faith and mutual Joys inſpir'd,
All took their Leave, and to their Cells retir'd.

CHAP.

---

(141) *Et licet morientis lectum peritiſſimi medicorum cingant, nullus juvare poteſt, niſi medicus è cælo.* Drexel.

Et abſterſurus eſt Deus omnem lacrymam ab oculis eorum, Rev. xxi. 4.

(142) Pſal. xxiii. 4.   (143) I. *Pet.* i. 9. II. *Tim.* iv. 7, 8.

(144) *Ezek.* i. 8.   (145) *O regnum beatitudinis ſempiteræ, ubi tu Domine ſpes es ſanctorum, & diadema gloriæ, facie ad faciem videris à ſanctis; lætificans eos undique in pace tua, quæ exſuperat omnem ſenſum.*   (146) *Novas ſemper harmonias vox meloda concrepat.*

(147) *Diſpar eſt gloria ſingulorum, ſed communis eſt lætitia omnium.*

(148) *Omne opus eorum laus Dei ſine fine, ſine defectione, ſine labore.* Meditat. & Sol. S. Aug.   (149) II. *Cor.* iv. 17. I. *Pet.* v. 4.

CHAP. X.

The Argument.

The Acts of Bu'no *here is prais'd,*
Who many Churches fair had rais'd;
To whom great Honour had been giv'n,
Before he dy'd, and went to Heav'n.

AFTER St. Win'frid was to Life reſtor'd,
  Bu'no became a Prieſt of mighty Fame:
And being call'd in Spirit by the LORD,
  His Will in diſtant Places to proclaim,
He for her Parents dear did fervent pray,
And unto them theſe pious Words did ſay.

"As you for CHRIST'S dear Sake a Church has giv'n,
  "At *Finhon*, where the Faithful GOD implore;
"So are you now rewarded by kind Heav'n,
  "And will be bleſs'd therein for evermore.
"An holy Man ſhall in my Place preſide;
"And let your Daughter's Virtues be your Guide.

"And you, fair Win'fred! ſtrive to run the Race,
  "As I have taught you with true Pains and Care:
"Virgins ſeleƈt, and be your Dwelling-Place
  "Round the ſaid Temple, in true Order there:
"And when for ſev'n Years thus you have obey'd,
"You will depart from thence, 'my heav'nly Maid!

"For Strangers will from foreign Countries come,
  "To be inſtruƈted in Religious Rules;
"Your Piety will found thro' *Chriſtendom*,
  "And your Example ſhine in all their Schools.
"Weep not, fair Daughter! tender Parents dear!
"Dry up thoſe Tears that on your Cheeks appear."

This

This faid, he led them to the cryſtal Fount,
  And, having pray'd a while, he thus begun:
Virgin, behold! GOD'S *Power will ſurmount!*
  See you thoſe Stones o'er which the Waters run?
'Twas from your Blood that they the Tincture gain'd,
When you the Crown of Martyrdom obtain'd.

Their ſanguine Spots can ne'er be waſh'd away: (150)
  And whoſoever three times journeys here,
With Souls devout, tho' Sickneſs them decay,
  Will find a gracious Anſwer to their Pray'r.
As near the Ocean I intend my Cell,
There's one Thing more that I to you muſt tell.

If once a Year you are diſpos'd to ſend
  A Token, lay it in this limpid Stream:
Ne'er fear but Providence will me befriend,
  Whereby I ſurely ſhall receive the ſame.
And now farewell; but tho' I bid you ſo,
Still I ſhall pray for you, where e'er I go.

So ſaid, they parted, and that Life ſhe led
  As he deſir'd; and when e'er ſhe ſent
A Parcel wrapt, 'twas at the Fountain's Head
  She laid the ſame, and ſwiftly on it went
Until it came towar'd the welcome Strand,
Which driven cloſe to Shore, came to his Hand.

As

---

(150) *There is at* Whitby *headless serpentine Stones, of which* Camden *thus writes.* Hildæ *autem precibus adscribit credulitas, tanquam illa commutâsset quæ primitiva Saxonum ecclesia, sacerdotum tonsuræ, & Paschalis juxta Romanum ritum celebrationi pro viribus obsistebat, synodo his de rebus anno 664 habita in monasterio suo, quod hoc in loco posuerat, & cui ipsa prima præfuit.*

[102]

As CHRIST well knew, that in a Fiſh's Mouth
  There might be found a Piece of Silver laid;
And order'd (151) *Peter* for to prove the Truth,
  Whereby that *Cæſar's* Tribute might be paid:
So did he ſay to his Apoſtles true,
They might thro' Faith do what they ſaw him do. (152)

Thus faithful Bu'NO, and St. WIN'FRID fair,
  As one directed, t'other did obey:
And Both in Sight of Heav'n was held ſo dear,
  As made obſequious prove the roaring Sea.
The Æſtuary is by *BRITONS* fam'd,
And the fair Creek *Port of the Veſtment nam'd*. (153)

So great the Virgin's Fame abroad had ſpread,
  That Lords and Biſhops came to *Guitherine:*
For that a Martyr dear ſhould loſe her Head,
  And live! did ſeem moſt wond'rous and divine:
But when the Fact before their Eyes was ſeen,
They more admir'd than did fair *Sheba's* Queen. (154)

Tho' importun'd, ſhe car'd not to reveal
  Her *Pure White Circle* round her Iv'ry Neck;
Until her Virgins Suit did more prevail,
  Whoſe dear Deſires ſhe thought not fit to check:
But when ſhe threw her ſable Veil aſide,
None could behold the ſame, but wept and cry'd.
                                              Ah!

---

(151) *Mat.* xvii. 27.   (152) JOH. xiv, 12. *Verily, verily, I say unto you, He that believeth on me, the works that I do, shall he do also; and greater works than these shall he do, because I go unto my Father.*

(153) In Welſh *Porth y Cassul*. The firſt Preſent was a fine wrought Veſtment, which St. *Bueno* placed in the Veſtry of the Pariſh Church of *Clynnog*, ſituated near the inlet from the Sea.

(154) II. *Chron.* ix. *from beginning to Ver.* 12.

Ah! wicked Prince, *they faid*, what flinty Heart,
  But your's, could act fo infamous a Crime?
Thus for to make fo good a Creature fmart;
  So innocent a Maid, yet fo fublime!
But yet fhe lives to prove when Martyrs bleed,
Their precious Blood becomes the Church's Seed. (155)

Then from their Cheeks the Tears would trickle down,
  As tho' they faw her circled in fad Fears;
Or fympathiz'd with her in ev'ry Moan,
  And Sigh fhe vented, when immerg'd in Cares:
Which made her weep, and alfo them confole,
With Praife to Heav'n, that thus had made her whole.

And is it You, *they faid*, that lovely Star,
  Which to your heav'nly Spoufe appears fo fair?
Whofe Light has led us fpangling from a-far,
  And brought us where true Virtues fhining are?
That in our holy Churches do refound!
And fhall we fay, that you at length we've found?

You, whom St. Bu'no did fo dear efteem,
  And told your moving from fair *Holy-Well?*
At whofe Deceafe, juft Heav'n did wifely deem
  That Eight Miles you fhould travel to the Cell
Of Deifer! and then to *Henthlant* neat,
Where venerable Saturn keep his Seat?

O what extatic Joys your Mind muft fill,
  Blefs'd Virgin! when he did direct you here:
Where Bloody Tyrants have no Pow'r to kill,
  And nothing more prevails than heav'nly Pray'r:
Where GOD'S true Word to Sin becomes a Sword;
Who, pleas'd, looks down to fee Himfelf ador'd.
                                                What

---

(155) *Sanguis martyrum, semen Ecclesiæ.*

What lovely Things of you can we now fay,
  Fair Patronefs, and Glory of our Land!
Since we're affur'd for us you'll ever pray,
  And Bleffings draw from the Almighty's Hand:
Long live, dear Creature! live till hence you foar,
On Angels Wings, to live for evermore.

The modeft Virgin blufh'd to hear fuch Praife,
  Which more increas'd their high Efteem and Love:
She bore the fame, becaufe fhe'd not difpleafe;
  But gave the Glory to the Pow'r above:
And in Return fhe had fuch Favours giv'n,
That each Beholder judg'd Her fit for Heav'n.

For fev'ral Years, whilft WIN'FRED was rever'd
  At *Finhon's* Dwelling, BU'NO was employ'd
In founding Churches, whilft the People heard
  Sweet Preaching, that their Souls were overjoy'd:
And many Converts came, from diftant Lands,
To feek for Baptifm at his facred Hands.

Thus did his Life and Miracles accord,
  In whom was kindled fuch an holy Flame,
He travell'd far to ferve his bleffed Lord;
  And when fo done, again to *Cambria* came,
No Labour fpar'd he precious Souls to bring,
By Heav'nly Knowledge, to the Heav'nly KING.

King CADVAN much efteem'd this holy Prieft,
  Who at one Time appear'd before his Throne;
And found fuch Goodnefs in his royal Breaft,
  As rais'd his Spirits more to beg a Boon.
Which he defign'd; a Monaftry to build:
To which Requeft the pious Prince did yield.

The END of the Third PART.

British PIETY Display'd

In the GLORIOUS

LIFE, Suffering, and DEATH

Of the Blessed

St. WINEFRED:

A Noble VIRGIN, martyr'd for her renowned Chastity, in *Wales:* Where, at Her Celebrated FOUNTAIN, called HOLY-WELL, many afflicted Persons have been happily freed from their miserable Distempers in past Centuries: The salutiferous Quality of which Water, continuing in the present Age, occasions its FAME to be spread in far-distant Kingdoms.

✠✠✠✠✠✠✠✠✠✠✠✠✠✠✠✠✠✠

Ecclesia nunquam florentior, quam cum afflictior inter cruces & gladios suorum martyrum pugnas & victorias spectavit.— Natura rerum ad Deum nos erigit. Quam magnifica sunt Opera Tua, DOMINE!

"*DEUS ter Optimus Maximus in aquis summas excel-*
"*lentissimas recondivit vires salutares, quarum tanta est*
"*præstantia ut longè multumque omnibus aliis remediorum*
"*generibus sint superiores.*" That is, *The Most Glorious and Omnipotent* GOD *has conceal'd the greatest and most excellent salubrious Efficacy in the Waters; which have so prevalent a Power, that they are far superior to all other Kinds of Remedies.*

✠✠✠✠✠✠✠✠✠✠✠✠✠✠✠✠✠✠

PART *the Fourth.*

✠✠✠✠✠✠✠✠✠✠✠✠✠✠✠✠✠✠

YORK: Printed and Sold by the Author THO. GENT, in *Petergate, Anno Dom.* MDCCXLII.

As CHRIST, when young, was clasp'd within the Arms
Of Heav'n's blest Virgin, and secur'd from Harms;
So oft it happens, that the Just protect
The Innocent, and not their Cause neglect:
Speak in Defence to Magistrates of Towns;
And for Truth's Sake disvalue Smiles or Frowns.
Thus Bu'no acted with religious Heart,
As you will find perusing of this Part:
Which I have strove, with no small Pains, to make
The Reading pleasant for the Reader's Sake:
And hope 'twill last for Ages yet to come,
Since to serve Others I my Life consume.

"Aliis serviens meipsum contero."

The Fourth PART of
The Holy LIFE and DEATH of
S. WINEFRED.

Continuation of the Tenth CHAPTER.

Containing a further ACCOUNT of St. BUNO's Piety.

THE King's fair Son, CADWALLON, did bestow
   Some (156) Lands likewise the Structure to enlarge.
Whilst the Foundations laying were below,
   A Gentlewoman did the work discharge.
A little Child was clasp'd within her Arms;
When with these Words she thus the Saint alarms:

BU'NO, *she said*, the Land is none of your's;
   But this sweet Infant's, by Inheritance.
He answer'd, Lady, He that Wrong procures,
   Deserves no Good from Men, or Heav'n's Defence.
Come to the Palace, where your Eyes may see
The royal Prince, who sign'd this Gift to me.

So

---

(156) *Historians write, They were called* Gwareddog.

So at (157) *Caermarthen* on a Day they met,
  The young Man fitting near his Father's Throne.
'Twas wrong, ſaid B u ' N O, me, alas! to treat,
  In granting Lands, which were not, Sir, your own.
Return the homag'd Scepter, which I gave
To hold with greater Right than what I have.

Vex'd was the Prince, and fir'd at the Heart:
  Nor would give back what B u ' N o had requir'd.
The Prieſt, thus griev'd, did excommunicate
  The royal Youth, and from the Court retir'd.
The noble (158) *Gwiddant*, hearing the Complaint,
Call'd for his Steed, and overtook the Saint.

Stay, holy Man! he ſaid, your Words recall,
  And for our aged King, his Son, and me,
Offer your Pray'rs: Accept what now I ſhall
  Out of my own Eſtate free grant to thee:
A Townſhip fair, to build, and there implore
Bleſſings from Heav'n, ne'er to be troubled more.

The Saint thus ſoften'd at the Noble's Speech,
  Bleſs'd him as *David* did fair (159) *Abigail;*
Pleading for *Nabal*, that moſt ſurly Leech,
  By Riches curs'd, and like by them to fail:
Your Offer, Sir, ſaid B u ' N o, I receive:
May Heav'n reward, and add to what you have!

Then

---

(157)   Or Caernarvon, *called* Cear Seiont, *and by the* Roman *Emperor* ANTONINUS Segontium; *where a Church was dedicated in Honour of St.* SIMPLICIUS.

(158)   *He was Couſin German to Prince* CADWELLON, *or* CADWALLON, &c.   *St.* Bu'no *also came of royal Extract, in* Montgomeryſhire, *at the Fall of the River* Rhyw, *that runs into* Severn, *and thence called* Aberhyw.   *St.* Gundeleius *was his Grandfather, and St.* Dangeſius *his Tutor.   His Father* Binſi *deſcended from* Cadel *Prince of* Gleſiwig; *his Mother from* Anna, *Queen of the* Picts, *Sister to the great K.* Arthur.

(159)   I. SAM. xxv. 32, 33, &c.   *And blessed be thou, &c.*

Then did he (160) build a Church moſt neat and fair,
  The Iſles croſs-ways, and ſtately to behold;
With lofty Turrets ſoaring in the Air,
  Whoſe Spires did glitter like to burniſh'd Gold:
And ſoon he rais'd a Monaſtry of Fame,
Which to his Praiſe was called by his Name.

Here with the Clergy, ſweetly ſpending Time,
  Did them aſſiſt in ſerving of the Poor.
The Comfortleſs he chear'd with Thoughts ſublime,
  And mov'd the Rich to give ſome of their Store;
Since CHRIST would largely balance ſuch a Sum,
When he in Glory as their Judge did come.

Thus having lived to a good old Age,
  A bright Example to the Juſt around;
And Death at length had mov'd him from Earth's Stage,
  A noble (161) Sepulchre his Body found:
Whilſt his Remembrance do's with Honour laſt, (162)
Which Time thro' rolling Ages ne'er could blaſt.

CHAP.

---

(160) *Some disagree when it was erected; but from the* MONASTICON, *'tis certain the Place was called* Clunok Vaus, *or* Vaur, *or* Klynog-Vaur, *in* Caernarvonſhire, *almoſt as large as St.* DAVID'S *Cathedral. A new Church was erected contiguous to it.*

(161) *He dy'd in* 660. *His Memory in the* Engliſh MARTYROLOGY *is celebrated on the* 14th *of* January.

(162) *In memoria æterna erit juſtus.* His Body was bury'd in the Pariſh Church, near *Porth y Caſſul,* or the Port of the Veſtment, by reaſon of the Token ſent from *S. WINEFRED,* where the Sea runs up as an Inlet. His Tomb is ſaid to be remaining; and her Hiſtory was moſt curiouſly painted in the Glaſs Windows thereof.

CHAP. XI.

The Argument.

How WINEFRED *did yield her Breath,*
With her Tranflation after Death;
And from far diftant Parts did come
Pilgrims, who vifited her Tomb.

THE lovely Virgin, more and more renown'd,
   For thofe bright Virtues which adorn'd her Mind;
In ev'ry Duty like the reft was found,
   And doing Good to *All* fhe knew inclin'd;
Thofe who were tempted quickly fhe'd perceive;
And, thro' GOD'S Help, moft ghoftly Councels gave.

More by Intreaty, than by harfh Command,
   She over all did fweet Obedience gain;
To hear her Praifes fhe would never ftand,
   But rather Pray'rs from Pilgrims poor obtain.
For nothing that fuperfluous appear'd,
But what was only neceffary, car'd.

Patience with Perfeverance crown'd her Mind,
   And frequent Invocations grac'd her Tongue;
Her Extafies and Raptures were refin'd,
   Her Voice like Angel's when fweet *Hymns* fhe fung:
Her Love to JESUS did all Hearts inflame;
She always figh'd, when e'er fhe heard his Name.

And as *GOD'S wonderful in all his Saints,*
   Mirac'lous Cures fhe often did perform;
Sick People eas'd of all their fad Complaints,
   And even thofe who did thro' Madnefs ftorm.
Nay, her Difcourfe did Malefactors turn,
And make them for their great Offences mourn.

As

As late one Night St. WIN'FRED (164) kneel'd at Pray'rs:
She feem'd encircled as with Rays of Light;
When to her wond'rous Joy, there, lo! appears
(165) Her LORD fhe thought, thro' Faith, before her Sight:
Who fignify'd that Death was drawing near,
And bid her for her latter End prepare.

"*Thy Will be done,*" my deareft LORD! faid fhe,
Your Sight's delightful to my longing Mind:
Pleas'd at Releafement from Captivity,
Now my Defire I firmly hope to find.
"*Thy Kingdom come*"! Who can thy blefs'd Words fay,
Yet wifh for Earth's Enjoyments, here to ftay? (166)

Alas! fweet LORD! dire Sins ftrive to furround,
And from Temptations none are fcarcely free! (167)
Thy Number, foon, accomplifhed, be found!
'Mongft whom, I truft, thou haft felected me!
Thy precious Arms will thine in Safety clofe:
O let my Soul with thee find blefs'd Repofe.

Fear

---

(164) *Beati servi illi, quos cum venerit Dominus, invenerit vigilantes.*

(165) Thus did our Bleffed Saviour appear unto St. PAUL in *Jerusalem,* Acts xxii. ver. 18 to 21. And another time, when he gave Encouragement to bear Witnefs of Him in *Rome,* Cap. xxiii. 11. Befides, Church Hiftory tells us of *that Miracle of Grace, and Nature's Beauty, the fair Saint* Potamiana, *(martyr'd about the Year* 205, *along with the Virgin* Herhais) *who appeared the third Night after Execution to* Bafilides *the Soldier, who with Tears had been obliged to conduct her to the Flames; when, holding a starry Diadem over his head, she inspired him to Christianity, by which he obtain'd the Crown of Martyrdom. About the same time S.* Perpetua *had a Vision a little before she suffer'd, of a narrow golden Ladder edg'd with Knives, &c.* And Zoe, *who had been hung by the Hair, and suffocated, the succeeding Night encouraged S.* Sebaftian; *who was cruelly wounded with Arrows, and most barbarously whipt to Death.*

(166) *Quid rogamus & petimus, ut* adveniat regnum cœlorum, *si captivitas terrena delectat?*

(167) *Nemo tam beatus vivit, quin plurimis obnoxius vivat periculis; & raro periculum sine periculo vitatur.* DREX.

Fear not, faid CHRIST; I ne'er forfake my own,
  But come to ferve them in their greateft Need;
Angels fhall guide thee to my Father's Throne;
  A fecond Time thou fhalt not for me bleed.
Watch for the Hour of Death, to waft thee o'er
Where (168) Safety dwells, ne'er to be fhip-wreck'd more.

My Lord, *faid fhe*, my Father! All in All!
  Sweet are the Words that from my Spoufe I hear.
I'll wait, obey the only happy'ft Call,
  That can tranflate me to an higher Sphere! (169)
Tho' Nature mourns, for Change of Joy it weeps;
And each alternate Paffion Vigil keeps.

That I may enter in Heav'n's furtheft Gate, (170)
  Where doubtful Spirits can't my Soul turmoil; (171)
Both Day and Night I fhall my Bridegroom wait,
  My Lamp fupply with conftant flowing Oil.
O happy Moment! when from hence I fever,
Once more, thro' Death, to live with Thee for ever! (172)

To St. ELERIUS fhe her Vifion told,
  And fome time after to her Virgins dear!
The News fo dampt them, like a fhiv'ring Cold,
  That for a while they could not fhed a Tear.
But when that Grief was fettled in its Throne,
Then Show'rs and Streams did from their Eyes run down.

Weep

---

(168) *Fœlix littus! securus portus! in quo nemo, nisi volens, naufragatur.*

(169) *Finis calamitatum, transitus ad immortalitatem.*

(170) PSAL. LV. 6. *and* LXIII. *also* PSAL. LXXXIV.

(171) HEB. XI. 25.

(172) *Quemadmodum desiderat cervus ad fontes aquarum, ita desiderat anima mea ad te, Deus! Cupio dissolvi & esse cum Christo.* Vid. *Psal.* xlii. 1. and *Phil.* i. 23.

Weep not, *said she*, 'tis my Creator's Will,
  To follow dear THEONIA to Reſt;
Nor think but what I ſhall be uſeful ſtill;
  My Pray'rs for you ſhall be amongſt the Bleſt.
Unto my heav'nly Spouſe I am to go;
Then joy with me, ſince He will have it ſo.

O good ELERIUS, dear Confeſſor! come,
  The Sacrament let me with Hope receive;
Since 'tis the only ſure *Viaticum*,
  To guide my better Part beyond the Grave.
Virgins, be mindful; think of what has paſt,
That you and I may meet in Heav'n at laſt.

O let my Body near THEONIA lye
  Cloſe as you may to that bleſt *Matron's* Side.
So ſaid, ſhe look'd around with tender Eye,
  Bleſs'd them once more, then cloſ'd her Lids, and dy'd.
Peaceful, ſhe breath'd her laſt within their Arms:
And as ſhe liv'd, ſo dy'd with Angel's Charms. (173)

Whilſt doleful Sounds came from the Paſſing-Bell,
  An (174) ancient Cuſtom calling all to Pray'rs;
And *Requiems* ſing, as good Hiſtorians tell,
  When precious Souls are eaſed from their Cares:
So nothing was there wanting to reveal
The piercing Grief that ev'ry one did feel.

No

---

(173) *Mr.* GAUTHER *writes, That she deceaſed* Anno CHRISTI 664, *on the 4th Day before the Nones of* November. *(The Nones, or 6th Day, after the* Kalends: *Which latter is the 1st Day after the Months of* March, May, June, *and* October; *in the reſt the 4th.) Others place her Death much later.*

(174) *Quod cum illa audiſſet, suscitavit cunctas ſorores & in eccleſiam convocatas, orationibus & psalmis pro anima · matris operam dare monuit."*
BED. Ven.

For fuch a Saint, who had fo high excell'd,
  Moft moving Accents thro' the Buildings rung;
No piteous Eye but what with Waters well'd,
  No Praife was wanting from each grateful Tongue.
She's gone! they cry'd, where Heav'nly Joy's in Store;
But gone from us, alas! for evermore!

The good ELERIUS faid the Fun'ral Pray'rs,
  And others fung the Dirge fweet and divine;
The (†) Grave, all humid with their falling Tears,
  Became illuftrious thro' the Virgin's Shrine:
For Miracles, moft evident difplay'd,
Did raife the Glory of this virtuous Maid.

The Prieft, as (175) One afferts, did then retire
  Into a Defart; Others (176) write, to *France:*
There, near a (177) River, but a Fountain nigher,
  A (178) Chapel to GOD'S Honour did advance.
But, willing for to lay his Bones in *Wales*
Amongft the Saints, he to fair *Cambria* fails.

Not long, methinks, he after this did live (179)
  On Earth, but went to meet the Saint in Heav'n;
Where his blefs'd Soul did certainly receive
  Thofe juft Rewards that to the Saints are giv'n:
Whilft in the Church his Memory did bloom,
For Wonders wrought to Pilgrims at his Tomb. (180)

Long

(†) *It was near to that of* Theonia, *where former Saints were interred. Amongst 'em were* S. Chæbeus *of* Anglefea, *and* S. Senan; *one at her Head, the other at her Side, both famous for Miracles.*

(175) PITS *in* ELER.   (176) MALBRANQUE, &c.

(177) Lifaine. *This and the Fountain* (fays CRESSY) *in ancient times afforded great Benefit and Help to the Inhabitants of* the adjacent *Places and Strangers.   But* (179) *the same Gentleman does not, through Obscurity of Writers, ascertain the exact time of his Death.*   (178) Luxueil.

(180) *In a Church erected to his Name and Memory.*

Long lay S. *WIN'FRED'S* Corpſe in *Guitherine*,
　To which all Sorts of Pilgrims did reſort :
Amongſt them Nobles viſited her Shrine,
　To ſeek for Bleſſings from the heav'nly Court.
And as her Well was honour'd ; ſo her Tomb,
For Wonders done, appeared freſh in Bloom.

For as a Lab'rer ſtruck an ancient Oak,
　Near to the Church, where Pilgrims often pray'd,
His Hand and Ax were faſten'd with the Stroke,
　That might have ſpoilt the beauty of the Shade :
But as in Tears, projected from the Ground,
He begg'd Remittance, ſo he Mercy found.

The very Thieves, when they had Miſchiefs done,
　Were terrify'd with horrid gloomy Thoughts ;
Brought to confeſs before the Altar Stone,
　And there deteſt their ſacrilegious Fau'ts :
Or elſe deep Vengeance, thro' tormenting Pains,
Enwrapt their Bodies, like to burning Chains.

A certain (181) Prieſt, in Firſt King *William's* Reign,
　Had ſuch Diſtempers none could truly tell,
Until two Brethren, ſent to eaſe his Pain,
　Went to the Chapel of fair *Holy-Well ;*
Where ſaying Pray'rs, as order'd in a Dream,
From that bleſs'd Hour he moſt ſound became.

A Carpenter, who had a Daughter dear,
　Born blind, and us'd to mourn her Loss of Sight ;
When Fame had touch'd the Organs of her Ear,
　The Cures there done, beyond dim Reaſon's Light ;
She begg'd her Sire to lead her to the Place,
And then as unto Heav'n ſhe told her Caſe.

　　　　　　　　　　　　　　　　　　O pity

---

(181) *Belonging to a famous Monastery begun A.D.* 1087, *by Earl* ROGER *of* Montgomery, *(to whom the Conqueror had given* Shropſhire *) and his pious Lady, at* Shrewſbury, *near* Severn.

O pity me, she said, *a Virgin poor !*
  That can't thy Wonders view ; but yet conceive,
By what I've heard, dear God ! thy wondrous Pow'r
  To faithful Mortals, very near their Grave.
So said, she in the Stream did bathe her Head,
And after that was to the Chapel led.

Most of that Night she pray'd, for *Win'frid's* Sake,
  That GOD her seal'd-up Eye-lids would unclose:
And that her grateful Soul would Off'rings make,
  When, lo! soft Slumber gave her sweet Repose;
And, whilst awaking from angelick Dreams, (182)
She view'd, what oft she'd felt, *Sol's* radiant Beams. (183)
                                                  'Twas

---

(182) *And upon the* handmaids *in those days will I pour out my spirit,* JOEL ii. Part of Ver. 29. *And in* 32 Ver. *Whosoever shall call on the Name of the LORD, shall be delivered, &c.*

(183) The Miracles, related by St. AUG. *de Civit.* Dei, Lib. xxii. Cap. 8, are very surprizing ; and the more, because he says he was a
                                                  Witness

'Twas in the ° Year 'Lev'n Hundred Thirty Eight,
  The Abbot (184) HERBERT sent 7 Monks to *Wales;*
They went to *Bangor's* See, where DANIEL sat
  Of old as Bishop, and their Suit reveals
To mitred DAVID, who most courteous sent
  Them to a Lord, to further their Intent.

That Nobleman did think their Errand good,
  Thus the bless'd Virgin's Relicks to desire;
But seem'd afraid the People Umbrage shou'd
  Take in their Hearts, if Heav'n did not inspire.
So with his Words they joyful did appear;
  And yet immediate fell in sudden Fear.

Nor

Witness to some of them: A blind Man and Woman receiving Sight; the wonderful Cures of *Innocentius* and *Innocentia;* of a converted Physician; paralytick Persons eased; Places and Dæmoniacs dispossessed; the Oppressed wonderfully relieved in extreme Penury, Sickness, &c. All these by visiting the revealed Graves or Shrines of Saints, with Acts agreeable to their Conversion and Faith, by holy Baptism, Prayer, and Charity. And, writing of the miraculous Cure (at *Uzali,* near *Utica*) of the noble Lady *Petronia,* who was much devoted to St. *Stephen,* and living in this Father's Time, he has these remarkable Words: *Non credunt hoc, qui etiam Dominum JESUM per integra virginalia matris enixum, & ad discipulos ostiis clausis ingressum fuisse non credunt. Sed hoc certè quærant, & si verum invenerint, illa credant. Clarissima fœmina est, nobiliter nata, nobiliter nupta,* Carthagine *habitat: ampla civitas, ampla persona, rem quærentes latere non sinunt. Martyr certè ipse, quo impetrante illa sanata est, in filium permanentis virginis credidit, in eum qui ostiis clausis ad discipulos ingressus est, credidit. Postremò, propter quod omnia ista dicuntur à nobis, in eum qui ascendit in cælum cum carne, in qua resurrexerat, credidit: & ideo per eum tanta fiunt, quia pro ista fide animam posuit. Fiunt ergo etiam nunc multa miracula: eodem Deo faciente per quos vult, & quemadmodum vult, &c.*

 (*) 1138.

 (184) Who presided over the aforesaid Monastery.

Nor without Caufe: For many ftood againft
   The Meffengers, 'till (185) Vifions made it known,
That Heav'n, who's honour'd, glorifies the Saints,
   And which on this Tranflation fet them on:
So when allow'd to enter Holy Ifle,
With great Devotion there they pafs'd a while.

They faw the healing Oyl flow from her Tomb,
   Which, like (186) *Glyceria's*, wond'rous Cures perform'd:
They fmelt the Odours fweet that did perfume;
   And, ftruck with Wonder, feem'd like Men transform'd.
Now they rejoic'd, then figh'd, or vented Moans;
And kifs'd, with Love and Reverence, the Stones.

In fineft Linnen they her Bones infold,
   And, whilft returning Home, did Wonders do;
Then in St. *Giles's* Church, fair to behold,
   They on the Altar plac'd to publick View.
One Night a poor fick Youth, who did invoke, (187)
Slumb'ring nigh Morn, was heal'd when he awoke.
                                                    When

---

   (185) St. *Cyprian*, lib. iv. fays, *That the Vision of the LORD foretold the eighth Persecution.* Theodorus, *when in extreme Torture, was comforted by an Angel in Form of a blooming Youth. Remarkable was that Vision to King* Edwin, *written in the History of* York; *of that to the noble Virgin* Cæcilia; *the Apparitions to* S. Sebaftian, Lucina, *and several others; particularly of the Martyr* Thecla *to the Emperor* Zeno, *as written by the noble* Evagrius Scholafticus, lib. iii. c. 8. *An extraordinary Vision (resembling our Saviour's to* S. Paul, Acts ix. 3, *&c.) was that to* Genefius, *a Comedian, in the reign of* Dioclefian, *whilst ridiculing the Sacrament of Baptism: Which converting him from a wicked Player to a glorious Martyr, he suffered the greatest Torments, and made his last Exit from the Theatre of this Life with the Applause of the cœlestial Inhabitants.—Most of these STARS shewing that this World was but like Mount* Calvary, *which wou'd present 'em with nothing but Crosses and Spectacles of Misery; encouraging them to suffer Death to gain Heaven, which Kingdom cannot be shaken.*

   (186) *A Virgin, martyr'd at* Heraclea; *from whose Body a Medicinal Oyl proceeding, that perform'd miraculous Cures, occasioned the Emperor* Mauritius *to visit her Church in that City, and to repair what had been destroy'd by the cruel Barbarians.*

   (187) *The young Man was, it seems, almost bent double; and having been long time in that miserable Condition, his sudden Relaxation and Recovery became wonderful to the People.*

When in Proceffion thefe dear Relicks were
    Removing to Earl *Roger's* Monaftry;
When e'er they paft, the Streets were dry and clear,
    Whilft Rains bedew'd the reft of *Shrewsbury:*
And in the Church of PETER and St. PAUL,
On the high Altar, to be feen by All,

They plac'd the Saint's Remains, in fplendid Shrine,
    Where People vifited with tender Love;
And as their Faith, fo Miracles divine
    Did very often to their Comforts prove:
Both Souls and Bodies found fweet Solace here,
Who came with Hearts devout, and Minds fincere.

Archbifhop (188) HENRY, who rul'd *Cantium's* See,
    Was fo much moved when he heard her Fame,
That in a learn'd conventual Synod, he
    A Feaft did on *November* Third proclaim.
In Fourteen Hundred Twenty it was done,
The annual Time when fhe her Race had run.

In ° Sixteen Hundred Six, a famous Knight,
    Sir ROGER BODENHAM, of *Bath* fo fair,
Thro' Quartan Ague, became fo ftrange a Sight,
    No Leper foul could worfe than him appear.
His (189) Doctor learn'd, a choice and skilful Man,
Did all that Mortal cou'd, or ever can.

Sienna

° 1606.

(188) *Henry Chickley*, the 63d from St. *Augustine*, a great Benefactor. He erected part of the South Steeple; founded a Collegiate Church at *Higham-Ferrars*, where he was born; two *Universities* at *Oxon*, &c. dy'd *An.* 1443, and lies in a ftately Monument on the N. Side of the Cathedral in *Canterbury*.

Sienna boafted where he was profefs'd :
   Padua for Practice, and in divers Parts
Of *Italy*, and *England*, was carrefs'd ;
   For all that knew him lov'd him in their Hearts.
He to *Augufta's* College, where he'd been, (190)
Sent the Knight's Cafe, and what was done therein.

That learned Train return'd an anfwer ftraight,
   Nothing in Nature could afford a Cure !
Whilft he, diftrefs'd ! feem'd only Death to wait ;
   His Friends Advice true Comfort did procure :
Good Sir ! *faid they*, pray bathe in WIN'FRED's Well.
Remember (191) N A M A A N : Heav'n can Men excell.

'Tis very true, *faid he;* and I'll try there.
   So faid, his trufty Servants did attend ;
And, whilft he wafh'd him in the Waters clear,
   Upon a fudden found himfelf to mend !
How great the Joys that center'd in his Heart,
To find the Cure that was unknown to Art ! (192)

His Family G O D ' S wond'rous Goodnefs prais'd ;
   Others, who held the lep'rous Knight in Scorn,
Were at themfelves for fuch a Sin difpleas'd,
   Since now his Flefh, like to a Child new-born,
All Clean and fweet, appear'd before their Eyes !
Whilft grateful Sounds like Arrows pierc'd the Skies.

                                                    'Twas

---

(189) *John David Rhes*, born in *Wales*, of worthy Parents.

(190) In the College of Phyficians, *London*, where he had been Reader to moft of that learned and illuftrious Body.

(191) II. *Kings* v. 14. *Then went he down, and dipped, &c.*

(192) The Witneffes of this Cure were Sir *Roger's* Lady ; Mrs. *Mary Bodenham*, his Daughter-in-Law ; *William Green*, and his Spoufe ; *Richard Bray*, *John Henley*, and other Attendants ; particularly Mr. *Thomas Beale*, Steward, who carry'd the Report of the Knight's Cafe to the College of Phyficians.

'Twas * Sixteen Hundred Thirty, when a Wretch
　　The Saint derided, and her Pilgrims dear;
As if the Devil did his Soul bewitch,
　　Whilſt to his End he was approaching near!
For the next Day the Jury found him dead, (193)
And Verdict gave, GOD'S *Judgment on him laid.*

Some, † fev'n Years after, who had much defac'd
　　The Virgin's Image; and the Iron Beams
Had took away, which pious People plac'd
　　That Pilgrims might ſupport them in the Streams;
Their ſacrilegious Deeds did Heav'n offend,
As made them hapleſs at their latter End.

About that Time a Wonder did commence;
　　Mrs. JANE WAKEMAN, with a Cancer griev'd;
When Doctors gave Opinion to this Senſe,
　　By Amputation ſhe ſhould be reliev'd;
Or elſe muſt wait a loathſome, ling'ring Death,
And in a nauſeous Stench reſign her Breath:

To cut it off ſhe car'd not to agree;
　　But, in *June* Sixteen Hundred Thirty Eight,
Left *London* City, and down haſten'd ſhe
　　To *Win'fred's* Well, to gain a better State.
And as the flowing Streams ſhe enter'd in,
To ceaſe from running did her Sores begin.

　　　　　　　　　　　　　　　　　　　　The

---

　　　　　　* 1630.　　　† 1637.

(193) So did a Judgment fall on two Brothers of the Name of *Styles*, mention'd in the Appendix, *Pag.* 28. of my Second Volume of Antiquities, concerning the Abbey of *Kirkstal*.

The third Time did the Gentlewoman heal
　To the Surprize of her beloved Spoufe, (194)
Joyful to fee what GOD did fo reveal,
　That both to Heav'n might offer up their Vows!
Three Children afterwards to him fhe bore;
Then quitted Life to live for evermore.

And fome * Years after this divine Relief,
　Once Mrs. CLEC a Pilgrimage did take
On Foot from *Worcefter*, to eafe her Grief,
　That many Years did her uneafy make:
At *Kiderminfter* call'd on Coufin COOK,
And told the Reafon fhe her Journey took.

A Bed-rid Woman, kept on Parifh-Pay,
　Heard what fhe faid in an adjoining Room;
And calling, as departing on her Way,
　The pious Pilgrim back again did come:
To whom the Woman faid, *This Penny take,*
And give it fome poor Creature for my Sake.

But tell fuch in the Holy-Well to go,
　And pray fincere that I my Limbs may gain:
My Faith does tell me Heav'n will grant it fo,
　And that I fhall be eafed of my Pain,
If 'tis but done, as I cou'd wifh to do;
And this dear Miftrefs! I befeech of you.

'Twas done, and inftantaneous was fhe feen
　Perfect and well by all who dwelt around;
Which Mr. BRIDGES, who'd High-Sheriff been,
　Recorded as a Miracle profound;
And Mrs. CLEC, returning, was amaz'd,
As fhe on the late Bed-rid Woman gaz'd.

　　　　　　　　　　　　　　　　　　Mifs

---

* 1647.

(194) Mr. *John Wakeman*, in *Roughley*, of *Horsham* Parifh. He faw the dead Wretch, who had abufed the Pilgrims.

Mifs MARY NUMAN, when but five Years old,
　Thro' Ague and Fever all her Limbs did lofe.
Of her fad Pains the reigning King was told,
　And his Phyficians utmoft Skill did ufe:
Touch'd by the Monarch; then to *Bath* fhe went,
And unto *Scotia's* faireft Springs was fent.

She fail'd to *France;* in fecond Grape-Prefs put;
　Touch'd by that Country's King to eafe her Pain;
Did vifit *Sichem;* Places moft devout;
　Amongft the reft was at fair *Aquifgrane*:
In *Belgia* too, where an *Italian* Prince
Advice did give, but not her Cure evince.

In * *Lufitanian* Baths fhe oft did lave;
　But ftill a Cripple prov'd as at the firft;
And twice St. *Win'fred's* Well did her receive,
　Which made her think her Cafe to be the worft;
'Till calling to her Mind what BU'NO faid,
"THREE VISITS *fhould unto the Well be made*":

'Twas Sixteen Hundred Sixty Six, in *June*,
　She came again; and, as a tender Child,
Was put therein; when, bathing, very foon
　Found that her faithful Heart was not beguil'd.
Sore Pains fhe felt; but then they were not vain;
For ev'ry Joint mov'd to its Place again.

No diflocated Bones fad Forms difplay:
　But on her Feet with comely Gefture ftood!
And, when fhe had been led a little Way,
　Walk'd of herfelf within the ftreaming Flood.
She wept for Joy, thank'd Heav'n for being heal'd,
And foon to fair *Hibernia's* Ifle fhe fail'd.

　　　　　　　　　　　　　　　　　　HUGH

---

* *Portugal.*

HUGH WILLIAMS, but a lad of nine Years old,
  Try'd once to leap quite o'er the limpid Well;
But, as tho' punifh'd for a Crime too bold,
  He prov'd too weak, and in the Water fell:
All gave him o'er for drown'd; or, yet as ill,
Thought kill'd beneath the Pavement and the Mill.

There were about two Inches Space between,
  And yet efcap'd thro' Means none certain knew:
For by a Youth a fifhing he was feen
  Creep from a Ditch, with only lofs of Shoe!
Except a little Skin from Ancle torn,
An Indication what he might have borne!

CORNELIUS NICH'LAS, aged feventeen Years,
  Struck by a Blaft, liv'd in corroding Pain;
'Till, in a Barrow plac'd, to eafe his Cares,
  The tender-hearted *Welfh* drove him amain
To the fair Well; when, bathing in the Stream,
His Strength return'd, and he moft found became.

So ROGER WHETSTONE, fixty Years of Age,
  Much indifpos'd, repaired to the Well; º
To wafh with others car'd not to engage,
  But drank the Water, and afleep he fell.
When he awoke, his Crutches threw afide,
And thus in joyful Raptures out he cry'd:

Thrice happy Streams, that thus have fet me free!
  How fhall I tell the Joys that fill my Heart?
Bleft Tongue that hither has directed me!
  To raife my Soul, and eafe my Body's Smart!
Delightful Spring! Comfort of the Opprefs'd,
O may thy Streams for evermore be bleft!
                                        Long

                   º *A. C.* 1667.

Long have have I liv'd in *Sidmore*, many Years,
  And moſt induſtrious earn'd my daily Bread,
Until that Sickneſs fill'd me full of Cares;
  And then my Hands could ſcarce ſupport my Head!
When, being much reduc'd, I grew ſo poor,
That I was forc'd to beg from Door to Door.

Ten Days I have been coming to this Place;
  And if Ten Hundred, ſure 'tis worth my Pains:
For what is Life depriv'd of Health, or Grace?
  Or can Wealth equal happy Pilgrims Gains?
Oh! that mine Eyes may ſtill be running o're,
Thro' Gratitude, 'till I can weep no more!

Tremendous Being! who rules over all,
  And whom the holy Virgin did obey;
My Soul of thy moſt wond'rous Mercy ſhall
  Give Teſtimony to my dying Day:
That ev'ry People may draw near to THEE,
And praiſe Thy Name by what they ſee of me,

Then, with exploring Eyes, when he eſpy'd
  The sanguine Stones, he beat his aged Heart:
His flowing Tears did with the Waters glide:
  He knew not how to ſtay, or well depart:
The People joy'd to find his Strength renew'd;
And yet they wept to ſee his Cheeks bedew'd.

Thus mighty Wonders can th'ALMIGHTY work
  Unto the Lame, the Dumb, the Deaf, or Blind:
He cures Diſtempers, which in Bodies lurk;
  And to his faithful Creatures is moſt kind.
Above the World's Philoſophy He knows;
And to the Humbleſt greateſt Pity ſhows.

Now let us love CHRIST'S Church with all our Hearts,
  'Tis orthodox, moſt faithful, and divine!
And let our Pray'rs aſcend like quiv'ring Darts;
  That, as in Suff'rings did Her Martyrs ſhine;
So may She triumph in the Realms above,
Where all is Peace, and Harmony, and Love.

Non nobis, Domine, non nobis, ſed Nomini Tuo da gloriam.
PSAL. cxv. 1.

CHAP. XII.

The Argument.

St. WINEFRED'S *furpaſſing Well,* (195)
Of which the learned Doctors tell:
Diſeaſes run to vaſt Extreams,
That ſtill are cured by the Streams.
Judgments from either mundane Cauſe,
Or Miracle, 'bove Nature's Laws:
How GOD, *who is Omnipotence,*
Oft acts beyond all human Senſe.

WITHIN a little Church, near which the Saint
  Was decollated by the Heathen Prince;
Moſt curious Artiſts did her Hiſt'ry paint,
  Fair on the Glaſs, the World for to convince:
At leaſt diſplay Tradition from an old,
Deliver'd down by Pen, in Words oft told.

Cloſe

---

(195) 'Tis in *Flintshire*, not far from *Desert* Caſtle, ſuppoſed to be ſo called from its Solitude. And here I cannot omit the very Words of CAMDEN: *Sub hoc* Haliwell, i.e. *fons sacer,* WENEFRIDÆ *virginis memoria quæ* ſtuprum per vim *oblatum ibi morte luit, & musco gratissimi odoris longè est celeberrimus, ex quo emanat fluviolus statim eximius, párque molæ agendæ, tanto impetu proruit.* Several have expatiated, with Enlargements in their Tranſlations; of which I ſhall quote only that of the Bp. of *London,* viz. *Under this Place I view'd* Holy-Well, *a small Town, where there's a Well much celebrated for the Memory of* Win'fred, *a Christian Virgin, ravish'd here, and beheaded by a Tyrant; as also for the Moss it yields of a very sweet Scent. Out of the Well a small Brook flows (or rather breaks forth thro' the Stones, on which are seen I know not what kind of Blood-Spots) and runs with such a violent Course, that immediately it's able to turn about a Mill.* But a later Writer aſſerts, *That the said* SPRING *in* VIEW *turns* THREE *Mills in* Breaſt; *and several Mills below them that never wanted Water.*

Clofe to the fame a pretty Chapel ftands, (196)
  Of curious Stone, well wrought, as Authors tell;
Or from a Rock, which choice laborious Hands
  Had hewn exactly, fhading o'er the Well:
Whofe lovely Waters beauteoufly do fhine,
Tranflucent, like to (197) *living* Streams divine. (198)

Here Pilgrims from remoteft Parts refort,
  And fhivering in the Streams do mingle Tears;
When looking up towards the heav'nly Court,
  They pierce the Heav'ns with moft pathetick Pray'rs:
When, lo! the Heat of blefs'd fupernal Love,
Superior to the piercing Cold do's prove.

Courageoufly they fink beneath the Streams,
  With Vows alacrious in tranfporting wife,
That Heav'n might help them in their worft Extreams,
  And fend down Bleffings from the arched Skies:
Not only make their Bodies clean and found,
But deck their Souls with piety profound.

Now

---

(196) Dedicated to the Memory of St. WINEFRED: Her Life was written firft by St. *Elerius* aforefaid; from him *Robertus Salopiensis*, (in *Latin*) who added her Tranflation, dedicated to another *Benedictine* Prior GUARINUS of *Worcester*, and approved by *Baronius*, *Pitts*, *Possevinus*, and *Surius*. The learned Mr. *John Flood*, Mr. *Cressy*, and fome others, have treated of this bleffed Virgin; and I hope what I have done with a pious Intent will not be unacceptable to my kind Readers.

(197) *Joh.* iv. 10, 11, 14. and Chap. vii. Ver. 38.

(198) *Rev.* vii. 17, and Chapter xxii. 1. Verfe 17.

Now more they fee than once they only heard,
   A Spring in Wales had done unnumber'd Cures;
FAITH here is ſtrengthen'd; REASON undebarr'd,
   In finding what the Pow'r divine procures.
CHRIST to His CHURCH will *Ever* prove a Friend,
Since promis'd to be with them *to the End.* (199)

---

(199) *Mat.* xxviii. 20. *I am with you alway, &c.*

———

The END of the Fourth PART.

British PIETY Display'd
In the GLORIOUS
LIFE, Suffering, and DEATH
Of the Blessed

St. WINEFRED:

A Noble VIRGIN, martyr'd for her renowned Chastity, in *Wales:* Where, at Her Celebrated FOUNTAIN, called HOLY-WELL, many afflicted Persons have been happily freed from their miserable Distempers in past Centuries: The salutiferous Quality of which Water, continuing in the present Age, occasions its FAME to be spread in far-distant Kingdoms.

Ecclesia nunquam florentior, quam cum afflictior inter cruces & gladios suorum martyrum pugnas & victorias spectavit.— Natura rerum ad Deum nos erigit. Quam magnifica sunt Opera Tua, D O M I N E !

"*DEUS ter Optimus Maximus in aquis summas excel-* "*lentissimas recondidit vires salutares, quarum tanta est* "*præstantia ut longè multumque omnibus aliis remediorum* "*generibus sint superiores.*" That is, *The Most Glorious and Omnipotent* GOD *has conceal'd the greatest and most excellent salubrious Efficacy in the Waters; which have so prevalent a Power, that they are far superior to all other Kinds of Remedies.*

PART *the Fifth.*

YORK: Printed and Sold by the Author THO. GENT, in *Petergate, Anno Dom.* MDCCXLII.

The Fifth PART OF
The Holy LIFE and DEATH of
S. WINEFRED.

Continuation of the Twelfth CHAPTER.

THO' to St. *Win'frid's* Streams the Sick do come,
   Where late lame Perfons Crutches leave behind;
Tho' Weak find Strength fo as to travel Home; (200)
   And precious Sight is given to the Blind:
Moft leprous Perfons cleans'd, and fo renew'd,
As once more blefs'd with new-born Flefh and Blood:

Yet Men will think fome fubterraneous Stream,
   By Miners turned from its ancient Courfe,
Was the firft Caufe; thro' Rains lefs clear became;
   Or bluifh Colour, ftill made worfe and worfe:
As tho' fome Mines of Lead lay in its Way; (201)
Or elfe proceeded from an harden'd Clay.

That learn'd (202) GIRALDUS never heard its Praife;
   And, confequently, was not in his Time:
Who liv'd Five Hundred Years fince *Bu'no's* Days,
   When He and *Win'frid* flourifh'd in their Prime:
Nor view'd he any Pilgrims in their Weeds,
Who gave Account of fuch amazing Deeds.
                                                                                            But

---

(200) Efpecially thofe newly recover'd of the *Small Pox*.

(201) "The fubterraneous Family of Minerals is a coagulable (or "*congealed)* fat Humidity; a *Mixture* of Fire, Air, and *pure Earth* over-"caft with Water." *So writes a Gentleman.*

(202) *Cambrensis*, fo call'd for his being a Native of *Wales*. His Chriftian Name was *Sylvester*. That this *Man* could adore both the falling and rifing Sun, by the Death of K. *Henry* II. and Succeffion of King *Richard* I., this is afcrib'd unto him:

But others fay, That AUTHOR did but dream,
   When writing of the (203) Silver Veins below;
Or had no Mind to fpread the Virgin's Fame,
   Like (204) One concealing what he well might know:
Nor could the Monks fo ftrange a wonder tell,
If GOD'S great Power had not caus'd her Well. (205)

This fubtle, fluid FORCE appears divine,
   They fay; and is a Miracle indeed:
Will not allow the Story of the Mine;
   Or that it fhould from any Caufe proceed,
But HIM, who Nature and its Laws did make, (206)
That fhew'd this Wonder for His Martyr's Sake.

Thus

Miro cano, sol occubuit, nox nulla sequuta.
The former Prince, whofe Life he wrote, had call'd him from his Travels to be his Secretary; and fent him as Tutor to his Son *John* in *Ireland*. He not only exhibited the Actions of his Pupil, but alfo the Hiftory of that Nation with great Applaufe. The like Praife he obtain'd by his *Itinerarium* of *Wales* and *Britain*, with a Chronicle of Englifh Tranfactions, &c.

(203) *Propè hunc locum, Giraldi ætate, erat ut ipse scribit,* "dives "vena, *fructuosumque* argenti *scrutinium*, ubi pecuniam fcrutando itum eft "in vifcera terræ." THAT IS, *Near unto this Place in the Time of* Giraldus,— *There was a rich and profitable Vein of Silver; in searching after which more diligently, no Pains were spared to enter into the very Bowels of the Earth.*

(204) *Tho' the learned Works of Venerable* BEDE, *an* Englifh Saxon, *are highly approved of by several Authors; yet they do not seem well pleased that he confined himself to treat only of his Country Saints; quite omitting those of the ancient* Britons, *(and of* Ireland, *except St.* FURSIUS, *who built a Monastery in* Suffolk *near the Sea, thro' the Favour of King* SIGHBERT) *amongst whom I find to have been many pious and illustrious Personages, such as* S. Urfula, S. David, *St.* Dubricius, *St.* Patricius, S. Kentigern, *Bishop of St.* Afaph, S. Sampfon, S. Theliau, S. Juftinian, *&c.*

(205) Et dixit *DEUS*, cujus nomen fanctificetur; Fecimus ex Aqua omnem rem. *Ex Lib. sacro.*

(206) "The ALMIGHTY, on account of His dominion, is called "*Lord God*, pantocrator, *or Universal Ruler.* [*Du*, an Arabic Word, (in "the oblique cafe *di*) fignifies only *Lord*, from which a learned "Gentleman has derived *Deus.*] He is Eternal, Infinite, Omnipotent, "Omnifcient, &c.

Thus, hon'ring HER, HIS Goodnefs *ftill* is fhown.
　Frefh Wonders caufe his Power more to fhine;
And that to all devoted Hearts is known,
　Whereby to Pray'rs and Praifes they incline;
When, for her Sake, each wounded Soul implores;
And, with ftrong Faith, revifits Seas and Shores.

As grateful Patients, long thro' Pains opprefs'd,
　Recall to Mind THOSE who have giv'n Relief;
And hon'ring Them, like Guardian Angels blefs'd,
　With moving Words, exprefs their former Grief:
So when heal'd Pilgrims think of *Win'frid's* Well,
They weep thro' Love, and of her Virtues tell.

Tokens moft dear! For as learn'd Doctors melt
　In Love to thofe who love Them and their Art:
So Heav'n has often for our Suff'rings felt
　Grief fympathetick, like a tender Heart:
For mutual Joys will evermore abound,
Where due refpect or Adoration's found.

Far be (207) *Lucretius'* Thoughts, like rocky Shelves,
　That GOD of Human Nature takes no Care;
Or that fupernal Powers, of Themfelves,
　Live undifturb'd, or fprung at firft from *Fear*, (208)
Which proves, if ‡ *Nature nothing doth in vain.*
As *Fear* in *All*, fo GOD on Earth will reign.

Did

---

‡ Arift.

(207) TITUS LUCRETIUS CARUS, a *Roman*, who taught the Doctrine of EPICURUS, a temperate Man, that placed the *summum bonum* in mental Felicity, but unhappily deny'd divine Providence. "*Tully* corrected *his* "Writings. VIRGIL eagerly ftudied them, as *Macrobius* and *Gellius* "witnefs; the latter, like *Ovid*, calling him *Poetam ingenio & facundia* "*præcellentem*; and *Cornelius Nepos* hath placed him *inter elegantissimos* "*Poetas.*" M. *Gravina*, who lately at *Rome* publifhed a Book concerning Poetry, does not approve thefe Words of *Quintilian*: Nam Macer & *Lucretius* legendi quidem, fed non ut phrafin, id eft corpus eloquentiæ

faciant

Did not TIBERIUS, that *wife* Emp'ror dread
The Stings of Confcience which did often wound? (209)
So *poor* CALIG'LA crept beneath the Bed,
When Lightning blaz'd, and Thunder did refound?
And WOLSEY, near his Death, betray'd fad Fears,
As if that *GOD forfook him in gray Hairs!* (210)

But that there is Reward and Punifhment, (211)
Throughout the Scriptures, Inftances are found:
To Hell great, *learned*, wicked Souls were fent;
And thofe, lefs *knowing*, in bright Glory crown'd: (212)
Judgments and Mercies in the World have been;
As have been *heard, felt, underftood*, and *feen*.

What

---

faciant: Elegantes in fua quifque materia, fed alter humilis, alter difficilis.—On the contrary, *Gravina* fays, he was a very great Poet; of furprizing Facility, and full of Majefty mix'd with Sweetnefs, confidering the intricate Subjects he wrote upon. And tho' fome perfons have ftyled him what I care not to repeat after them: Yet Archbifhop *Tillotson*, who has moft learnedly preach'd and wrote againft Atheifm; while he profeffes him to have been but a bad Maker and Contriver of the World, however admires his Compofition. His *fortuitous* Beginning of the Univerfe, tho' abfurd, that great Divine fays is very elegantly expreffed;

    Sed quibus ille modis conjectus, &c. Lib. 5. Pag. 142.
Englifhed by the Rev. Mr. *Creech*, pag. 153. Edit. 5. of *Epicurean* Philofophy; to both, or either of which, I refer my Reader.

  (208) *Primum in orbe Deos fecit Timor.*

  (209) *C. Sueton. Tranq.* TIBER. Cap. 63. *And tho' he had small regard to Religion; yet he was exceedingly afraid of Thunder.* "Tonitrua tamen præter modum expavefcebat." *So it's less to be wonder'd in the Tyrant his Successor.*

  (210) Upon the account of that great Cardinal, fee my Octavo Hiftory of York, pag. 80. But this, and the two former Inftances, are *pertinently* mention'd by the aforefaid Archbifhop againft the Opinions of fuch who may think Religion invented by *Politicians, and a Juggle of State to cozen* the poor ignorant *People into Obedience.*

  (211) Archbifhop *Dawes* has fully written of a future State, fufficient to convince a *corrupt* and *treacherous* generation, almoft ruin'd thro' Party Feud and Animofity.

    (212) *Surgunt indocti, & cælum rapiunt, &c.* AUG.

What GOD defigns, Earth's Power can't put by;
 And, when he pleafes, Bleffings can withdraw:
Both give, and take; grant Favours, and deny;
 Pleafe, or afflict; His Will muft be our Law.
When Mortals finn'd; or if repenting were,
His Gifts withdrew, or did His Bounties fhare.

† Thus when LYSIMACHUS, did, at *Epire*, (213)
 An Impoft raife on the *Tragafæan* Salt;
Heav'n was difpleas'd at fuch at bafe Defire,
 And made it vanifh for the Taxer's Fault:
But when he did the publick Right reftore,
It came as freely as it did before.

The Gardens of (214) ŒNOTRIA, moft fair,
 Where beft *Calabria's* Manna did defcend;
When by the King of *Naples* clofed were,
 That People might be tax'd to ferve his End:
GOD took away the Bleffings he had giv'n,
And till the Tribute ceas'd, none came from Heav'n.

So when (215) ANTIGONUS upon the Sick,
 Who came to drink at fair *Edepfum's* Spring,
A Rate did lay; the royal Mifer's Trick,
 Heav'n did refent as an unkingly Thing:
The new-fprung healthful Waters fled amain,
And inftantaneous perifh'd all his Gain.

Thus

---

† *Those three Examples, following the above Mark, I have selected from an excellent Book, intituled,* Holy Living and Dying, *Pag.* 171, *written by* JEREMY TAYLOR, *a learned Bishop.*

(213) *A Country in* Greece, *bounded E. by* Achaia; *on the N. by* Macedonia; *has the Mountains* Acroceraunii *on the W. and the* Ionian Sea *on the S.*—Tragafæa *is a Region belonging to* Epire.

(214) *The Name of* Italy, *from* ŒNOTRIUS, *King of the* Sabines.— Calabria *is an Island that lies on the upper Part, and so very plentiful as to bring forth choice Fruit twice every Year.*

(215) *Several Kings of* Syria *were of this royal Name.*

Thus as a Friend can't fee a Friend opprefs'd;
  Or like a Parent who defends his Child:
So neither Heav'n will flight us when diftrefs'd,
  But yield Protection, when by Foes *beguil'd!*
Foes moft *deceitful*, (like to *crooked* Reeds)
Who Villains *live*, and *perifh* thro' their Deeds.

And as poor honeft Pris'ners in a Jayl,
  By vile Betrayers barbaroufly thrown,
When fome kind Providence affordeth Bayl,
  From which *Timonean* Harpyes long were flown!
And now exult with Joy that they can fee
That precious Thing once more, call'd LIBERTY:

So, in a myftick Senfe, the Wonders wrought, (216)
  With Sighs for heav'nly Streams the Juft infpire; (217)
And ftrike the Soul, from *Satan* freed, with Thought
  Of grateful Love, and *what* we fhou'd defire! (218)
Juft as a Bird efcap'd eludes the Snare;
Takes the right Way, and fings that all may hear.

Or as a Perfon foon reftor'd to Sight,
  Looks round, amaz'd, and thinks he fweetly dreams;
Surpriz'd with Raptures at bright *Phœbus*' Light,
  Skies, Meadows, Groves, Plains, Mountains, Vales, and Streams!
So oft' to Mental Sight Heav'n's Views appear,
Strange and portentive like what *Jofeph's* were. (219)

Why

---

(216) *The springs of water were seen, and the foundations of the world were discover'd at thy chiding, O Lord.* Pfal. xviii. 15.

(217) Now "*to the pleasing Springs above I'll go;*
"*The Springs that in the* heav'nly Canaan *flow.*"

(218) "*Quo sitiens igitur peterem de flumine lympham,*
"*Cùm meo tam varium viscera virus edit?*
"*Ah! nisi Te nullo sitis hæc placatur ab haustu,*
"*Tu potes hanc solus fonte domare sitim.*
"*Scis etenim, mea lux, quam te, meus ardor anheles*
"*Cervus ut irrigui fontis anhelat aquas.*" HER.

(219) *And Jofeph dreamed a dream, &c.* GEN. xxxviii. 5.

Why do we wonder (219) GOD has Wonders ſhown?
  What can't He do, who is Omnipotence?
Did not his Servant MOSES force hard Stone (220)
  Even to ſtream for *Iſrael's* Life's Defence?
Nay, (221) Oyl and Honey flinty Rocks did yield,
  That He might His ſelected People ſhield!

Did not ELISHA give the ⁰ *Shunnamite*,
  When unexpected, a moſt lovely Son?
And, when ‡ cold Death had took her Heart's Delight,
  ‖ Recall'd ſwift Life, a longer Race to run!
So PETER *Tabitha* did § wondrous raiſe;
And *Eutychus*, thro' PAUL, † liv'd Heav'n to praiſe.

Prophets, Apoſtles, Martyrs; ſhining Men!
  What have not they perform'd thro' ſtedfaſt Faith?
That Virtue, ſo high-prais'd by ſacred Pen,
  Mountains to move, as plain the Scripture ſaith; (222)
Slain ev'n with Breath ſuch who would Ill maintain, ††
Which ſhew'd their Pow'r, thro' GOD, was not in vain.

When CHRIST was dying, *Sol* did loſe its Light:
  The Temple rent, Graves open'd, Dead aroſe!
Earth groan'd and trembl'd, as in horrid Fright;
  And Heav'n itſelf did fearful Signs diſcloſe:
Who then can doubt, by what good Writers tell, ‡‡
But that that the DEITY can form a *Well?*

Did

---

* II. *Kings* iv. 17.   ‡ 20.   ‖ 35.   § *Acts* ix. 40.   † xx. 10.

(219) ISA. xl. 12. *Who hath measured the Waters, &c.*

(220) Rock *Horeb*, Exod. xvii. 6.   (221) *Deut.* xxxii. 13.

(222) *Mat.* xvii. 20.   †† *Acts* v. 5th and 10th *Verses.*

‡‡ For *One*, see *Dorotheus* of the Prophets, who is commended by *Eusebius*. He lived in the Time of *Diocletian*, &c. He was Minister of the Church of *Antioch*. By Reason his Work was so compendious, he intitul'd it *Synopsis*.

Did *Jewish* Doctors learn'd ISAIAH praife, (223)
  That GOD, thro' him, had wrought *Siloam's* Stream?
And to that Martyr dear a Tomb did raife, (224)
  That, by his Pray'rs, they might enjoy the fame?
Sure faithful *Britons* to their Praife may own
As *clear* a Spring, and Saint of fair Renown.

Whilft WIN'FRED liv'd on Earth, there many came;
  And, by their Pray'rs, with Her's, were fpeedy cur'd:
Nay, after Death, fuch, who had heard her Fame,
  But unto painful Travels not innur'd;
Or too far diftant throughout *Chriftendom*,
And had not Strength, or Wealth, nor Pow'r to come:

Her Spirit would in Vifion oft appear;
  Tell for thofe lovely red-fpot Stones to fend;
Which, being thrown in Cups of Waters clear,
  And drank thereof, would their Diftempers mend:
Such, mindful of thefe vifionary Dreams,
Were certain cur'd, when in the worft Extreams.

†CHRIST'S Apparition firft converted *Saul*,
  But 'twas a ⁰ Vifion *Ananias* fent:
A Vifion too, behold! had *praying* PAUL, ‡
  And with *new Light* the ‖ *Holy Ghoft* was fent.
So to St. *Peter*, and *Cornelius*, dear §
To Heav'n above, Heav'n's Angels did appear.

                                                    Dreams

---

  (223) He was fawn afunder in the Reign of *Manasses*.
  (224) His Monument is near thofe of the Kings of *Jerusalem*.
  † *Acts* ix. 3.   ⁰ 10.   ‡ 12.   ‖ 17, 18.   § *Acts* x. 3, 11, &c.

Dreams often warn us; such when Guardians wait,
  For whom we pray they *may surround our Bed;* (225)
Thefe, under G O D, preferve our happy State;
  By them to certain Glory we are led:
'Tis they, they chiefly, evil Spirits chace;
Fore-arm our Thoughts, or let them reft in Peace.

Thus when Light's ftreaky Rays o'er Darknefs peep,
  And *Chanticleer's* fhrill Notes *ill* Spirits fright; (226)
The Innocent, in waking from their Sleep,
  In blifsful Hopes find fpirit'al Delight:
The dear remember'd Vifions, whilft they pray,
Rife as the Sun, and flourifh with the Day.

Where is the Harm, (ye pious, learn'd Divines!)
  To think, in awful Silence of the Night,
A fair ingliding Virgin kneeling fhines,
  'Midst Rays, more bright than Gold, before our Sight!
And fhews us Streams and Chapels where to find
Cures for the wounded Body, or the Mind?

To

---

(225) *Let thy holy Angels pitch their Tents about* my *Bed, &c. (or our* Beds). See the *Companion to the Altar,* Page 74.

(226) *See in my Octavo History of* York, *Page* 145, *concerning this Tradition, begun in the* 4th *Century, about* afflicted *or* ill *Spirits being frighted away at the Crowing of the Cock: However, it was a good Angel that delivered* PETER *out of Prison in the Night,* Acts xii. 9. *And undoubtedly an holy One, even GOD, that wrestled with* JACOB; *who said,* Let me go, for the day breaketh, *Gen.* xxxii. 26. *Good Angels appear both Day and Night. In the Even Two were entertained by* Lot; *who, in the Morning, set him without the City,* Gen. xix. 1. to 16. *Those were Spectres of the Night that appeared to trembling* Job, *valiant* Brutus, *religions* Anthony, *and other eminent Personages mentioned by* LAVATOR *in his Book* de Spectris. *Whilst some assert, That our departing Souls, thro'* a *particular Judgment, will immediately enter into an intermediate State 'till the general Tribunal, when their final Sentences are to be pronounced for or against them: Others allow not only from* Ethnick *Antiquity, but frequently since the Promulgation of the Gospel, even in latter Ages, that known Apparitions have been seen; of which they have given some Instances. But whether they properly appear'd, or that other Spirits supply'd their Places, I humbly leave my kind Readers to determine.*

To pray no Harms againſt us may prevail;
  Or Friendſhip turn to Hatred moſt unjuſt:
No cruel Hands our kindeſt Hearts aſſail,
  Nor faithleſs Kindred to betray their Truſt:
And when forſaken, languiſhing thro' Grief,
To point the Way wherein to ſeek Relief!

To think bleſs'd Angels bid us weep no more;
  But for a better State in Heav'n prepare;
Think how they ſmile and beckon as they ſoar,
  And unſeen Choirs of Saints melodious hear!
Are theſe inſomnial Airs? Or rather Gleams
Of Lights from Heav'n, tho' ſhaded in our Dreams?

When Miracles have ſo long lain obſcure,
  Why now reviv'd, *few* Friends have I to tell;
But that true Virtue urg'd me on, I'm ſure,
  Like when I wrote of YORK, 'tis known full well.
O may this WORK with its kind PEOPLE take,
As well as Others, for St. *WIN'FRED'S* Sake!

Hail, *publick* FRIEND! lov'd by fair *B—rl—gton*,
  Since I muſt call You by no other Name;
Behold St. *Win'frid's* Life, which, when begun,
  Kind, You approv'd!—that ſet my Soul a-flame!
May Your's, when Death in Swan-like Strains you ſing,
'Midſt Joys expreſsleſs, mount on Angel's Wing!

May bleſs'd *ELIZA*, Comfort of your Breaſt
  When living, meet you with St. *Win'fred's* Ghoſt;
And never part until YE all find Reſt,
  Thro' Seas of Air, upon the heav'nly Coaſt;
Unleſs it be, thro' GOD'S Command to do
A Guardian's Part, as Angels do for You.

Let not my wand'ring Thoughts the leaft offend,
  Since to learn'd Judgments I fhall e'er give Place.
The *Soul's* Extenfion blifsful Hopes attend,
  Swift, as on Turtle's Wings, that fly to Peace.
Err, fure *mine* may; like thofe who rove thro' Dark,
'Till, with Faith's Branch, it finds Religion's Ark.

Return, O Mufe, from dear St. *Win'frid's* Ghoft,
  To clofe my darling Subject of her Spring:
An endlefs Theme! Joy to fair *Flintia's* Coaft;
  Where faithful Patients her high Praifes fing:
Humbly mount Heav'n thro' Extafies and Pray'rs;
Which GOD, that fees, thro' CHRIST, in Mercy, hears.

                                        O *Scarb'rough*

O *Scarb'rough!* did thy Waters firſt proceed
From fuch a Virgin, thro' divine Command,
Thy pendent Cliffs might not have done ill Deed
To thy fair Town, and fmoothly-moving Sand:
But fince thy Springs are found, and cleans'd thy Shore,
Be kind to All, and Heav'n's great Pow'r adore.*

Some learn'd Phyſicians have been heard declare,
That no Place can exceed St. *Winfred's* Well:
Not *Jordan's* Streams, nor various Spaws that are;
Nor the hot *am'rous* BATHS of *la Chapelle*. (227)
I will not fay *compare;* tho', fince divine,
Fair *Holy-Well* above the *moſt* may ſhine,

For

---

* GENT alludes in this Verse to a curious Event which happened a short Time before the publication of the Life of S. WINEFRED. In the Month of December, 1737, the Staith or Sea-Wall of the Spa at Scarborough, composed of a large Body of Stone bound by Timber, gave way in an extraordinary Manner. A great Mass of the Cliff, containing nearly an Acre of pasture Land, with the Cattle grazing upon it, sank perpendicularly several Yards; whilst the Earth and Sand beneath the Cliff rose North and South of the Staith for a Length of above one hundred Yards to a Height of 6-7 Yards above its former Level. The Spa Well rose at first with the Mass of Earth, but soon ceased to flow, and it was only in 1740 that the Mineral Spring was again discovered and the Spa re-opened. *(Note by the Editor.)*

(227) *Aix la Chapelle, Aquisgranum,* or *Aachen,* a City in *Westphalia,* belonging to *Germany.* See fome Account at the End of the firſt Volume of my Hiſtory of *England,* amongſt the Additions treating of an Emperor, Pag. 257. The hot mineral Waters, on which account it is much frequented, are convey'd by Pipes into 28 Baths, where Perfons find Relief in all *chronical,* or *inveterate, slow,* and almoſt *immoveable* Diſtempers; and are of very great Service to Pofterity, if we may believe the following Epigram made of its procreative Vertues.

" Vidit *Aquisgranum,* terras dum luſtrat & urbes,
" Alma *Venus;* geniumque loci mirata lacufque,
" Hoc, dixit, locus est haud dignior ullus amore.
" Jam valeant arcus, ignitaque ſpicula. Poſthac
" Unda cupidineis incendet pectora flammis.
" Sic fatur, natumque vocans, jubet ire natatum,
" Cærulaque ardentem deferre in balnea tædam.
" Exequitur mandata puer: cum lampade in undas
" Infilit,

For Here not only *Hearing* to the Ears,
And *Fruitfulnefs* is given to the Womb: (228)
Not only pleafant *Sight*, and *Speech* that chears; (229)
Dear unto *Thofe* born, haplefs, *deaf,* and *dumb!*
But, thro' *thefe* Streams convulfive Pangs depart;
And Dæmons fly each *Sin's* poffeffed Heart. (230)

If this we ponder, lefs we've Caufe to own
Some Things in Nature, tho' they curious feem:
For if not ufeful, little Vertue's known;
If hurtful, why fhould they deferve Efteem:
Unlefs it be, thro' Contraft, to declare
What Men may ufe, and what they fhould forbear.

One Fountain carries Death within the Stream, (231)
Another, if but touch'd, the Country drowns; (232)
A Third ingenders *Evils,* moft extreme, (233)
A Fourth makes wife Folk drunk as foolifh Clowns. (234)
A fterile Fifth deftroys the fruitful Womb, (235)
And a blind Sixth proves like *Cimmeria's* Gloom. (236)
So

"Infilit, & niveæ fparguntur gurgite pennæ.
"Dum natat, algentes cecidit fcintilla per undas,
"Incaluitque vadum. Liquidæ contagia flammæ
"Senfit pofteritas. Quicunque hic lavit, amavit."

(228) "DEUS DAT INCREMENTUM."
(229) "Sanctorum patrociniis terra lætatur."
(230) "Martyrum orationibus propitiatur DEUS populi peccatis." *Confess. S.* AUGUST, *de Sanctis.*

(231) *In Islandiâ est fons, qui rem quamlibet injectam in lapidem transmutat: & alius, qui gustatus* MORTEM *adfert.*

(232) *In Hyberniâ est fons, cujus aqua pilis aspersa illos canos reddit. Est & alius, quo si quis abluatur, non canescit. Est & alius qui,* tactus ab homine, ftatim totam provinciam inundat. *These Wonders* Giraldus *acknowledges to have heard in his Time.*

(233) *Amongst the* Alps, *that certainly gives the King's Evil.*

(234) *In Paphlagoniâ est fons vinei saporis, qui potantes facit temulentos.*

(235) *In Siciliâ est fons acetosus, quo indigenæ utuntur pro aceto. Ibidem sunt duo fontes, quorum unus fœcundat sterilem, alter fœcundam facit sterilem.*

(236) *In* Italy. *But in* Sardinia *are different Fountains that cause and cure Blindness.*

So *Ethiopia's* red-ſtream'd Fountain makes
  The thirſty Stranger turn directly mad: (237)
Much like *Avernus* or *Tartarean* Lakes,
  Where nothing reigns but Grief, or Torments ſad!
But let us tell the Vertues of what Springs
Seem to promote the Happineſs of Things.

What tho' one Well an unctious Surface grace, (238)
  Or from another uſeful Waters flow; (239)
Or *Lybia's* Fountain freezing in hot Days, (240)
  And in hard Nights like boiling Liquids glow;
Or *Egypt's*, which extinguiſh and cauſe Fire;
Or cold *Illyria's* burn, that all admire!

What tho' fair *Carls-bad* Streams o'er *flinty* Stones,
  In fair *Bohemia*, pleaſantly do run;
Whoſe Virgin-nitrous Salt each Patient owns
  Has *gentle* Powers that *ſome* Cures have done;
For which they're ſtyled Baths of CAROLINE, (241)
As dear to them, and held in part divine.

What tho' a Fountain of fam'd *Paleſtine*,
  Bleſs'd *Idumæa's* call'd, Three Months appears
Like raging Waves; then, turning red, combine
  The other Three to ſtrike the Mind with Fears:
For Three Months more do ſhow a lovely Green,
And the laſt Three like cleareſt Cryſtal ſeen:

What

---

(237) In *Æthiopiâ est fons ruber, è quo bibit, fit lymphaticus.*

(238) In *Scotiâ, &c.*   (239) In *Sicily*, as aforeſaid.

(240) In *Lybiâ est fons, qui Sole orto & occaso est tepidus, in meridie frigidus, media nocte calidissimus. Dicitur fons Solis.—Apud Garamantes fons est tam algens interdiu, ut bibi non queat, tam calidus nocte, ut ferri non possit ipsius caliditas.*   Vid. Alſted. *Cursus Philosophici*, Pag. 1422, &c.

(241) *In Bohemia* commendabiles ſunt Thermæ CAROLINÆ. A Diſſertation upon thoſe hot acid mineral Waters, which had their Original from Mines abounding with *Pyrites*, or *Flint* Stones, was *A.D.* 1708. publiſhed at *Wolfenbuttel*, &c. by a digniſy'd Phyſician, under the following Title: *Sacræ Majestati Regis* AUGUSTI *dicata de Thermis CAROLINIS Commentatio, qua omnium Origo Fontium calidorum itemque acidorum ex Pyrite ostenditur. Auctore* Joanne Gothofredo Bergero, *Archiatro Regio & Profeſſore Medico.* (In 4to. Pag. 157.)

What tho' *Mount-Falcon's* Spring doth petrify,
  Whence ſtoney Rinds proceed, and Boughs with Leaves;
And from hot Baths, which do contiguous lie,
  The ſickly Patient long'd-for Health receives:
Tho' Medicinal Herbs do bleſs the Land,
Where ſtout *Venetia's* Sons bear juſt Command:

Yet All theſe can't compare with *Win'fred's* Well:
  Their Streams but partly heal; but Her's the *whole*.
Heav'n, for her Sake, who did all Vice repell,
  Cures *ev'ry* Pilgrim, comforts *ev'ry* Soul!
To *Flintia*, then, may Thoſe diſtreſs'd repair,
And ſeek true Health, ſince they may find it there.

The Catholicks, unſhaken in their Belief,
  With flowing Tears for tender Mercy cry:
They think the Saint, who gives to All Relief,
  Will pray for *Them* to the Bleſs'd TRINITY.
The *LITANIES*, (241a) exhibited, reveal
That *Love* and *Pow'r*, they own, to *pray*, and *heal*.

                                                    And,

✠

(241a.) LORD, have Mercy upon us.
         Christ, have Mercy upon us.
Lord, have Mercy upon us.
God, the Father of Heaven, have Mercy upon us.
God, the Son, Redeemer of Mankind, have mercy upon us.
God, the Holy Ghost, have Mercy upon us.
Holy Trinity, One God, have Mercy upon us.
Holy *Mary*,
Holy Mother of God,
Holy Virgin of Virgins,
O Blessed St. *Wenefride*,
O Humble and Mild Virgin,
O Glorious Spouse of Christ,
O Devout and Charitable Virgin,
O Sweet Comforter of the Afflicted,
O Singular Example of Chastity,   O Radiant

⎫
⎬ *Pray for us.*
⎭

And, sure, whatever Happiness can be
In Heav'n or Earth, All wish for to acquire.
We are like Pilgrims to Eternity,
And might be lost, or in our Journey tire,
Thro' Sin's foul Burden, if we sought not Aid
From Christ, as they do by this shining Maid.

'Tis

O Radiant Star,
O Fairest Flower of the British Nation,
O Admirable and Elected Vessel,
O Mirror of Chastity,
O Mirror of Devotion,
O Mirror of Piety,
O Bright Lamb of Sanctity,
O Golden Image of Angelical Purity,
O Hope and Safety of distressed Pilgrims,
} *Pray for us.*

That we may be deliver'd from all Disorder'd Passions of the Mind,
That we may be delivered from the Deceits of the World, Flesh and Devil,
That we may be deliver'd from all Occasions of Sin,
That we may be delivered from Plague, Famine and War,
That we may be delivered from the Wrath of God, and Eternal Damnation.
That we and all Sinners may have true Contrition, and full Remission of our Sins,
That all Schismaticks, Hereticks, and Infidels may be Converted to the Holy Catholick and Apostolical Faith,
That we may always hate Sin, and overcome all Temptations,
That we may despise all worldly Vanities and Delights,
That we all may ever fear God, and fulfil his Holy Will,
That we may have both Spiritual and Corporal Health,
That we may devoutly affect Chastity and Purity of Life,
That we may fervently love Humility and Mildness,
That we may delight in pious Prayer, Fasting and Charitable Alms,
That we may discreetly and fervently continue in the Exercise of Godliness,
That we may cheerfully and constantly suffer for the Love of Christ,
} *O Holy Virgin, and Martyr, Pray for us.*

That

'Tis fcarce deny'd, that Heav'n hears ev'ry Pray'r,
  And Hymn that's offer'd, tho' it be to Saints:
So we may learn, from Signs and Tokens clear,
  By fudden Cures in many fad Complaints!
And may not Joy, like *good* Enthufiafm, range
O'er boundlefs Scenes for fuch a rapturous Change?

And if we can but gain an happy End;
  If GOD is with our Off'rings fatisfy'd:
What matters much, how, or by whom, we fend;
  Since Pray'rs conjoin'd thro' CHRIST are not deny'd?
For when ftrong Faith and Love in Woes appear,
No Sigh's unheard, nor drops in vain one Tear.

But

That the Souls in Purgatory, and all Afflicted Persons, may obtain heavenly Consolations,

That our Benefactors, and all that labour to save Souls, may be blessed with abundance of Grace and everlasting Life,

That we may enjoy true Peace, and endless Felicity,

That God of His abundant Mercy will vouchsafe to bless this our Pilgrimage,

That by thy pious Intercession it may be to the perfect Health of our Souls and Bodies,

That thou wilt vouchsafe to grant our Requests,

O Blessed *Winefride!*

} *Holy Virgin and Martyr, pray for us.*

LET US PRAY.

A LMIGHTY *and Everlasting God, who hast adorned St.* Winefride, *with the Reward of Virginity: Grant, we beseech thee, by her Pious Intercession to set aside the Delights of the World, and obtain with her the Throne of Everlasting Glory.* Through Jesus Christ, *Thy Son, who with Thee liveth and reigneth in the Unity of the Holy Ghost, for ever.* Amen.

Another Prayer.

A LMIGHTY and everlasting God, we humbly beseech thee, that blessed S. *Wenefride* may obtain for us such Spiritual and Temporal Benefits as are expedient for Thy Holy Service, and our eternal Salvation. Through our Lord *Jesus Christ*, thy Son, who with thee and the Holy Ghost liveth and reigneth ever one God, World without end. *Amen.*

But should our Pray'rs for Months or Years seem vain,
  Let not Impatience give to Heav'n Offence:
Tho' Angels fly us, think it not Disdain;
  Nor blame an over-ruling Providence.
Powers divine, when they think fit will give
Those proper Virtues how to die, or live.

As when from various Ports poor Passengers
  Send up their ardent Pray'rs for wish'd-for Gales;
GOD, tho' He ev'ry craving Mortal hears,
  Yet at one Time not ev'ry Pray'r prevails:
But if they to His Will divine agree,
At last He sends All where they wish to be:

Ev'n

The Hymn of S. Wenefride.

AS fragrant Rose in pleasant Spring,
  To God's own Son a Spouse most dear,
And Martyr rare of Christ our King,
  Saint *Wenefride* did flourish here.
Descended well of *BRITISH RACE*,
  In Faith was firm, in Hope secure;
With Holy Works and Soul in Grace,
  From Worldly Filth preserved pure.
Cradock this Sacred Maid did kill,
  And him Hell swallowed presently,
Where Tears in vain do run down still,
  'Mongst burning Flames incessantly.
A Token sure of this strange Thing,
  Bespotted all with Bloody Red,
A Well by God's Command doth spring,
  Where Tyrant's Sword cut off her Head.
Here Wonders great God's Hand doth work:
  The Blind doth see, the Dumb doth speak;
Diseases, which in Bodies lurk,
  Are cured where Faith is not weak.
O glorious Virgin *Wenefride*,
  To us the raging Sea appease,
And free us so from Satan's dread,
  That he on us may never seize.   *Amen.*

Ev'n fo 'tis here: Tho' All would Health attain,
  And ev'ry Soul defires to find Relief:
Heav'n firft will fearch their Faith before their Pain,
  And eafe the Humbleft of their fharpeft Grief:
At length give Joy to All who weep and mourn,
And to their Homes with Gufts of Blifs return.

Two Hundred Forty Tons S. *Win'fred's* Well
  And comely (242) Ciftern, do together hold;
But, when difcharg'd, as worthy Perfons tell,
  Two Minutes do reftore the Number told:
Scarce Alteration of the Weather taints it;
And to the Eye moft clear Heav'n's Power paints it.

More than one Hundred Tons the Spring doth rife,
  In ev'ry Minute 'twixt the clofe-laid Stones; (243)
Which with their sanguine Spots do ftrike the Eyes,
  And wound the Heart with fympathetick Moans:
                                                For

A Prayer to S. Wenefride.

O BLESSED S. *Wenefride*, O Glorious Virgin and Martyr, who hast admirably beautified with the Purple of thy Blood the rare Purity of thy Innocent Life, whom God has so specially chosen, so highly privileged, and so wonderfully restored to Life again, gracing thee with the Honour of a living Martyr, causing a Fountain miraculously to spring bearing a perpetual Memory of thy name, for the Relief of all diseased and distressed Pilgrims, who shall devoutly beg thy powerful Intercession: O Blessed S. *Wenefride*, hear the Prayers, and receive the humble Supplications, of thy poor devoted Pilgrims; and obtain, that, by thy pious Intercession, God of his infinite Mercy will be pleased to grant us a full Pardon and Remission of our Sins, and a Blessing to this our Pilgrimage; and that we may increase and persevere in God's Grace, and enjoy Him eternally in Heaven. This we beg of thee, O blessed Virgin and Martyr for *Jesus Christ* our Lord and Saviour's Sake. *Amen.*

(242) Or Bafon, being 4 Feet in depth. The Water feems to boil, as tho' in an extraordinary hot Caldron.

(243) The Experiment was made *A.D.* 1731, before the Reverend Minifter, feveral learned Perfonages, and others.

For here no other Argument's allow'd,
But that the Red came from the Virgin's Blood.

Some Blood-Stones, of a reddifh Iron Hue, (244)
  In *Germany* and *Britain's* Ifle are feen:
A diff'rent Sort, but of kind Nature too, (245)
  Shews fanguine Veins ftreak'd in a dufky Green:
But Her's, for wond'rous Beauty, in clear Streams,
None can excell from *Tyber* unto *Thames*.

Each bleeding Stone, with downy Mofs embrac'd,
  Like Incenfe fmells; as Wall-lov'd Ivy feems;
And fince all are in lovely Order plac'd,
  United Beauties gild the cryftal Streams.
Like flow'ry Pots fome look, in *Flora's* Prime,
When Meadows, Groves, and Gardens look fublime.

And tho' the Streams with dimpling Eddies play,
  Not far they run, but in Mæanders twine:
But where 'tis deeper, fmoother make their Way,
  And like bright Cryftal do the Waters fhine. (246)
So quick the Vafe emits, fo faft it fills,
As to fupply feven large and ufeful Mills.

And thus it has obtain'd fo great Renown,
  That, as to *Bath*, great Quality refort;
So from a Village to a Market-Town,
  Is *Holy-Well*, or rather like a Court:
Where kind Affiftance to the Poor is giv'n,
Who pray for Bleffings to defcend from Heav'n.

Hail,

---

(244) See Dr. *Quincy's* Difpenfatory, Edit. 8. pag. 111. under *Lapis Hæmatites*; good in *Hæmorrhages*, or *Bloody Eruptions*.

(245) The *Heliotropium*, the true Blood-Stone of the Ancients. It is fo called, becaufe it changeth the Sun-Beams by Reflexion, if caft into Water; if out of it, like a Burning-Glafs, we may fee the Sun's Eclipfe, and *Motion* of the *Moon*.

(246) The Water is fo tranfparent, that the fmalleft Piece of Money, or even a Pin's Head, may be feen at the Bottom; and the Fragrancy of the circling Mofs is look'd upon as a divine Effufion, in refpect of the Saint's angelical Virtues.

Hail, PATRONESS, divine! blefs'd Saint renown'd!
May blooming Youth and Virgins fair attend,
Whilft Hymns of Praife, with Mufick's Charms, refound
　Thy Life, harmonious, and thy precious End;
Thy Angel's State; thy Country fam'd thro' Thee;
Efteem'd by *All*, and lov'd moft dear by *Me*. (247).

St GEORGE within our fair Cathedral ftands, (248)
　As tho' he with a bloody *Dragon* fights;
Worfe than abforbing *Brutes*, who fwallow Lands,
　Or hinder good Men to renew their Rights:
And thus his Image, which Time long has fpar'd,
For fair *Sabrina's* Sake, fhews him rever'd.

If not *Britannia's* Guardian dear confeft,
　How comes that Saint's Refemblance to be feen,
In fhining Armour, glitt'ring on the Breaft
　Of every valiant KING, and lovely QUEEN?
Long may He be rever'd, whilft Truth prevails;
And fight for *England*, whilft She prays for *Wales*.

---

(247) *In my juvenile Years, being driven by Storms into* Douglas, *in the Isle of* Man, *I met with such kind Usage from the Family of Mr.* Corris, *Mr.* Kendale, *and other Inhabitants, that on a lofty prominent Rock near the Place I was, as it were, inspired to write some Stanza's in their deserved Praise; And, afterwards, forc'd, thro' contrary Winds, towards the extremest Promontory or Westerly Corner in the most Northerly Part of* North-Wales, *in the Isle of* Mona, *or* Anglefey; *I was obliged to land at a Place (famous of old thro'* St. KIBY, *a pious Hermit) called* Holy-Head. *In my tiresome Journey from thence to* Weft Chefter, *I must needs own, what thro' false Report I did not expect in this Manner to observe, That I never found a* more *hospitable and good-natur'd People to distressed Pilgrims, or Strangers.*

(248) For a compendious Account of this Guardian Champion of *England*, I refer my kind Reader to my Hiftory of *York*, Pag. 31. where I treat of its magnificent Cathedral, juftly fo call'd, thro' the extraordinary Care of a moft illuftrious DEAN, and other worthy Dignitaries of the Church.

The END *of the* Fifth PART.

British PIETY Display'd
In the GLORIOUS
LIFE, Suffering, and DEATH
Of the Blessed

St. WINEFRED:

A Noble VIRGIN, martyr'd for her renowned Chastity, in *Wales:* Where, at Her Celebrated FOUNTAIN, called HOLY-WELL, many afflicted Persons have been happily freed from their miserable Distempers in past Centuries: The salutiferous Quality of which Water, continuing in the present Age, occasions its FAME to be spread in far-distant Kingdoms.

Ecclesia nunquam florentior, quam cum afflictior inter cruces & gladios suorum martyrum pugnas & victorias spectavit.— Natura rerum ad Deum nos erigit. Quam magnifica sunt Opera Tua, DOMINE!

"*DEUS ter Optimus Maximus in aquis summas excellentissimas recondivit vires salutares, quarum tanta est præstantia ut longè multumque omnibus aliis remediorum generibus sint superiores.*" That is, *The Most Glorious and Omnipotent* GOD *has conceal'd the greatest and most excellent salubrious Efficacy in the Waters; which have so prevalent a Power, that they are far superior to all other Kinds of Remedies.*

YORK: Printed and Sold by the Author THO. GENT, in *Petergate, Anno Dom.* MDCCXLII.

I thought it convenient to add the following Epitome, *in order to oblige* fome *Readers; who either may think it more eafy to be underflood, or affift them the better to perufe what has been pioufly written concerning the Holy Life of this celebrated Virgin.*

ST. WINEFRED, the Daughter of Lord THEWITH and Lady WENLO, was born in the troublefome Reign of King CADWALLOWN. As ſhe grew up, ſhe appear'd a perfect Beauty; and no Care was wanting in her Education. After the King dy'd, he was quickly fucceeded by ELUITH, the Second of that Name. Then flouriſh'd a very religious Prieſt, called BUENO, who fprung from noble Parentage. Whilſt he was paying a Vifit to his Relations in *Flintſhire*, in a particular manner he ſhew'd his Refpect to the aforefaid Lord *Thewith*, his Brother-in-Law, whofe Spoufe was his Sifter. In a long Difcourfe with him, he befought a Piece of Ground, that he might erect a Church upon for the Good of Souls in general; and to pray for the Happinefs of the Family in particular. The good Lord quickly condefcended to the pious Requeſt. Nay, he gave him the Manor he then liv'd in; making Choice of a fit Dwelling upon an Hill, not far from the Place: And befought the Saint to educate his fair Daughter. The Building immediately was promoted, and the Nobleman carry'd Baſkets with Materials to encourage others to follow on the Work. When it was finiſhed, there appear'd in all a conſtant Harmony in Devotion. The Child was much taken with St. BUENO's Preaching; and, by his Perfuafions, having won her to embrace a Life of Virginity, the Confent of her tender Parents was obtain'd, altho' they had defign'd to have given her in Marriage to fome worthy Perfonage in that Country. After this, no Creature could be more devout than the young Virgin. She became inflam'd with the Love of JESUS. Prayers iſſued from her Heart. She wept with

thofe

thofe that mourn'd, was liberal in her Alms to the Poor; and never a Word proceeded from her Lips but what was angelically divine.

One Sunday, while the Family was at Church, her being not well occafion'd her to ſtay at home. She was fuddenly furpriz'd at the unfeafonable Vifit of Prince *Caradoc*. When ſhe modeſtly aſked him, What his Pleafure was? He begun to boaſt of his being Son to King ALAN; and of his vaſt Riches, which ſhould be at her Service, if ſhe would but conform to his Embraces. Struck to the Quick with juſt Anger and Difdain, ſhe bluſh'd, and held down her Head: But, recovering her fainting Spirits, ſhe told him, That he might efpoufe a far more noble Lady than ſhe was; and that, undoubtedly, he was able to perform thofe great Endowments he had promifed, in Cafe he did her the Honour of mutually entering into a connubial State: Yet befought him to wait the Return of her dear Parents, which would be to all their Satisfaction, when Things were acted in a lawful Manner. But the haughty Prince, accounting his Will to be a Law, fuppofed himfelf like another CALIGULA, who was accuſtom'd to ufe this infamous Expreffion: *Memento omnia mihi, & in omnes licere.* So, faid he, *Remember, that 'tis lawful for me to ufe all* WOMEN, in Love-Affairs, *juſt as I pleafe;* and now, fair Lady, I will enjoy you. Thus the Villain, burning with Luſt, and impatient of Delay, began to be violently rude; fo that ſhe was oblig'd to have Regard to a pious Strategem. She wept, and conjur'd him, by all the Tyes of Honour and Generofity; by his Veneration to the Heathen Gods, if he had no Regard to the bleſſed JESUS, to whom ſhe was efpoufed in the Spirit, through her Vow of perpetual Virginity; that he would not further attempt to violate her Chaſtity, which was dearer to her than Life itſelf. But the wicked Prince, who was deaf to all pious Intreaty, and, like an untam'd Brute, profecuting his falacious Intention; ſhe then feem'd to comply with his Defires; but befought him,

fince

since he appear'd unwilling to tarry for the coming home of her dear Parents, that, at least, he would permit her to enter into her Closet, the better to adorn herself for his princely Enjoyment; and that she would make all the haste possible to answer his desired and fervent Expectations.

No sooner was she parted, but as it were a Gleam of Lightning she softly attain'd to a private Portal; out of which, as fast as her tender Feet would permit her, she ran towards the Church: But the Prince, fearing her Delay might frustrate his Design, quickly burst open the Door of her Chamber, which he thought a more proper Place for his Fruition. Finding her gone, the Fire of Indignation became added to that of his Lust. Has she deceiv'd me? Never will I forgive this Affront! cry'd the foolish, vain Prince; and, like a Coward, who would assault an innocent Lady, he drew his Sword, as he espy'd her from the Window. Down the Stairs he leapt with Fury; and, as a Wolf of Prey, with greater Strength and Speed than the harmless Virgin was endow'd with, he overtook the weeping Lady just as she was descending the Hill. Then, brandishing his Weapon like a simple Tragedian, and as such using the most illiterate Expressions, as tho' Life and Reputation were in his wilful Power, or to be adjudg'd safe and unstrain'd according to the ridiculous Sentence of a most arbitrary Villain, he thus foolishly roar'd out: Dost thou scorn me, false and deceitful Creature! thus vainly to fly from the superlative Happiness of being embraced in my princely Arms! What do'st thou deserve for this most heinous Contempt of my Person, honoured by every charming Lady, excepting thee? Be obsequiously quick, thou treacherous Damsel, in yielding to my Desires; or, by *Jupiter*, (who enjoy'd his beloved *Io*, the charming Princess *Alcmena*, and other terrestrial Beauties) I'll soon prevent thy second running from me, by separating thy deceitful Head from off thy fair Shoulders? Don't you see my Dagger is unsheath'd for the same Purpose? Be wise, therefore, while you may; and

do

do not thro' Perverfenefs, give me any further troublefome Provocation. But the noble Virgin, wiping off her pearly Tears, prefently appear'd as if fhe was in no manner intimidated, altho' the Blade almoft touched her milk-white Neck, which he held there by way of Terror. "Prince, *faid* "*fhe*, I moft humbly befeech your Pardon that I cannot pre-
"tend to accept you as my Husband; which, perhaps, with
"other Ufage I might have done, had I not, as I told you
"before, been confecrated, by way of Efpoufal, entirely to be
"devoted to the fupernal Embraces of my Bleffed Saviour·
"From my Infancy, as foon as I had the leaft Senfe to difcern
"how amiable He was; and with what Meeknefs he fuffer'd
"his moft precious Blood to be fhed for my Salvation; which
"He has alfo done for You, my Lord, if you pleafe but to
"repent, and be converted; indeed, I became fo enamour'd
"with his divine Sweetnefs, (for who could be otherwife that
"truly confiders the wonderful Series of his heav'nly Life, in
"which he was often deny'd a Place even to lay down his
"facred Head with Safety!) that I was eafily perfuaded to
"enter into that Contract, which, in my ferious Opinion, no
"Power upon Earth can, or at leaft ought, to diffolve. Did you
"but know what a Comfort He has been to my languifhing
"Soul, how He has preferved me from the Snares of Tempta-
"tion, fupported me under the moft grievous Pains thro' In-
"difpofitions I am fometimes fubject to, and even now raifes
"my Soul, tho' perhaps you think I may tremble under your
"heavy Difpleafure; fure I am, you would be of my Mind in
"placing your Love on Him alfo, who would lead you by the
"right Hand, keep your Feet from falling, dry up your
"penitential Tears, and conduct you to Glory. O may thefe
"pious Arguments of mine, moft noble Prince! have far
"greater Power over you to embrace a Life of Chaftity, than
"your fad Threatnings to affright me from my profeffed Vir-
"tue! But if Heaven, to try my Conftancy, thinks not fit to
"grant me this Petition for your Converfion; and that, as I

fear

"fear by your Countenance, your Heart, like *Pharoah's*, will
"prove fo harden'd as to have no Regard to the Laws of
"Heaven, or the Innocency of a diftreffed Maiden, which every
"worthy Knight is obliged, by their foverign Order, inftead of
"violating, to defend; here, behold, I ftand as a prepared
"Victim, willing to be facrificed at your Pleafure, rather
"than, by Menaces, be compell'd to hazard, indeed, both
"our Salvation. Believe me, O Prince! the Lofs of Life
"is of very little Value to that of my Virginity. I neither
"can, or will, forfeit my Title to the Love of my dearest
"Saviour: And if I prefently am to exift no more on Earth
"through the Effects of your cruel Paffion here; I know
"that my Redeemer liveth, who has promifed again to
"raife me with his Saints, and will be a moft merciful
"Judge, and kind Lord, to my precious happy Soul here-
"after."

What a pious and heroic Example is here recorded to eftablifh the Conftancy of blooming innocent Virgins to future Ages, as long as this World fhall endure!

The cruel Youth by her pathetick Speech was quite prevented from making any Reply to the injur'd Lady. She guefs'd his fatal Refolution; and, in refigned Humility to GOD, funk gently on her tender Knees, with her fmall white Fingers prettily infolded; the Tears gliding down her beautiful Cheeks; whilft her foft melodious Voice, in the moft moving Accents, was imploring Heaven to look upon her!—What Tyrant could have beheld fuch an affecting Sight, and not have relented? But raging Pride had got an abfolute Dominion over all the tender Emotions that are fufceptible to human Nature. For a while he trembled, and vainly urged her to comply; but fhe did not regard him: And whilft fhe was repeating, *JESU! have Mercy*— the mercilefs villain ftruck her fo forcibly on her beautiful Neck, that feparated her lovely Head from her well-fhap'd
Body:

Body: Which, tho' they mutually fell bleeding to the Ground; yet quickly became, for a while, as it were by a particular Providence, a confiderable Way, parted afunder!

Whilft the horrid Prince was wiping his Sword on the Grafs, he found the late glittering Steel had receiv'd fuch a fanguinary Tincture as was out of his Power to remove. Immediately, while the Blood furrounded him in circling Streamlets, as tho' confining him to a certain Space 'till condign Punifhment fhould be inflicted on him, he loft all Motion to go off undifcover'd: And when he had leapt over the sanguine Rivulet, he could move not much farther than the Margin thereof. Then, as if the Earth wept at the Horror of the Action, a Spring burft forth as it were from its opening Veins; the mingling Streams of which, flowing down the Hill, never appear'd a more beautiful Conjunction! In the mean while, the Head, no way unlovely thro' the ufual ghaftly Form of Death, rowl'd gently on the defcending Glebe 'till it reached the very Church Door, and fo proceeded to the Font, as if to declare, that IT was now baptiz'd with Blood as well as by Water. The People were ftruck with Amazement! The holy Prieft, defcending from the Altar, took up the precious Head, and accompany'd the mournful Parents with Tears. After which, they afcended the Hill, and found the princely Murderer ftanding fome little diftance from the holy Virgin's bleeding Body, as tho' without Power, or Concern. Villain! faid Bu'no, could neither thy Birth, her Innocency, or the fear of Judgment, keep thee from this nefandous Crime. Haft thou polluted the Sabbath, and offended thy Maker, without fhewing the leaft Sign of Repentance? I pray GOD immediately to punifh with Vengeance thy great Cruelty, moft deteftable to Heaven and Earth. He had fcarce faid thefe Words, but the Wretch fell down, quickly difappeared, and was fnatch'd away into a woful Eternity.

The

The holy Prieſt, taking Notice of the miraculous Fountain, placed the Head near to the Body; and, covering both with his Mantle, return'd into the Church, to end divine Service. This done, they all went again to the Place where ſhe lay: And after he had told them of her angelical Virtues, he earneſtly beſought Heav'n to reſtore her to Life. Accordingly, GOD was pleaſed to work a Miracle, by a wonderful Re-union: She aroſe on her Feet, and ſaluted the weeping Spectators; who obſerving a white Circle round her Neck, they chang'd her Name from BRUENA to WINEFRED.

Her Well became in great Eſtimation for moſt wonderful Cures: The Stones at the Bottom were tinctur'd with her Blood; from which a pretty cemented Moſs emitted a charming Smell like Incenſe, or ſweeteſt Perfume.

After her Refuſcitation from Death, ſhe took upon her a religious Habit; and her Parents, thro' St. *Bueno's* Advice, building fair Habitations round the Church, they ſoon became the Dwellings of young, noble and religious Virgins, who ſubmitted themſelves to the eaſy Yoke of CHRIST, under the Directions of their pious Daughter, whoſe Fame was ſpread to diſtant Nations.

In the meantime BUENO had founded a Monaſtery near the Sea Shore; and dy'd about the ſeventh Year of her being Abbeſs near *Finhon*. The Prieſt, DEIFER, who was her Confeſſor, had a Viſion that commanded him to tell WINEFRED to go to an holy Hermit, named SATURN, who ſhould direct her where to reſide. She having a fore-knowledge of what was reveal'd, anticipated the good Man's Journey by travelling to his Cell, 8 Miles from *Holy Well*;. and accordingly, as he told her, ſhe haſted to holy SATURN. That Hermit, having met her with great Reſpect, conducted her to his Chapel, and then accompany'd her ſome Part of the Way to the Valley of *Clutina*. At parting, he told her of the famous Abbey

Abbey built by St. ELERIUS, who would place her over pious Virgins, among whom fhe fhould fpend the Remainder of her Days. Thither fhe bent her Courfe; and was in Proceffion met by the Saint, conducted to the Convent, and on the Death of the Abbefs THEONEA was befought to take the holy Office upon her. Thro' GOD'S Affiftance fhe cured the Bodies of fick Perfons; and by her Wifdom comforted afflicted Minds. At length, as one Night fhe was ardently praying, fhe faw our Bleffed Saviour, who told her, that her Diffolution was drawing near; and bid her prepare for an happy Change. She received the Summons with Refignation, acquainted St. ELERIUS of the Vifion, which he did to the Virgins, who appear'd in melting Tears: But having comforted them with Hopes of a happy Meeting, fhe meekly refign'd her precious Soul to Him that made and preferv'd it. With great Lamentations of the Inhabitants fhe was interr'd at *Gutherine;* after which feveral devout Perfons were miraculoufly cur'd at her Tomb, thro' faithful and ardent Prayers; which fhew'd how dear fhe was to Almighty God, in accepting their Devotion perform'd in Honour of the bleffed Martyr: And in her Office of nine Leffons was this Prayer:

O Almighty and Everlafting GOD, who haft honoured the bleffed Virgin Saint WINEFRED *with the Reward of Virginity; grant to us, we befeech Thee, by* † *her Interceffion, that we may defpife the Allurements of this World, and together with her obtain the Seat of everlafting Glory.* Amen.

To conclude: We may remember to have read, that St. BUENO told the lovely Sufferer, If *the Well did not anfwer Expectations in a* firft *and* fecond *Pilgrimage; the* THIRD Vifit, *as if to try the perfevering Virtue of devout afflicted Perfons, would infallibly cure all their Grievances.* I wifh my kind Readers, when they have carefully perufed this little Book *twice* thorough at their leifure Hours, that THEY would be pleafed·

to

---

† Angelos preces noftras offerre Deo.

to allow it the Honour of a *third* Reading: Not only to weigh more maturely the Effects of what has proceeded from serious Contemplation, join'd with laborious Study, in order to delight Them; but that they might the more esteem the Merits of the fair Sufferer, and admire at the wonderful Effusion of her Spring, which have in past Times demanded Tributes of deserv'd Praise from the Pens of several Authors, as now they have done from this of mine, and Press too. And, thus, humbly taking my Leave, permit me to pray, That from the Tri-une Source of Highest Divinity may flow down on our precious Souls such clear cœlestial Streams that may wash off every polluted Stain, and make them whiter than Mountain Snow! May they pass with Safety, guarded by tutelar Angels, thro' this sorrowful Vale of Tears! May they be accepted in their proper Mansions amongst the blessed Company of Spirits, thro' the most glorious Merits of a crucify'd Saviour! And when, finally, He shall sit on the Throne of Judgment, attended by the heavenly Hierarchy of Saints and Angels; may We receive that blisful Sentence, foretold us in holy Scripture, to be most happy in His Presence to all Eternity; for which End his most precious Blood was shed upon the Cross.

An I N D E X *of the* Chief Paffages, &c.

A.

❖❖❖ POOR lame Youth, named Cornelius Nicholas, (Son of John,
❖ A ❖ of *Tremaine* Parish, *Cardiganshire*, about 2 Miles off the County
❖❖❖ Town) having, on *Dec.* 21, 1673, been struck so by a sudden
Blast; was cut, lanc'd, anointed, &c. But all in vain, 'till, being
put in the Well, *Friday, June* 12, 1674, he quickly recovered; to
the Admiration of the Beholders, who praised Almighty GOD *for
His Love to the Saints.* Part IV. Pag. 125.

Afflictions, Part I. page 50.; Part III. pages 94. 96. 98. 99.

Alan, King, Father to Prince Caradoc. Part I. p. 41.

Ambrosius, a most famous King. *Part* I. page 41.

Anger, how allay'd in others, as well as ourselves, thro' Vertue of that
great Humility taught by the Example of the Ever-blessed JESUS,
Part *I.* 49. —— That no Provocations should move us to *sinful*
Wrath; which, like tempestous Winds to floating Vessels, might
destroy our present and eternal Happiness, Part III. 94.

Anglia, Preface, pag. 40.

Anthony, Hermit. *Part* II. page 73. and V. pag. 140.

Antigonus, King, offends Heaven. *Part* V. pag. 136.

Apparitions, Part II. 71. Part IV. pag. 112. 119. and V. 139.

Aquisgrane, Part IV. page 124. and Part V. pag. 143.

Arthur, A famous King, Part IV. 109. See a full Account in my
English History, from Pag. 37 to 54.

Arwaker, (Edm.) translates *Pia Desideria,* Pref. p. 40.

Atalantis, by Lord Bacon, delightful to peruse, Pref. p. 39.

Aurora, *Titan's Daughter,* her Beauty compared, I. 42. Her Morning's
Splendor seen before Sun-Rise, II. 75.

Author

Author of this Book, who writ the Original by a Sort of Inspiration on Recovery from Sickness, his Desire it may be acceptable to the Publick, considering his Misfortunes, (One of which was the loss of an Estate thro' ‡ *repeated*—Death—which is generally more kind than to cause the *sudden* Destruction of *whole* Families, and for the most part *mercifully* proves to the *Gain* of the Living) Pref. 40. His Love to the People of YORK, amongst whom he has dwelt many Years, Part V. 141. His Remembrance of a kind Friend, who has much encouraged him in his pious Undertakings, *ib*. And his just Character of *Wales*, for the great Humanity and Civility shewn to him by the Inhabitants. Pag. 152.

AYWGI, or BINSI. Part I. page 44. and Part IV. pag. 109.

B.

Basingwerke, a *Cistercian* Abbey, situated about half a Mile from *Holy-Well*, of which Miracle some ONLY *suppose* the Monks to have been Inventors; and *wretchedly* mistake about the Foundation of the Monastery, It was begun in 1131. RANULPH Earl of *Chester* and his Barons, King HENRY II., the Princes LLEWELLIN and DAVID of *North-Wales*, were Benefactors. Part V. p. 133.

Base Actions always to be exposed with Safety; tho' not the Committers of them, 'till offended Heaven and Justice more visibly bring them to Shame, &c. Part III. 94.

BODENHAM, *Sir* ROGER, wonderfully cured, when given over for incureable by learned Physicians. Part IV. 120.

BRIDGES, Esq., High-Sheriff, records a Miracle. Part IV. 123.

BRUENA, Lord *Thewith's* Daughter, Part I. 45. How her Name came to be called *Winefred*, Part II. 71.

BUENO

---

‡ To the *Manes* of the Reverend Mr. *R. HITCH;* a Gentleman when living who proved himself such by his kind *Letters* to the Author, in regard to his Family and Station.

> *L*AMENTED SHADE! *Thy Kindness done to* Me;
> *But, what was* dearer! PITY *shewn to M I N E!*
> *Tho' new amongst the shining Saints* You *be,*
> *Thy Fate We'll mourn, and venerate Your Shrine!*
> *'Till Heav'n, like You, who stopt our streaming Tears,*
> *Shall (thro' Death's Summons) free our Souls from Cares.*

INDEX to the several PARTS.

BUENO, *St.*, his Birth, and Parentage, *Part* I. p. 44., IV. 109., becomes an itinerary Priest, *Part* I. 44. In the Reign of King ELUITH II. he applies to Lord THEWITH for Land to erect a Church, which was granted, *ib.* p. 45. has the spiritual tuition of that Nobleman's Daughter, and obtains her Parents' Consent to live a sanctimonial Life, Pag. 47. Excellent Instructions that he gave her, Pag. 48 to 51. Whilst preparing to offer the Unbloody Sacrifice, is surpriz'd, and takes up the bleeding Head of the martyr'd Virgin, *Part* II. 65. Reprehends the Heathen Prince, and foretells the Punishment, which happen'd, 66. Works a great Miracle thro' Prayer, 67 to 70. Sails to *Hibernia*, 71. Returns to *Finhon*, gives Charge to *Winefred* there to instruct young Virgins, foretells her Call to *Guitherine*, takes his final Farewell, and orders her annual Tokens to be sent after a wonderful Manner, Part III. 101. Obtains Favour of King CADVAN to erect a Monastery, 104. But happens to disagree with Prince CADWALLON, 'till the Breach was made up by the noble GWIDDANT, Part IV. pages 108. 109. He builds a Church, and dies, 110.

C.

CADOC, a most pious Bishop, and Martyr, Part I. 44.

CADVAN, a good Christian King, Part III. 104.

CADWALLIN, a most wise aud valiant King, Part I. 41.

CADWALLON, Prince, very bountiful, Part IV. 108.

Cambria, or *Wales*, the BRITISH Settlement, Part I. 41.

Carpenter's Daughter, near *Holy-Well*, having been born blind, is led to the Well, and prays, Part IV. 116. She miraculously obtains her long'd-for Sight, ib. 117.

Charity, its Benefit, Part I. 48, and Part III. 97 and 99.

CHRISTOPHER, *St.*, remarkably described, Part III. 91.

Clunock Vaur, a most stately Monastery there, Part IV. 110.

Clutina's Vale, pleasantly describ'd, Part II. 78.

Conscience, a most terrible Accuser, Part I. page 59.

Contemplation, how it raises the Mind, Part III. 97.

Contempt of the Simple to be unregarded, Part III. 95.

Content, the great Happiness of it, Part III. page 96.

CRADOC

CRADOC, Prince, his strange Visit to *S. Winefred*, Part I. 52. Is more enflam'd by her innocent Answer, 53. Rudely attempts to ravish the beautiful Virgin, who prays for deliverance, 54. Pursues her whilst endeavouring to escape, and kills her, 57 to 60. He insults the Priest who advised him to Repentance, and is swallow'd in the Bowels of the Earth, Part II. 66.

D.

Demons banished through divine Power, Part V. 144.

Death, what it is, and as we make it, Part I. 50.

DEIFER, a Priest of eminent Godliness, Part II. 72.

Denbigh, a fruitful Province in *Wales*, Part II. 72. 79.

Derider of the Saint and Pilgrims, a Judgment upon him, and such wicked Persons like him, Part IV. 122.

Dreams, &c. often prove *real* Warnings, Part V. 140.

Dry Vale, or *Barren-Bottom*, water'd with the Streams of *Fountain*, or *Finhon*, as it is in the *Welsh*, Part II. 67.

E.

EDMUND, a famous King and Martyr, Part I. Pref. 39.

ELERIUS, *St.*, meets *S. Winefred*, and on the decease of the Abbess *Theonia* prevails with her to accept of the Office, Part II. 81. He administers the last Holy Sacraments, and buries her, IV. 114. 115. And dies soon after, ibid. 115.

Equinox, what it signifies, and when. Part II. 73.

Eternity, A Subject of the greatest Consideration, I. 51.

F.

Fear, A special Mark or Stamp of Divinity, Part V. 135.

Finhon, or *Fountain*, called *Holy-Well*, &c., Part III. 100. 104.

Fountains, various in their Causes and Effects, Part V. 144. 145.

Friendship, A most Heavenly Comparison, Part V. 137.

G.

GEORGE, St. tutelar Guardian of *England*, Part V. 152.

GENESIUS, A Comedian, converted from a ridiculous Buffoon, becomes a glorious Martyr, Part IV. page 119.

GIRALDUS

GIRALDUS *Cambrensis*, who he was, Part V. page 132.

GLYCERIA, A martyr'd Virgin, Part IV. page 119.

GOD ALMIGHTY, His Wonders; and the stupendous Actions of Apostles, Martyrs, &c. Part I. 49. II. 66; 73 to 76. III. 102, &c. IV. 117. V. 138, &c.

GUIDDANT, His pious and noble Generosity, Part IV. 109.

Guitherine, Part II. page 81. Part IV. page 116.

H.

Heaven, the Joys thereof, Part I. 47   II. 64. &c.   III. 99.   IV. 113. How favourable to the Sick and Oppressed, when human Assistances quite fail us, III. 98.

HERBERT, Abbot, sends for Holy Relicks, Part IV. 118.

Hermit's Cell, near *Henthlant*, described, Part II. 77.

Holy-Well, its powerful Vertues, Part III. 101. IV. 128.

House of Hospitality to entertain Pilgrims, Part II. 80.

HUGO, *Hermannus*, a learned and pious Writer, Pref. 40.

Humility, its powerful Charms, Part I. page 49.

Hymn, Litanies and Pray'rs, used at *Holy-Well*, V. 146 to 150.

J.

JESUS, His Sufferings most pathetically described, Part III. 88. He is said to appear to *Winefred*, and to warn her of her approaching Dissolution, IV. 112.

Jews, their Respect for the Prophet ISAIAH, V. 139. But their amazing Cruelty towards our Saviour, III. 89.

Impatience in Affliction much to be avoided, Part V. 149.

JOSEPH of *Arimathea*, an excellent Personage, III. 90.

JUAN, Bishop of *Osma*, an excellent Writer, Pref. 40.

Judgments, Part I. page 51. And Part II. page 68.

K.

KENTIGERN, Bishop of *Glascow* and St. *Asaph*, Part I. 44.

KENN, an excellent Bishop, and seraphical Poet, Pref. 39.

L.

Labour, how profitable to Body and Soul, I. 50. III. 97.

LANDATUS, Abbot, related to St. BUENO, Part I. 44.

Life,

Life, A Shadow, Vapour, &c., Part I. page 50.
LYSIMACHUS, His great Disappointment, Part V. 136.

M.

MARY, Blessed Virgin, Her Grief compar'd, Part III. 90.
Marriage State, when a Blessing, &c., Part III. 95.
Martyrs, their Sufferings represented, Part II. 84, &c.
MERLIN, a Prophet, Part I. 41. See an Account of his Prophecies in my History of *England*, page 35.
Minerals, from whence they do proceed, Part V. 132.
Miracles, Part II. page 69. Likewise Part V. page 136.
Musick, its wonderful Power, Part III. 98. 99.

N.

Nature, represented in most curious Work, Part II. 83.
NEMESIS, who she was, and why mentioned, I. 59.
NUMAN, *Miss* MARY, surprizingly cured. Witnessed by JOHN HUGHES *de Combe*, ROBERT PRICE *de Aelwyducha*, Mrs. *Degg*, Mrs. *Paling*, &c· Part IV. 124.

O.

Obedience, How necessary to Happiness, Part III. 93. IV. 111.

Oppressors, who unmercifully seize the Effects of their innocent Fellow-Creatures dying without Restitution and Repentance, are in great danger of being absorb'd in the Jaws of Destruction, Part III. 94. Compar'd to *beguiling* Foes, deceitful in supporting the Distressed like *crooked*, *weak*, *untuneable* or *silly* REEDS, Part V. 137. Oppressors worse than the Dragon slain by St. *George*, or that of MOOR of *Moor-Hall*; because Death generally ended the Miseries of those swallow'd up, along with Virgins, Pigs, Geese, Houses, Churches, &c. But these *slow, grinding* Vermin [plurally and ludicrously styl'd in the *Canting* Dictionary *Nickums* and *Nockys*, signifying the Compounds of *Sharpness* and *Dulness*] suffer the highly Injur'd and Oppressed long to languish between their *racking* and *devouring* Teeth, impurely to feed their insatiable Avarice and Cruelty, when they *wou'd* hinder honest, well-meaning People from *renewing* their Rights, or by defending *Villany*, V. 152.

INDEX to the several PARTS.

P.

Passing-Bell, its Tolling of great Antiquity, Part IV. 114.

Persecution, An Encouragement to bear it, Part III. 96.

Philosophy, according to the Doctrine of *Zoroaster*, II. 74.

Physicians, &c. worthy of great Respect, Part V. 134.

Pilgrims, their Admiration at St. *Winefred*, Part III. 102.

Plants, the various Kinds they produce, Part II. 73.

Pools of *Bethesda* and *Siloam*, Part II. 67. Part V. 139.

Poor People, how we ought to comfort them, Part I. 51. Taken great Care of by the pious Clergy, Part IV. 110.

Poverty, How good People reduc'd to that state through Misfortune or Oppression, ought to be treated with great Tenderness, in Imitation of the Saint, Part I. 43.

Prayer, How uttered with Resignation, Part I. 48. 50.

Presumption and *Despair* to be avoided' Part III. 98.

Priest, cured of complicated Distempers, Part IV. 116.

Q.

Queen *Rowena* miserably burnt in a Turret, Part I. 41.

R.

ROGER, Earl, of his Monastery, near *Severn*, IV. 120.

S.

Saints and Angels, their Knowledge of what is done on Earth agreeable to St. *Luke's* Gospel, xv. 7. who writes of cœlestial *Joy* OVER *one that repenteth*, V. 140, &c.

SATURN, A venerable Hermit, Part II. 72. His Knowledge of Nature, and Piety to GOD, 73. 74. 75. The Situation of his Hermitage, Chapel, &c., 77. Description of his Person, ib. He hastes to meet S. *Winefred*, conducts her towards the Valley of *Clutina*, gives proper Directions, blesses her, and bids farewell, 78, &c.

Scarborough, on its past Loss thro' the falling of the Cliff, and present Happiness in Recovery of the *Spaw*, V. 143.

Seasons of the Year pleasantly described, Part II. 83.

SENAN, a most religious Confessor, Part II. 71.

Shrewsbury, A remarkable Town, &c., Part IV. 120.

Sighs from the Soul for an happy Eternity, IV. 127.
Sinners for their Sacrilege brought to Repentance, IV. 116.
Soul, how preciously it ought to be regarded, I. 50.
Sufferings of the Saints and Martyrs represented, II. 84.

T.

TAYLOR, Bishop, His three remarkable Instances, V. 136.
THEONIA, Abbess, dying, is succeeded by S. *Winefred*, II. 81. 82.
THEWITH, or *Tivy*, a Lord, Part I. 42. 45. III. 100.

V.

VORTIGERN, a most unfortunate King, Part I. 41.

W.

WHETSTONE, ROGER, a Quaker, miraculously cur'd, Part IV. 125. His grateful Acknowledgement and Behaviour on the Banks of the Streams, ibid. His Cure was affirm'd by ROGER HILL, another Quaker in *Worcestershire*, Overseer of the Poor of *Bromesgrove* Parish, whose Daughter was also cured by the Water in *August* the same Year when the amazing Cure was wrought upon ROGER WHETSTONE, the Taylor.

WINEFRED, S., Her noble Birth and Education, Part I. 42. Her early Charity, and panting Desires toward Heaven, 43. Her incomparable Beauty, 46. She desires to be espoused to the blessed JESUS, 47. Receives holy Instructions from St. BUENO, 48 to 51. Is surprized thro' an unwelcome Visit from an Heathen Prince, 52. Her prudent Answer to his Demands, 53. Resists his Embraces, 54. Prays to be deliver'd, 55. Evades his Intentions, 56. Her pious Resolution, heavenly Arguments, and cruel Murder, 59, &c. Her Soul in the outward Courts of Heaven, Part II. 63. 64. Miraculously is reinstated with the Body, and is called by the aforesaid Name, 69. Her Confessors, 71. Goes to venerable SATURN, 72. Entertain'd in his Cell, 78. Lodges in an Hospital of Virgins, 80. Met by the Convent of *Witheriacus*, and on the Death of THEONIA becomes Abbess, 81. The beautiful Works of the Virgins, 82, &c. Her Chapel describ'd, Part III. 87 to 91. Tenderness shewn to the Distressed, &c., ibid. Her Exhortations, 93 to 99. She is much visited by Pilgrims, 102., &c. Her continu'd Goodness, Part IV. 111. Receives Warning of her Death, 112. Is comforted, tells ELERIUS of the Vision, her dying Request, Death and Burial amongst the Bodies of glorious Saints, 113 to 115.

Advertisement.
PETER-Gate, YORK.
MDCCXLIII.

To all Ingenious Lovers of Art *and* Induſtry.

HAVING, in the Year 1724, removed my Printing-Preſs and Letters from *London* to this ancient City, on the Occaſion of eſpouſing the Widow of Mr. *Charles Bourne*, Printer, Grandſon to the memorable Mr. JOHN WHITE; and ſince then follow'd my lawful Profeſſion, for the Preſervation of my Family, with uncommon Care and Induſtry, to the preſent Time: I take this happy Opportunity in giving Notice, That I am now removed into *PETER*-Gate, (that which is called the *Lower Part* of it) but a little Way from *Stone-Gate.*—I humbly hope, thro' Divine Aſſiſtance, that the favourable Munificence of my Friends, conſidering the Contingencies in Life, will generouſly extend to the Place of my new Settlement, *repair'd* to withſtand the *Inclemency* of the Weather, *freed* from all filthy Incumbrances, and by *credible* Apartments fit to entertain the better Sort of well-bred Lodgers, or Cuſtomers that *rightly* encourage the true typographical Artiſts; thoſe only that become ſuch by Vertue of *lawful* Indentures, &c., and not by *interloping, ſurreptitious* Methods, to the Ruin of honeſt Practitioners: Which Houſe in *Peter-Gate* is made as neceſſary for a *Printing Office*, as tho' it had been contrived *Two* Hundred Years ago: Where Books in *Greek, Latin,* and *Engliſh;* alſo *Mathematical* Work;

Warrants,

Warrants, Hand-Bills, &c. may be printed in a neat and correct Manner. Likewife all Sorts of curious Printing-Work, that Gentlemen and Others fhall have Occafion to ufe, can artfully be done to Satisfaction; Travellers furnifh'd with various Sorts of Chapmens Books; Paper, Pens and Ink to be fold; as alfo the celebrated *Daffey's* Elixir, with Pictures, and various other Sorts of Goods.

And as I have, with great Expence, ufed my Endeavours to fet forth whatever might be of Ufe or Ornament to this famous City, its beautiful Aynfty, and extenfive County; I have fome Reafon ftill to hope for further Encouragement, by exhibiting the following Books, collected and written by me, either thro' Knowledge obtain'd in painful Travel, or Communication of kind Friends, and wrought by careful Servants at my Prefs: *Viz.*

I. The Antient and Modern Hiftory of the famous City of YORK; and in a particular Manner of its Magnificent Cathedral, commonly called *York* Minfter. As alfo an Account of St. *Mary's* Abbey, and other antient Religious Houfes and Churches; the Places whereon they ftood, what Orders belong'd to them, and the Remains of thofe ancient Buildings that are yet to be feen: With a Defcription of thofe Churches now in Ufe, of their curioufly painted Windows, the Infcriptions carefully collected, and many of them tranflated: The Lives of the Archbifhops of this See: The Government of the Northern Parts under the *Romans*, efpecially by the Emperors *Severus* and *Conftantius*, who both dy'd in this City: Of the Kings of *England*, and other illuftrious Perfonages, who have honqur'd *York* with their Prefence: An Account of the Mayors and Bayliffs, Lord-Mayors and Sheriffs, (with feveral remarkable Tranfactions, not publifh'd before) from different Manufcripts, down to the Third Year of His prefent Majefty. Publifhed in the Year of our Bleffed Lord 1730. *Price* 4s.

II. The

II. The Hiſtory of the Loyal Town of *Rippon:* Introduc'd by a Poem on the ſurprizing Beauties of *Studley* Park, with a Defcription of the venerable Ruins of *Fountains-Abbey;* and another of the Pleaſures of a Country Life, by a Reverend Young Gentleman. With particular Accounts of Three of the Northern Saints in the Seventh Century, *Viz.* St. CUTHBERT, who lies interr'd in the Cathedral at *Durham;* St. WILFRID of *Rippon;* and St. JOHN of *Beverley.* The famous Charters of King ATHELSTANE, and other great Monarchs, (given by Them to the Church of *Rippon*) tranſlated: The various Times of rebuilding that Minſter, ſince its firſt Foundation: Its preſent happy State; with the Arms, Monuments, and Inſcriptions, alphabetically digeſted. An exact Liſt of the *Wakemen* and Mayors of the Town to the Year 1733, interſperſed with ſeveral remarkable Accidents: The Death of ſeveral eminent Perſons: In particular, ſome of the venerable Archbiſhops of this See, whoſe Tombs are partly defcrib'd, with proper References to the Hiſtory of YORK, for their Inſcriptions and Epitaphs, to which This is very ſupplemental. Adorn'd with many Cuts, preceded by a South-Weſt Profpect (and a new Plan) of *Rippon.* Beſides are added, Travels into other Parts of *Yorkſhire.* 1. *Beverley*, an Account of its Minſter: The Seal of St. *John*: The Beauty of St. *Mary's:* And a Liſt of the Mayors of the Town, ſince incorporated. 2. Remarks on *Pontefract.* 3. Of the Church at *Wakefield.* 4. Thoſe of *Leeds:* With a Viſit to *Kirkſtal,* and *Kirkham.* 5. An Account of *Keighley.* 6. State of *Skipton* Caſtle, &c. 7. *Knaresborough.* Of the Church and its Monuments; St. *Robert's* Chapel, &c. 8. Towns near to YORK: As, *Tadcaſter, Bilbrough, Bolton-Percy; Howlden; Selby, Wiſtow, Cawood* Church and Caſtle; *Acaſter* and *Biſhopſthorpe; Acomb, Nun-Monkton* and *Skelton,* &c. with their Antiquity and Inſcriptions: Alſo the Delights of a rural State. Publiſhed in 1733. Price 4s. 6d.

III. *Annales*

III. *Annales Regioduni Hullini:* Or, The History of the Royal and Beautiful Town of *Kingston-upon-Hull*, from the Original of it, through the Means of its illustrious Founder, King *Edward* the First: Who (being pleas'd with its beautiful Situation whilst hunting with his Nobles on the pleasant Banks of the River) erected the Town, *Anno Dom.* 1296. And from that remarkable Æra, the Vicissitudes of it are display'd, 'till the Year 1735. In which are included, All the most remarkable Transactions, Ecclesiastical, Civil and Military. The Erection of Churches, Convents, and Monasteries: with the Names of their Founders and Benefactors: Also a succinct Relation of the *De la Pole's* Family, from the first Mayor of that Name, to his Successors, who were advanc'd to be Earls and Dukes of *Suffolk*. The Monuments, Inscriptions, &c. of the Churches of *Holy Trinity* and St. *Mary*. The Names of the Mayors, Sheriffs, and Chamberlains; with what remarkable Accidents have befallen some of them in the Course of their Lives: Interspers'd with a Compendium of *British* History, especially what alludes to the Civil Wars, (for the better Illustration of such Things as most particularly concern'd the Town in those troublesome Times;) and since then, with Regard to the Revolution. Set forth in 1735. Price 5s.

Lately Published,

IV. *Historia Compendiosa* A N G L I C A N A :

Or, A *Compendious* and *Delightful*

History of England:

WHEREIN IS CONTAINED,

An Account of its Rulers, or Kings, from about the Year of the Creation 2851, in the Time of the Prophet *Samuel*, to the Year of Salvation, 1741. Adorn'd with Portraitures, at length, of those Monarchs, who have sway'd the British Sceptre since the Conquest: The History of the Kings of *France* and *Scotland*: Particularly of the

latter

BOOKS *publiſhed* by T. GENT, *of* YORK. 175

latter Kingdom, from the Reign of the famous King FERGUS, *Anno Mundi* 3618, 'till King JAMES the Firſt united that Crown to the Engliſh Diadem: And an impartial Account of the Roman Pontiffs, from St. *Peter's* Crucifixion, to the preſent Pope *Benedict* XIV.

AS LIKEWISE

V. A fuccinct History of *ROME*, from its Foundation by ROMULUS 'till the Fall of *K. Tarquin*, occaſion'd by the Rape of the chaſte *LUCRETIA*: An Account of the Conſulate, Triumvirate, Higher and Lower Empires; the Removal of the Imperial Seat to *Constantinople;* Diviſion of the Eaſtern and Weſtern Empires; Diſſolution of the former by the *Turks;* with the Riſe of the *Mahometans*, and the Lives of their mighty Emperors, to the Year of our LORD 1742.

To which is annex'd,

An APPENDIX, relating to the City of YORK, and of thoſe illuſtrious Perſonages that have proved ineſtimable Bleſſings to this extenſive County: Particularly a mournful Tribute due to the ever-beloved Memory of the late Right Hon. CHARLES HOWARD Earl of *Carlisle*; and likewise to the precious Remembrance of the most incomparable Lady ELIZABETH HASTINGS. A Review of the Churches in YORK, ſhewing their Dimenſions; with modern Inſcriptions and Epitaphs over the Graves of eminent Perſons of both Sexes, who in Life have been juſtly celebrated for Learning, Hoſpitality, Virtue, Temper, Beauty and Piety. A further hiſtorical Account of *Pontefract*, and its once ſtupendous Caſtle, adorn'd with lofty Towers, more than ever yet has been exhibited; with the various Revolutions of its ancient Glory, and the ſurprizing Valour of its laſt moſt remarkable Defenders. A new Hiſtory, divided into Chapters, of the ancient St. ROBERT of *Knaresborough*; with the exact Dimenſions of his Chapel within a Rock near the pleaſant Streams of the River *Nid*. The Lamentation over ADONIS from the Original *Greek* of BION of *Smyrna*, which is exhibited beneath the Engliſh Tranſlation. With Indexes to the Whole, illuſtrated with explanatory Notes, deſcribing remote Parts of the Earth; Kings famous in ancient Mythology; Founders of States and Monarchies; and many curious Obſervations proper to entertain the ingenious Reader. In Two Volumes. 6s.

SOLI DEO HONOR ET GLORIA.

NAMES *of the* SUBSCRIBERS, *who, generously, by their Encouragement, set this Work to the Press.*

Mr. Chas. Alexander, of Colne.

B.
Miſs Nancy Banks.
Mr. Francis Bell.
Mrs. Mary Binns.
Mr. Marmaduke Bullock.
Mrs. Elizabeth Bullock.
Mrs. Ruth Burton.
Mr. Benjamin Burton.
Mr. John Bonſor, 2 *Books*.
Mrs. Frances Brookes.

C.
Mr. Richard Chandler.
Mr. Stephen Clarke.
Mrs. Mary Clarke.
Mr. William Cook.
Mrs. Mary Conyers.
Mr. James Coats.
Mrs. Mary Curtis.

D.
Mr. Francis Drake.
Mr. William Dickinſon.
Mrs. Mary Dickinſon.
Miſs Frances Dowbiggin.
Miſs Jenny Dowbiggin.

E.
Mr. J. Elſtone.
Mr. John Evans.

F.
Mr. Thomas Fawcett.
Mr. Peter Fawcett.
Mrs. Ann Fawcett.
Mrs. Alice Fawcett.

G.
Mr. George Gray.

H.
Mr. William Hall.
Mr. John Hamilton.
Mrs. Anne Harling.
Mr. George Harriſon.
Mr. Francis Haſſelgrave.
Mr. George Heartley.
Mr. Edward Hill.
Mr. H. Hindley, 3 *Books*.
Mr. Richard Howworth.
Mr. John Hopkins.
Mr. Thomas Houlden.
Mr. Robert Humphreys.
Mrs. Anne Hunt.

J.
Mr. John Jackſon.
Mrs. Magdalen Jackſon.
Mr. Francis Jackſon.

Mr. John Jefferſon.
Mrs. Elizabeth Juſtice.

K.
Mr. Thomas Kayley.
Mrs. Mary Kiddſon.
Mr. Knowlton, 21 *Books*.
Mr. Charles Knowlton.

L.
Mr. Thomas Laſhley.
Mr. John Lambert.
Miss Jenny Lambert.
Mr. John Lofthouſe.
Mr. William Long.

M.
Mrs. Iſabell Mitchel.
Mr. Robert Moon.

N.
Mr. Joſhua Nickſon.

O.
Mr. Thomas Oliver.
Mr. Marmaduke Oliver.

P.
Mr. William Paul.
Mr. William Potter.
Mrs. Anne Potter.

R.
Miſs Polly Ralph.
Mr. Thomas Riley.
Mr. George Reynoldſon.
Mr. John Roberts.
Mr. John Ruſſel.

S.
Mr. John Seynor.
Mr. George Skelton.
Mrs. Elizabeth Skinner.

T.
Mr. James Taylor.
Mr. John Tate.
Mr. Thomas Tredwell.

V.
Mrs. Elizabeth Vanner.
Maſter Richard Vevers.

W.
Mr. Cæſar Ward.
Mr. William Warrin.
Mr. John Webſter.
Mr. David Wood, Jun.
Mr. John Wood.
Mr. William Wood.
Mr. George Wright.

Y.
Mr. Joſeph Yarrow.

THE HISTORY

OF THE

LIFE and MIRACLES

Of our Blessed SAVIOUR,

JESUS CHRIST;

From His Birth to His Crucifixion.

AS ALSO, THE

LIVES, SUFFERINGS and DEATH

OF THE

EVANGELISTS and APOSTLES.

Taken from the Holy Scriptures, and the Learned Writings of Eminent Divines of the CHURCH to these Times. With explanatory Notes, relating to those Prophets, who foretold of our Blessed Saviour's Coming upon the Earth. By T. G.

Also the Respect, even of Heathens, shewn to our Blessed Saviour: As a Letter of Invitation sent to CHRIST by King AGBARUS; with our Saviour's Answer. And another Letter sent by PUBLIUS LENTULUS to the Senate of ROME concerning our Redeemer's Person, Doctrine, Miracles, and Behaviour.

Done into VERSE, for the Delight and Improvement of the weakest Capacity, and not unworthy the Perusal of the most knowing. The like never comprehended in so small a Volume before, and is particularly adapted to the Memory of Children.

YORK: *Printed and Sold by* THO. GENT.

To the Eternal Fountain of Goodnefs
JESUS CHRIST,
The Saviour of Mankind.

FOUNTAIN *of Fountains! let thy Streams*
  Diſtil into my thirſty Soul:
O Sun of Heav'n, impart thy Beams,
  To which SOL'S radiant Beams are foul;
That ſo, while I preſume to ſing,
  Thy quick'ning Spirit may inſpire,
With rapturous Joy; and with the Wing
  Of ſweet Devotion mount me higher.

Thy Life and Death's too too divine
  For any mortal Man to write:
Yet, Bleſſed Lord! I accept each Line,
  Which Love and Duty do excite;
Drawn from the Pens of Holy Men,
  Who did with Thee on Earth converſe;
Who con'd thy Actions, where, and when,
  And thy Original rehearſe.

Yet, farther, Lord, I thee beſeech,
  To help me through this falling Life;
Humble, like Thee, to be in Speech;
  Like Thee, behave through Cares and Strife;
That, when Death comes, to eaſe our Woes,
  We may enjoy thy Heavenly Sight;
With Pleaſure ſee this Veil difcloſe,
  And live with Thee, our Soul's Delight.

The LIVES of the Bleſſed JESUS, and His APOSTLES, &c.

CHAP. I.

ALMOST Four Thouſand Years had paſt,
  Whilſt Sin had ſpread invenom'd Wings,
'Till in AUGUSTUS' Reign, at laſt,
  Appear'd the Glorious KING of KINGS.

Like to the DAWN, * *AURORA* fair,
  The Bleſſed † VIRGIN may be ſtyl'd;
But, as the DAY, more bright and clear,
  Such was the Heavenly INFANT mild.

Thus GOD His Promiſe did fulfill,
  What ‡ PROPHETS long of CHRIST foretold:
MARY obey'd the Heavenly Will,   *Luk.* I. 38.
  Which JOSEPH's Viſion did unfold.   *Mat.* I. 20, &c.

When Great AUGUSTUS rul'd in Rome,
  The Thirty Seventh of Herod's Reign,
JOSEPH and MARY, to the Town
  Of Bethlem, in Judea, came.   *Luk.* II. 4.
                                        The

---

* *Quæ est ista quæ progreditur quasi Aurora consurgens.* i.e. What is ſhe that goeth forth as a riſing Morning? *Serm.* of John *Bishop of* Rocheſter.

† *When the Virgin* Mary *conceived by the Holy Ghost, she was but fifteen Years of Age.*

‡ Isaiah, *who is call'd the Evangelical Prophet.* Hoſea, *of his flying into Ægypt.* Micah, *of his Birth.* Jeremiah, *of his springing from Jacob.* Daniel, *that he should put a Period to the Oblations of the Levitical Priests.* Hagai, *animating the People with the Desire of all Nations.* Malachi, *the Restoration of Jerusalem.* John Baptiſt, *(Son of Zechariah the Priest and his Wife Elizabeth) that he should turn the Hearts of the Fathers to the Children.* Zachary, Viſitavit nos Oriens ex Alto: Illuminare his qui in Tenebris & in Umbra Mortis ſedent. *i.e. To give Light unto them that sit in Darkness, and in the Shadow of Death.*

The Inns were fill'd, so they constrain'd
  To Stables, cut from harden'd Rocks;
One of them chose, a Manger gain'd,　　　　*ver.* 7.
  Where, feeding near them, was the Ox.

Here, without Pain, as without Sin,
  The Holy Virgin's brought to Bed!
The Infant fair, without, within,
  In swadling Clothes reclines its Head.

Alas! sweet Child! was there no other,
  No better Place to lay thy Head?
No softer Bed for thy dear Mother,
  But both obscurely here be laid?

Yet, what to Great Ones were conceal'd,
  To Shepherds, near where David kept　　　*ver.* 8.
His Sheep; to these Heaven first reveal'd
  Glad Tydings, whilst all others slept.

An ANGEL bright, encircled round
  With Glories transparently clear:
"Shepherds, (said He) Let Joys abound;
  "Let now attentive be your Ear.

"A SAVIOUR to the World is born,
  "A Babe to Humane Eyes display'd,
"All poorly wrapt in swathing Bands,
  "And in a Manger laid."

'Thus spake the Angel, and forthwith
  'Appear'd a shining Throng
'Of ANGELS, praising GOD, and thus
  'Began their joyful SONG.

"All Glory be to GOD on High,
  "And to the Earth be Peace:
"Good Will from Heaven to mortal Men
  "Begin, and never cease."

　　　　　　　　　　　　　　　　Thrice

Thrice happy, happy Shepherds then,
  To hear, fuch as the Angels fung
When GOD created Heaven and Men, *Job* XXXVIII. 7.
  Such their Redemption loudly rung.

When to the higher Heavens they flew,
  And Shadows fill'd their lightfome Space;
With Joy the watchful Shepherds knew,
  By Angel's Guide, to find the Place.

Thro' every Village, which they pafs'd,
  Proclaim'd the Joyful happy Sound.
Words upon Words, like Echoes grac'd,
  When they 'gainft Rocks and Hills rebound.

Kings of CHALDEA, PERSIAN Lands,
  And of ARABIA's Defarts wild,
A Bright Cæleftial STAR demands
  Their Journey to the Heavenly Child.

Unwearied Steps their Travels blefs,
  They come to fair Jerufalem;
KING OF THE JEWS, they CHRIST exprefs,
  Who ought to wear the Diadem.

Thence paffing unto Bethlehem Town,
  The Star, obfequious, ftopt above:
Proftrate the Eaftern Kings fell down,
  And fhew'd their Loyalty and Love.

Thofe Products, which their Countries yield,
  Bright fhining Gold, and Odours fweet;
What grac'd their Perfons, or the Field,   *Mat.*
  They laid 'em at our Saviour's Feet.   II. 11.

HEROD enrag'd, when well he knew
  His Sanhedrim's prognoftick Tale;
In Blood he would his Hands imbrue,
  That over CHRIST he might prevail.   *ver.* 16.

Alas!

*Alas! what horrid dread Alarms,
  What mournful Sights did fill the Plain!
The Children, dragg'd from Mothers Arms,
  Were stuck on Spears, or cut in twain!

But all in vain, the Heav'nly Power
  Doth shield the Son of Heav'n from Ill;
And after, Worms did him devour,   JOSEPHUS.
Who would our Blest Redeemer kill

CHAP. II. *Of our Redeemer's Life and Miracles.*

AT Twelve Years old, most strange to hear,
  He in the Temple plainly show'd,
To Jewish Doctors sitting there,   *Luke* II. 46. 47.
Such Knowledge like the Son of God.

When in Judea's Desart brought,   *Matt.* IV. *Luke* IV.
  Enabled forty Days to fast,   and *Mark* I.
In vain the Tempter did accost,
  And ‡ lost his Labour to the last.   ‡ MILTON.

Not the fair Temple's highest Spire,
  Nor Pisgah's Mountain could him charm;
CHRIST forc'd the Tempter to retire,
  And of his Weapons did disarm.

Soon after he Disciples gain'd,
  And still to make himself divine,
At Cana's Feast, his Power maintain'd,
  He turn'd their § Water into Wine.

Those, who would buy, and who wou'd sell,
  He drove from off the Temple's Floor. *John* II. 15.
With Woman, at Samaria's Well,   *John* IV. 7.
  Discours'd of living Water's Store.
                                                                               The

---

* *In this Massacre, a Son of King* HEROD'S, *then at Nurse, was slain with the rest.*

§ John ii. 7, &c. *Some say the six Water-Pots held eighteen hundred Quarts.*

The Son of Chuza, Herod's Steward,   *ver.* 46, &c.
   Our Saviour with a Word did heal:
That, and the Father's Faith, reſtor'd
   What the Youth's Safety did reveal.

Peter and Andrew, James and John,   *Luk.* V.
   To theſe while on the Silver Main,
His Power commands the finny Throng,
   When as before they fiſh'd in vain.

A poor Man by a Dæmon griev'd,   *Luk.* IV. 33.
   With Sin, and Satan's Power Stung;
He from convulſive Pains reliev'd,
   For which Chriſt's Fame was loudly rung.

Peter's Wife's Mother he reſtor'd   *Mat.* VIII. 15.
   From ſcorching Fever's burning Heat;
The laying of his Hand, or Word,
   Heal'd all Infirmities compleat.

° Betheſda's Pool, could not do more,
   In curing thoſe, who enter'd in;
Chriſt did the Impotent reſtore,
   And heal'd the believing Soul from Sin.   *Luk.* VII. 50.

He cur'd the lame Man's wither'd Hand;   *Mark* III. 5.
   Numbers, who touch'd him, found Relief;   *ver.* 10.
Spirits impure, at his Command,
   Were diſpoſſeſs'd to Satan's Grief.   *Matt.* VIII. 16.

Near Galilee, a Widow's Son,   *Luk.* VII. 12.
   Deceas'd, was borne upon a Byer;
Chriſt ſpoke the Word, the Work was done,
   The Youth aroſe, whilſt all admire.   *v.* 14, 15.

---

* *A famous Pool, S.E. Part of* Jerusalem, *which washing the Sacrifices,
'twas thought a descending Angel gave it a healing Quality.*

A poor Demoniac, blind and dumb,   *Mat.* XII. 22.
  Reſtor'd to Uſe of Speech and Sight,
Declares him to be David's Son,
  Againſt blaſpheming Jewiſh Spite.

Embark'd upon the raging Sea,   *Mat.* VIII. *ver.*
  While his Diſciples were afraid,   23 to 27.
Both Winds and Waves our Lord obey,
  In Cliffs and Mountains hide their Head.

Two Creatures poor, poſſeſs'd in Mind,   *ver.* 28
  One with a Legion wounded ſore;   to 32.
Chriſt made thoſe Devils enter Swine,
  And trouble theſe two Men no more.

JAIRUS'S Daughter he reſtor'd,   *Mark* V. 42.
  Altho' embrac'd by Death's cold Hand:
Two blind Men but implor'd the Lord,   *Mat.* IX.
  And they by Faith their Sight regain'd.   29, 30.

A Multitude by Chriſt was fed,   *Mat.* XV. 36. 37, &c.
  With two ſmall Fiſhes, Loaves but ſeven;
He on the Sea, as Braſs, did tread;   *Joh.* VI. 19.
  A Dæmon was from Virgin driven.   *Mark* VII. 29. 30.

He cur'd a Man both deaf and dumb.   *Mark* VII. 33.
  His Fingers put into his Ears,   34. 35.
With Spittle laid upon his Tongue,
  The wond'ring Patient ſpeaks and hears.

On Tabor's lofty Mountain bleak,   *Luk.* IX. *ver.*
  Our Saviour was intent in Prayer;   28 to 31.
There MOSES and ELIAS ſpeak,
  There cloath'd in Glory did appear.

The Apoſtles heard a Voice from Heaven,
  "Hear him, my pleas'd beloved Son!"   *ver.* 35.
No greater Sign could ſure be given,
  Nor more amazing Wonders done.

A poor

A poor Man's Child, by Spirit vile,   *Mat.* XVII. 15.
  Alternate thrown in Streams and Fire;
JESUS! He took him but a while,
  And Hell's infernal Troops retire.

A wicked Spirit, of evil Kind,   *Luk.* XIII., *v.* 12. 13.
  Abus'd a Woman eighteen Years:
A Man too, who had been born blind,   *Joh.* IX. 7.
  Chrift eafes them of both their Cares.

Four Days was LAZARUS in his Tomb,   *Joh.* XI.
  'Till Jefus call'd him out from thence.   17. *to* 44.
This prov'd the Great Meffiah come,
  And fhew'd divine Omnipotence.

Many the Scriptures do declare
  Of Wonders great beyond my Verfe;
Which not the Books that written are,
  Or fhould be writ, could full rehearfe.   *Joh.* XXI. 25.

CHAP. III.   *Containing our Saviour's Sufferings and Afcenfion.*

YE Priefts and Scribes, moft unbelov'd,
  As much as falfe Things are to true:
The Earth felt Earthquakes; how unmov'd,
  How could you, Monfters, how could you?

King AGBARUS a Letter fent
  Unto our Bleffed Saviour dear:
Words that are holy, permanent,
  And do require attentive Ear.

✦ ✦ ✦ ✧

King AGBARUS'S Letter.

"OF thee I've heard, and of thy Fame,
  "Beyond all Natural, Human Skill;
"Thou cur'ft the Leprous, Blind and Lame,
  "And cafts out Devils, thro' thy Will.

                            "I hearing

"I hearing thefe, my Belief is this,
 "Thou muft be God, or elfe His Son:
"For in this World, none fure there is,
 "Can do thofe Wonders thou haft done.

"Wherefore fince I do underftand
 "The Jews do ftrive to work thee Hate:
"Come, come, thou Bleffed! out of Hand,
 "Come to my City, fmall, but neat.

"Twill ferve us both; you welcome are,
 "And glad I'll be to fee thy Sight." *
Pleas'd with the King, our Saviour dear
 This kindly Anfwer did indite:

✦ ✦ ✦ ✦

Our Saviour's Anfwer to King AGBARUS.

"BLEST are thou, O AGBARUS, King,
 "In whofe Heart Faith divinely reigns;
"And me, thy Saviour, yet unfeen,
 "My Honour undefil'd maintains.

"Tis writ of me, They which have feen,
 "Should never on me ftedfaft believe;
"That thofe, who have not happy been
 "In feeing me, fhould believe, and live.

"But as to what thou feem'ft intent,
 "Thefe are to intimate to thee,
"I muft return to Him that fent,
 "When all Things are fulfill'd of me.

"Yet after my Afcent to Heaven,
 "A Bleft DISCIPLE thee fhall cure;
"Thy fad Diftemper quite be driven,
 "New Life be given, found and pure.

"And

---

* *This Letter, and the Answer to it, was translated by EUSEBIUS, out of the Records of EDESSA, written in the Syrian Tongue.*

"And not to thee, O King, alone,
 "But unto all who round thee wait;
"Knowledge thro' Me fhall blefs thy Throne,
 "And bring Thee to my Father's Gate."

Thus Lentulus, in Tiberius Time,   *Josephus.*
 Governour of JUDEA fair,
A Letter wrote to thofe of Rome,
 Concerning Chrift our Saviour dear.

✦ ✦ ✦ ✦

Publius Lentulus's Letter.

"IN our Days a Man appear'd,
  "Still living, JESUS call'd by Name;
"Who as a Prophet is rever'd,
  "Nay, call'd God's Son, of Heavenly Frame.

"The Dead he raifes, Sicknefs heals,
  "A Man of Stature, comely, tall!
"Rev'rence his Countenance reveals,
  "Which caufes Fear, yet Love withall.

"His Hair of Chefnut Colour ripe,
  "And plain down almoft to his Ears:
"From thence 'tis fomewhat curl'd, more bright,
  "O'er Shoulders, waving, it appears.

"Mid'ft of his Head, a Seam of Hair,
  "Goes parting like a Nazarite:
"Smooth doth his lovely Face appear,
  "Which, mix'd with Red, attracts the Sight.

"His Nofe and Mouth fo comely, fair,
  "Nothing can reprehended be;
"His Beard thick, colour'd like his Hair,
  "Eyes grey, and quick with Majefty.

"When

"When he reproves, he's then fevere,
    "Counfelling, you'd think an Angel fpeaks;
"Tho' grave his Speech, yet charms the Ear
    "Of him, who his lov'd Doctrine feeks.

"No one has feen this good Man laugh,
    "But weeping, fearing others' Harms;
"His Body ftrait, of beauteous Shape:
    "Delectable his Hands and Arms

"In Speaking, temp'rate, modeft, wife;
    "A Man for fing'lar Beauty; when
"We look, we find him, with Surprize,
    "Exceeding far the * Sons of Men."

Thus Heathens, of our Bleffed Lord,
    Wrote with refpective Eloquence,
Whilft cruel JEWS, to be abhorr'd,
    Blafphem'd divine Omnipotence.

If we now mark his Life and Death,
    Our Tears fhould prove like falling Show'rs,
For his dear Sake, who, when on Earth,
    Shed melting heaven-like Tears for our's.

PALM SUNDAY.

The JEWS, now mad, our Lord to fee,
    And People's Hands with Palms replete,
To vote his Death they all agree,
    Whofe Power they view'd fublime and great.

MONDAY.

The Fig-Tree falls a Sacrifice,
    Becaufe no Old Fruit grew thereon:
The Money-Changers out he drives,
    Who in the Temple were a Throng.

TUES.

---

* Psalm 45. 2. *Fairer than the Children of Men.* Besides this, *Josephus* gives a great Character of our Blessed Saviour.

TUESDAY.

JESUS difputes his Power there,
  Defeats the Scribes and learned Men;
To Mountain Olivet doth repair,
  And tells of Wonders how, and when.

After doth wafh th' Apoftles' Feet,
  Declares the Traytor JUDAS vile;
To him he gives the Sop to eat,
  That treach'rous Wretch, who fhould beguile.

WEDNESDAY.

The Priefts affemble, JUDAS goes,
  Betrays his Lord for wretched Gold:
For * thirty Pieces heap'd on Woes,
  When he his Bleft Redeemer fold.

THURSDAY.

At Night the Supper forth was fet,
  When Bread was given, Wine it flow'd:
To Gethfemane Chrift went, and wept,
  And pray'd 'till he fweat Drops of Blood.

Near which, the JEWS did apprehend
  Our Lord, betray'd by JUDAS Kifs;
The Apoftles fly, and PETER then
  Deny'd his Bleffed Mafter thrice.

Good FRIDAY.

Next Morning, *Pilate* would releafe,
  But all the cruel JEWS faid, No!
Then mock'd, they robe him in Difgrace,
  And fend to *Herod* too and fro.

That

---

* They were called Staders, or Shekles of the Sanctuary, which amount to Three Pounds Fifteen Shil. of our Money.

That Chrift, (O ftrange it is to tell!)
Should Subftitute his Heav'nly Frame,
With Mocks and Scourges here fhould dwell,
And on the Crofs expofed in Shame!

Between two Thieves be crucify'd,   *Luk.* XXIII. 33.
Pierce'd thro' his Side, his Hands, and Feet!
Bleeding, whilft curfed *Jews* deride,   ver. 35.
Could Cruelty be more compleat?

Yet,

Yet, far from calling Vengeance due,
 Chrift prays for them, whofe Sins were moft.
Forgive......they know not what they do!   ver. 34.
 Then bowing, yielded up the Ghoft.

The Temple rends, the Rocks are fplit, *Mat.* XXVII. 51.
 While different Orders change their Place:
The † bright Sun, as with Horror fmit,
 In Deteftation, veil'd its Face.

O who can tell the Virgin's Grief!
 A Sword feem'd piercing to her Heart: *Luk.* II.
Her Son, the Lord o'er Heaven and Earth,   35.
 To feel for us fuch bitter Smart!

Cruel Longinus! could'ft thou bore
 Thy Saviour's Side, with fharpen'd Spear?
'Tis well thou didft; 'tis one Wound more,
 In which our Sins immerged are.

Thrice happy ° Jofeph, then to greet,
 With melting Eye, thy Saviour dear!
In Linnen wrapt, with Spices fweet,
 To lay him in thy Sepulcher!

SATURDAY.

On this Day Pilate fent a Guard
 To watch our Saviour's filent Tomb,
Becaufe that JESUS had declar'd
 The Third Day he from thence would come.

EASTER

---

† When Dioniosius the Areopagite, was at Athens, and perceived the wonderful Eclipse, he cryed out, Aut Deus naturæ paritur, aut Mundi machina dissolvetur. That is, Either the God of Nature suffers, or the Frame of this World is dissolved.

° This Joseph was the Son of one Matthias, at Arimathea, and was a Pharisee, 'till our Saviour preach'd his Doctrine. The Sepulchre was made for himself, 8 Foot long, situated about 180 Foot from Mount Calvary

EASTER SUNDAY.

When Mary Magdalen, with more,
    Went the next Morn, to pay their laſt
To Him, whom they in Life adore,
    Were at th' amazing Sight aghaſt.

The Guards lay proſtrate, tho' as dead,
    No Stone was found againſt the Door!
The Napkin left, which bound Chriſt's Head,
    And Shroud that vail'd his Body o'er.

Inſtead of which, they ſtrait beheld
    Two Angels ſhine with Glory bright; *Luk.* XXIV. 4.
Back, ſent to Peter, they reveal'd
    Chriſt's Reſurrection, and their Sight.

Peter and John did thither go;   *Joh.* XX. 3.
    Return'd again: Mary behind,
Lamenting, JESUS let her know,   *ver.* 16.
    'Twas Him ſhe ſought, and ſooth'd her Mind.

To two Diſciples he appears,   *Luk.* XXIV. 15.
    As they walk'd to Emaus Town;
Who knew him not, 'till his Diſcourſe   *ver.* 31.
    Clear'd up their Eyes; then Him they own.

Back,

Calvary, and distant 1000 Paces from Mount Sion: It was cut out of a Rock: Our Saviour's Head was placed towards the West, with his Face to the East; a Custom to this Day in Use among the Christians. After Christ's Death, Joseph lived a solitary Life, 'till being adopted one of the 72 Disciples by St. Peter, after many Tribulations, he was ordain'd to preach the Gospel in England; where landing at Barrow-Bay in Somersetshire, he came from thence to Glastenbury, 3 Years after Christ's Death, aged 54, where he having set his Staff in the Earth, it turned into a blossoming Thorn, which to late Times was noted for budding Yearly on Christmas Day in the Morning, blossoming at Noon, and fading at Night. Joseph had with him twelve Companions, by whom the Abbey of Glastenbury was built; which in succeeding Ages was amply endow'd with Revenues, ornamented and honour'd by Princes and Kings.

Back to Jerufalem they hafte,
  Where Peter did his Saviour fee:
JESUS to all appears, and afks   *Luk.* XXIV.
  For Meat, and eats, to fhew 'twas He.   v. 41. &c.

Bids them, The Holy Ghoft receive.   *Joh.* XX. 22.
  But faithlefs Thomas was not there:
Who told of this, could not yet believe
  'Till JESUS did again appear.

Reach here thy Fingers, faith our Lord,   v. 27.
  And thruft thy Hands into my Side.
Thomas his Unbelief abhorr'd:
  My Lord! My God! he then reply'd.   v. 28.

Seven of the Apoftles fifh'd at Sea,
  And nothing all the Night they caught;
But at the Dawn of following Day,
  Our Lord did help them to a Draught. *Joh.* XXI. 6.

Peter with hafte did fwim therefore,
  And with the reft did hafte to Land:
Chrift dines with them upon the Shore,
  And gave to Peter ftrict Command.   *ver.* 15, 16, 17.

Another Time, our Lord appear'd   *Mat.* XXVIII. 16, &c.
  Upon a Galilean Mount;
Five Hundred Brethren there rever'd,
  Which all their Scruples did furmount.

There Power was given for to baptize,
  And preach the Gofpel every where;
That Devils ejected be likewife,   *Mark* III. 15.
  The Sick recover'd by their Care.

St. James too had our Lord's bleft Sight,   I *Cor.* XV. 7.
  When forty Days were almoft fpent;
O inexpreffed fweet Delight,
  Extatick Joy, and fweet Content!

                                              The

The Apoſtles privately being met,
  With others at Jeruſalem,
On the laſt Day, as They were ſet,
  Chriſt ſuddenly appear'd to them.

Promis'd the Holy Ghoſt with Speed,
  Them leads to Olivet's high Head,
Where more his Glory did exceed,
  He ſhew'd thoſe Wounds, which for us bled.

His Benediction then he gave,
  Whilſt they ador'd, with bended Knees;
With wiſhful Eyes they took their Leave,
  And ſaw him mounting by Degrees.

A Cloud enfolds the Heavenly God,
  Triumphantly he rides to Heaven;
And there He makes His Blest Abode,
  By whom Alone we are forgiven.

Mr. Eachard says, in his Ecclesiastical History, Vol. I. p. 217: "That our Lord ascended on the 14th Day of our Month May, the "9th Month of the 19th Year of the Emperor Tiberius, and in the "36th Year of his Age. And that if he was born (as Christians mostly "concur) on the 25th of December, the full Time of his Continuance "on Earth was precisely 36 Years and 5 Months; almost a Year more "than his Fore-runner John Baptist, who is commemorated the 24th "of June."

The LIVES of the Evangelists and Apostles.

St. MATTHEW, Evangelist and Apostle.

THRO' Persia, and throughout the Parthian Lands,
  He preach'd the Gospel of our Blessed Lord;
At Nuddabar, near Ethiopian Strands,
  He fell a Martyr for the Holy Word.
The horrid People cast him in a Flame,
  Which not consuming his most precious Life,
Quite thro' his bleeding Heart a Halbert came,
  And thus he left this World of Care and Strife.

This Evangelist was an Hebrew, Son of Alpheus, a Galilean, and of Mary, Kinswoman of the Blessed Virgin; and was also Collector of the Jews, 'till our Saviour call'd him at Capernaum. His Festival is on the 21st September.

St. MARK, the Evangelist.

IN Egypt, and in Africk's Countries wild,
  This Saint Christ's Doctrine boldly did maintain,
'Till, in fair Alexandria, beguil'd,
  By Pagans this Evangelist was slain.
With binding Cords those bloody Wretches ty'd
  His tender Feet, then dragg'd him on the Stones;
Thus bruis'd and bleeding, in that Cafe he dy'd,
  And yielded up his Soul with bitter Groans.

His Festival is on the 25th of April.

St. LUKE, the Evangelist.

THIS skilful Painter unto Christ did turn,
  Taught by St. Paul those Things that are divine:
And while his Heart with glowing Zeal did burn,
  He wrote his Gospel, fam'd in ev'ry Line:
Then preach'd in Egypt, Lybia, and in Greece,
  Until Barbarians hung him on a Tree;
Whose happy Soul did mount to Heavenly Bliss,
  And with his Master lives eternally.

His Festival is on the 18th of October.

St. JOHN, *the Evangelift and Apoftle.*

BY our dear Lord he was moſt lov'd, 'tis plain,
  Chriſt calls him Boanerges, Son of Thunder.
Some thought he ſhould live 'till he came again,
  Yet tho' he did not, here appears a Wonder.
Domitian, Emperor, caſt him into * Oyl,
  In horrid Caldron over burning Fire;
Cool turns the fame, and back the Flames recoil,
  As, lo! this Sight averts the Tyrant's Ire.
Howe'er to Patmos Iſle he's ſent a Slave:
  But, lo! what Angels ſeek him in the Mine!
What wond'rous Truths he wrote, Sights which Heav'n gave,
  And which, while e'er the World do's laſt, will ſhine,
'Till rolling Ages ſhall the fame declare.
At Epheſus this bleſt Beloved dy'd.
To Him our Lord bequeath'd his Mother dear,
  When He upon the Croſs was crucify'd.

His Festival is December 27.

* The Hiſtory of this holy Saint's being caſt into Oyl, with what was reveal'd to him, is excellently deſcribed in the painted Glaſs of the Eaſt Window in York Minſter, which equals (if not exceeds) any Church Window in this Kingdom; the Deſcription of which has been publiſhed in the History of York, compil'd by the Author of this little Book.

St. PETER, *the Apoftle.*

PETER by Herod was confin'd in Chains,
  But after, at Conſtantinople great,
He preach'd the Goſpel with pure Zeal and Pains,
  Converting Thouſands to a Bleſſed State.
But when to Rome this Saint again was come,
  The bloody Emperor Nero, in his Ire,
Did cauſe him for to ſuffer Martyrdom,
  And crucify'd he was to his † Deſire.

His Festival is June 29.

† *He was firſt ſcourg'd, and then crucify'd with his Head downwards, in Humility to his Bleſſed Maſter Chriſt Jeſus.*

St. ANDREW, the Apoſtle.

SCYTHIA, Gallatia, Nice, Chalcedon too,
   There preach'd the Goſpel with a fervent Heart;
But Petræus, Conſul, unto Heav'n ne'er true,
   He would convert, which caus'd his bitter Smart:
For which condemn'd, he to a Croſs was nail'd,
   Whereon, tho' painful, ſtill he preach'd the Word,
Two Days in ſuff'ring, yet his Voice prevail'd,
   And then expiring went unto the Lord.
His Festival is November 30.

St. JAMES the Great, Apoſtle.

HE was a fervent Preacher of the Word,
   And for the fame by Herod loſt his Head:
But Time will everlaſtingly record,
   Jeruſalem, the Place he ſuffered.
His Festival is July 25.

St. PHILIP, the Apoſtle.

IN Phrygian Land this Saint did much exclaim
   Againſt Idolatry; and Truth did preach
To Heathens, who on Pillar (to their Shame)
   Did hang him for the Doctrine he did teach.
His Festival is May 1.

St. BARTHOLOMEW, the Apoſtle.

IN the Armenian Climes this Saint he fell,
   B'ing flay'd alive by Tyrant King's Command,
Becauſe he preach'd againſt thoſe Sons of Hell,
   Whoſe Superſtition would the Truth withſtand.
His Festival is August 24.

St. THOMAS, the Apoſtle.

UNBELIEVING Thomas, once he was a Jew,
   But when converted, for his Saviour ſtood;
And tho' a while he doubted what was true,
   Yet ſoon convinc'd, for Chriſt would loſe his Blood.

To Perſians, Medes, Hyrcanians did he preach
  The Word of Truth moſt faithful, without Art,
'Till Indian Prieſts with cruel Spears did reach,
  And pierc'd the bleſt Apoſtle to the Heart.
     His Festival is December 21.

St. JAMES the Leſs, Apoſtle.

AFTER our Lord's Aſenſion he was choſe
  By the Apoſtles Biſhop of the Church;
The Scribes and Phariſees, his mortal Foes,
  Contriv'd to bring this good Man in the Lurch.
Unto the Pinacle of Temple fair,
  They went up with him, and thence threw him down;
Yet living, Men below with Clubs fevere
  His Brains did ſcatter on the Stoney Ground.
     His Festival is May 1.

St. SIMON, the Apoſtle.

A GALILEAN, of a fervent Zeal,
  In Egypt, Africk, Lybia, and Syrene,
In Mauritania, too, he did reveal
  The Word of God, which Tyrants did diſdain.
Some write, to Britain at the laſt he came,
  Where, like his Saviour, he was crucify'd:
Ah! pity that our Land his Blood ſhould ſtain,
  Where now the Word of Truth is glorify'd.
     His Festival is October 28, with St. Jude's.

St. JUDE, the Apoſtle.

'TWAS in Judea, Galilee, ſo fair,
  Samaria, Idume, Meſopotame;
The Word of Chriſt he would have Men revere,
  'Till at the length to Perſian Lands he came;
Then ty'd to Stake, ſwift Arrows they let fly,
  So thick as cover'd all his Body o'er:
Thus in a painful Manner did he die,
  For Chriſt his ſake, whom all the World adore,

St. MATTHIAS, the Apostle.

IN fair Judea he the Gospel preach'd,
   In Macedonia, Ethiopia too;
But while that in *Jerusalem* he teach'd,
   The *Jews*, accurst, with Stones this good Man slew.
      His Festival is February 24.

St. PAUL, the Apostle.

AT Tarsus born, was noble and well taught,
   And first a Persecutor of the Word;
'Till struck by Heav'n, by Light exceeding Thought,
   Became a Preacher for his blessed Lord.
Then sent to Rome, by Nero lost his Head,
   Faithful to Death this good Saint did remain:
And tho' his Perils were unnumbered;
   Now, past them all, with Jesus Christ doth reign.
      His Festival is June 29.

St. BARNABUS.

OF Levi's Tribe, and born in *Cyprus* Isle,
   Antioch City he did soon convert;
Some say, that Fortune more did on him smile
   Than others, who had felt most bitter Smart.
Yet learn'd Men unanimous declare
   That at Salmatia he was crucify'd,
Or ston'd; but either Way it doth appear,
   That for the blessed Word of Truth he dy'd.
      His Festival is June 11.

The Soul's Expostulation with our Blessed Saviour JESUS CHRIST.

ALAS! my Lord! when I consider of that wonderful Charity of thine, that thou, a God of eternal Majesty, should not disdain to be born and suffer for my sake; it melts my Heart to think how much I have offended thee. My dearest Redeemer, I acknowledge my Unworthiness, not fit to be called thy Son, ungratefully repaying thy Love, who for me and all Mankind passed thro' troublesome Seas of Calamities, Labours, and Persecutions. How didst thou pray to thy Father, insomuch that thy Tears congealed to Drops of Blood! How patiently didst thou offer thyself to Reproaches, Blasphemies and the
                                                                                         vilest

vilest Usage from the most ignominious among Mankind; led from Pilate to Herod, and from Herod to Pilate again; cloathed with a ridiculous Garment; bound to a Pillar, and scourg'd 'till a Torrent of Purple Blood ran trickling down thy Body; then adorn'd in Purple with a ludicrous Sceptre, and scornfully saluted; compell'd to bear the Burden of thy Cross; and last of all, crucify'd with exceeding Torment between Thieves; nailed thro' thy Hands and Feet, the Joints of thy Members dissolv'd, and all thy Body hanging upon four bleeding Wounds!

Oh! my Saviour! who can think of this, and not be wounded; but who can think of their Sins, and not be smitten, for causing thy Wounds to bleed again! I am sorry for my Offences, and for not making a right Use of thy Satisfaction. But thou, who art my Father, the inexhaustible Fountain of Mercies, behold me prostrate; and, according to my Belief, that no Crimes can exceed the Effects of thy bitter Passion, shew Pity upon me. I cast my inordinate Affections and Transgressions into the Furnace of thy divine Love. I am ready to dye rather than to offend thee again; and my purpose is through thy Grace to avoid whatever is displeasing to thee for the future. Inspire me, I beseech thee, to love thee with a fervent Love, and deep Compassion; to make Thee the Object of my Affections; to resign my self to thy Holy Will; and to be ready to suffer for thy sake any Injury and Contempt, any Tribulation and Misfortune whatever, even to be deprived of any sensible Consolation.

And if such should happen to me, as Persecution did happen to thy Apostles and Followers; amidst all such Troubles, adorn my Soul with thy Merits and Graces, as true Humility, Meekness, Patience and Charity, that my Senses may be restrain'd and the Nakedness of my Spirit be adorn'd with a perfect Purity.

O my God! in all the Adversites I have been subject to, whether in Poverty, Sickness, Temptation, or any other Extremity, I never found so effectual a Remedy, as in the Merits of thy Sufferings. My Life and Hope is in thy Death; and thy Death is my Health, Refuge and Resurrection. My Soul, which is espoused by Faith, and endowed with Spirit, thou, O JESUS! who hast dignified with thy Image, and redeemed by thy Blood, must surely inspire her to love thee, by whom she is so much beloved. With exceeding great Devotion, most ardent Affection and Fervour she desires to receive thee. How may she obtain a Union with Thee, O Lord, to find thee alone, to open her whole Heart to thee as she desires? Truly, thou art her Beloved, the choice among Thousands, in whom she taketh Pleasure to dwell all the Days of her Life. How do's she love to remember Thee in that Blessed Sacrament, thou thyself hast instituted. Thou art her only Peacemaker, in whom the truest Rest is to be found. You refresh all those that labour, and are heavy laden, infusing much Comfort against sundry Tribulations, and lifting them from the Depth of Self-Dejection to the Hope of thy Protection. Thou art a Fountain always sweet and overflowing, never failing to satisfy the thirsty Soul. So that tho' I labour in the Sweat of my Brow, vexed with Grief of Heart, burthen'd with Sins, troubled with Temptations, oppressed, intangled and enslaved with many evil Passions, and there seems none to deliver me; yet in Thee, my Saviour, I put my whole Trust, committing myself, and all that is mine, into thy Tuition, that thou may'st keep me and them safe; and, thro' thy abundant Mercy, bring us all to Life everlasting. *Amen.*

FINIS.

Divine Justice and Mercy Displayed.

Set forth in the unhappy Birth, wicked Life, and miferable End of that deceitful Apoftle,

JUDAS ISCARIOT;

Who, for thirty Pieces of Silver, betrayed and fold his LORD and MASTER,

JESUS CHRIST.

SHEWING,

I. His Mother's Dream after Conception; the Manner of his Birth; and the evident Marks of his future Shame.

II. How his Parents, inclofing him in a little Cheft, threw him into the Sea; where he was found by a King on the Coaft of *Iscariot*, who called him by that Name.

III. His Advancement to be a Privy-Counfellor; and how he unfortunately killed the King's Son.

IV. He flies to *Joppa;* and, unknowingly, flew his own Father; for which he was forced to abfcond a fecond Time.

V. Returning a Year after, he married his Mother; who knew him to be her Child by the particular Marks he had, and by his Declaration.

VI. And, laftly, feeming to repent of his wicked Actions, he followed our bleffed Saviour, and became one of his Apoftles; but after betray'd him into the Hands of the chief Priefts; and then, miferably hanging himfelf, his Bowels dropt out of his Belly.

With Meditations *on the* Life *and* Death *of our B.* Saviour.

―――――― *Quis talia fando*
Temperet à lacrymis? ―― VIRG. Lib. II.
But who the SUFFERINGS of *JESU* hears,
Can ceafe from Sighs, or ftop his falling Tears?

By Mr. THOMAS GENT, *Author of the* HISTORY *of* YORK, *in* 1730; *thofe of the fine Scriptural Great Eaftern WINDOW of the Magnificent Cathedral of St.*Peter; Rippon, *and* Hull; *a Paftoral Poem on the Death of the Earl of* Carlifle; *and of* Caftle-Howard, *St.* WINEFRED'S *Well,* &c. *Originally written in* LONDON *at the Age of* 18; *and late improved in* 80.

Y O R K:
Printed at the *New Printing - Office,* in *Fofgate,* 1772.
[Price Twopence.]

To the READER.

WHAT *here is writ, pathetically, shows*
  Young JUDAS' *strange and most stupendous Birth.*
It tells his Parents Sorrows, Grief, and Woes,
  For (what they knew) his sad untimely Death.
With Projects vain, they strive t' anticipate
The Thing, which was decreed by certain Fate.

Inclos'd in Wood, amid'st impetuous Waves,
  Where rolling Billows boist'rously do roam;
Where many Thousands find unfathom'd Graves;
  Ah! there the Infant's *banish'd from his home.*
But, lo! a royal KING *the Child did find;*
Endearing prov'd, like tend'rest Parent, kind.

Yet, when at Age, the Sov'reign's *Son he kill'd,*
  And then escaped to a Land unknown.
Here, by his Hands, his Father's Blood was spill'd,
  And wed his Mother when these Crimes were done!
Next turn'd Disciple; strange to think of this;
At last betray'd our SAVIOUR *with a Kiss!*

This is the ARGUMENT *of what I write;*
  Concluding with the Manner of his End:
The various Griefs and Passions I indite
  Of JESUS CHRIST, *our best and surest Friend.*
May none, like JUDAS, *ever interpose,*
To sell (as He was sold) the CHURCH, *His* Spouse.

Accept the darling Offspring of my Mind,
  When Ardour *strove to help my* Judgment *weak:*
For, now, you'll truer Satisfaction find;
  And I more LIFE *in Things I write, or speak;*
Since whate'er Scriptures *do afford I bring;*
How foul *a Traitor looks, how* FAIR *a* KING.

CHAP.

CHAP. I.

Of his Birth; the Dream of his Mother; and how he was unnaturally committed to the raging Ocean.

THAT, by the Means of *JUDAS*, CHRIST was flain,
 The *Sacred WRITINGS* tell us very plain; *
But no where fhews his ill fore-boding Birth,
Who prov'd the faddeft Wretch upon the Earth! †
 My prefent Tafk, far as TRADITION'S Truth,
Shall be improving LINES, begun in YOUTH;
From various AUTHORS; || who the Mind engage,
By Heaven infpir'd, and known from Age to Age.
 Cœleftial SENSE is beft, right underftood;
But, next, undoubted TESTIMONY'S good;
From whence bright Knowledge, like fair Rivers flow;
Or Dews, from HIGH, refrefhing ALL below.
 So 'twas of old, the *SACRIFICE* divine;
The *EUCHARIST*, in *Holy Bread* and *Wine*,
Was fair difplay'd, as what the CHURCH fhould deck,
By Sanction's Pow'r, thro' King MELCHIZEDEK. ‡
 An INSTITUTION, laftingly remember'd,
CHRIST'S nat'ral BODY on the Crofs fo render'd;
Held, by the LEARNED, conftantly to prove,
Appeafing *Anger*, and obtaining *LOVE!* ††
 But *Judas*' Name, that bears the fad Tranfgreffion, †°
Derived is from *Praife*, and *true Confeffion*.
PERSONS, fo ftyl'd, gave Rife to HISTORY:
From whom I'll mention which of them was He.°°

The

---

 * MAT. xxvi. 46.——xxvii. 3, 4, 5. Acts i. to 21. MARK xiv. 10. LUKE xxii. 3. JOHN xviii. 2.
 † MAT. xxvi. 23, 24, 25. MARK xiv. 18, 19, 20, 21. 42 to 46. LUKE xxii. 21, 22, 23, 47, 48. JOHN xiii. 18, 21 to 32.—xviii. 1, 2, 3, 4.
 || EUSEBIUS, JOSEPHUS, OROSIUS, SOZOMENES, &c.
 ‡ Gen. xiv. 18.
 †† *See* Dr. Marfhall, *St.* Cyprian; *and the Sacrifice at the Altar.*
 †* *See* JEHUDA, JUDA, &c., *in Table the First of the Ancient* Holy Bible.
 °° MAT. xxvi. 14. xxvii. 3. *Yet our Lord admitted him to taste of the Bread and Wine*, ver. 26. Mahomet *wrote, that one of the Name suffered on*

the

The firſt, call'd MACCHABÆUS, once did ſhine,
For Deeds of Valour, thro' all *Paleſtine;*
Prieſt of *Medine*, his Father, of high Note,
As from *JOSEPHUS* various Authors quote.

The ſecond, fam'd; a Carpenter by Trade;
Eſteem'd as Husband by a Bleſſed M A I D:
From Him, diſtinguiſh'd plain, in Holy Writ,
Far from Deception, *TREASON* to commit! *

But that *ISCARIOT* ‡, of ill-fated Style;
The grudging Miſer, prompted to beguile;
He ſeems decreed the Pattern of worſt Vice;
His God, the *Purſe;* the World, his *Paradiſe.*

Had *SENECA* then flouriſh'd, but to tell
How *Poverty* cou'd not with bright Souls dwell, ||
'Twould be in vain——for, ſure, 'twas pre-ordain'd,
His Crime in *this* Globe ſhould be ever ſtain'd.

Indeed, if we a ſolemn R E C O R D mind,
The SON of GOD as doom'd to Death we find!
Juſt as a Parent would, lamenting, ſtand, †
To ſee th' up-lifted Sword in Murd'rer's Hand!

But here a while, until the S E Q U E L brings,
By riper Thoughts, to judge of ſacred Things;
Let gradual Fate, portentive, bear the Sway,
Juſt as the Twilight uſhers in the Day.

This *Judas*, thirdly, born to Earth's Diſgrace,
That fawning Traitor, Shame to human Race;
Who was his Father? I come to explore.
A Tanner rich, who lived on *Joppa's* Shore.

Beauteous

---

the *Cross instead of Christ. Even that Impostor honour'd the Son of GOD as an holy Prophet; but* Tacitus *exhibited very unworthily of Christians in general, because their holy Tenets were contrary and averse to Heathenism.*

* See *St.* MAT. *as above.*——*And Ver.* 14, 15. *Likewise* JOHN xiv. 22.

‡ JOHN xiii. 27.

|| *Si ad naturam vixeris, nunquam eris pauper: si ad opinionem, nunquam dives.* Ad *Lucil.* Ep. XVI.

† II. ESDRAS, vii. 28, 29.

Beauteous the Country, blefs'd with aereal Gleams,
O'er *Jordan's* River, like *Kilkenny* Streams;
Limpid as Cryftal; fmoaklefs Flames arife;
Nor Mifts annoy the ambient facred Skies.

No gloomy Fog, offenfive Smoak, or Mud,
Difturb the Air, the Fire, or the Flood;
Infpiring POETS with delightful Themes;
So, like the cleareft, were fair *Jordan's* Streams.

But uncongeneal to parental Race,
And to the Nature of the holy Place,
He feem'd; where now the *Turkifh* Crefcents fhine,
With Worfhips ftain'd, that blemifh *Paleftine*.

Howe'er, his Mother was a noble DAME,
Styl'd in fome Books fair *BERENICE* by Name.°
What will not Riches do? Who *SIMON* priz'd;
And wed, becaufe he alfo merchandiz'd.

In foft Addrefs this tanning Vent'rer woo'd;
With mutual Love her fweet Careffes flow'd.
Nor then deem'd vain; when, blefs'd by nuptial Rites,
New Joys increas'd; more fervent their Delights!

But lafted fhort —— for near, when fhe conceiv'd,
By nightly Vifions fhe was forely griev'd.
SLEEP, dear Repofe! that lulls all Cares to Reft,
Had not one Charm to calm her troubled Breaft.

While, gradual, waking, follow'd Sighs and Groans,
As tho' diffolving with her piteous Moans:
To that Extent fo pungent were her Dreams,
Her fcreeching Voice did found like *Bedlam's* Screams!

The Husband, often ftung; but more, one Night:
"What is't," faid he, "that doth my Dear affright?"
She anfwer'd, "Jewel, were you but to feel
"My Grief; I'm fure, you'd foon the like reveal.

"My

---

* *Some write, She was the Daughter of* MACCHABÆUS, *of the Tribe of* ISSACHAR; *and that he employ'd Ships in trading from one Country to another; residing alternately, in pleasant populous Sea-Ports of the* Holy-Land, *or* PALESTINE; *that small Part, yet whose spreading Fame would prove by Decree sonorous over all the world, thro' the Birth of our dear Redeemer, and for the inestimable Blessing of our Salvation.*

"My tender Child, that moves now in the Womb!
"Oh! that he were but in the silent Tomb!
"But he'll spring forth, on purpose to betray
"The LORD of LIFE, whom cruel *Jews* will slay.
  "For this ungrateful Act, so black, so foul,
"I'm 'fraid just Vengeance will fall on his Soul.
"Howe'er, I'm sure, shou'd he make *JESU* bleed,
"His Body, pendent, must attone the Deed.
  "No Peace on Earth to ease a *wicked* Mind.
"They fly —— are lost —— to *hang*, or *drown*, inclin'd.
"His *Lot* the former, like AHITHOPHEL.*
"When *Conscience* Wounds, *Life* soon becomes an *Hell*.
  "What must we do? How from our Sorrows sever!
"As soon as born, (better that it were never!)
"Let gulphing Seas prevent such direful End,
"And drown those Woes that you and me attend."
  This said, the LADY bursted into Tears,
(Employ enough for him to ease her Cares!)
'Till both agreed to make the Child away,
And cause his Birth to prove its fun'ral Day.
  Not done —— for why, it scarce had seen the Light,
But, like an Angel, charming Mortal's Sight;
Symmetrious, in PARTS extern, it seem'd;
So sweet, so fair, a SERAPH might be deem'd.
  Pity return'd —— 'till on the Breast they view'd
Sign of the *Cross;* predicting, sure, the *Rood!*
Near that sad Mark, a *Gibbet*, ty'd with *Band*,
Amaz'd their Eyes, as, trembling, they did stand!
  Tho' these confirm'd the Mother's frightful Dream;
Yet Fondness turn'd her Mind from Death's Extreme.
"My Love," *she* cry'd, "a Thought has stricken me,
"To lose the Infant —— not its *Exit* see.
  "Tho' this be Sin, sure it is better far
"Than shed the Blood of such a blooming Star.
                                                 " My

---

* II. SAM. xxvii. 23.

"My Counfel is, Commit it to the Deep!"——
Thus fpoke, their Eyes bewell'd, and both did weep.
 But that indulgent Providence might fave;
Nor piercing Cold affect each threat'ning Wave;
A little ARK, or Cheft, they did provide,
With Happing warm, to keep out Wind and Tide.
 In this the thoughtlefs Sailor they inclofe.
But where's the Tongue can tell the Parent's Woes?
The fweet Child, fmiling in its Mammy's Face,
Frefh Drops inforce, afflicting her Embrace.
 "O cruel Mother! am I not?" *faid fhe.*
"Foolifh, to judge my Dream was Heav'n's Decree;
"And were I afcertain'd, how finful I,
"To doom my Child to *FATE"S* Uncertainty?
 "Strange! I fhould have a Notion of my own.
"What is this Lord of Life, this Pow'r unknown?
"Not *Greece*, nor *Rome*, as yet, can full declare:
"And yet I'm mov'd my Infant not to fpare.
 "*GOD* might reverfe what in my Sleep appear'd;
"And turn to Joys thofe Sorrows which I fear'd.
"My Pray'rs and Tears, like *Nineveh's* Defence,*
"Would more become, than doubt kind Providence.
 "Am I an HULDAH? Or, as HANNAH, bright?
"Have I prophetick Gifts, or *Second* Sight?
"Shall I prove like CASSANDRA, fad, for *Troy?*
"Or change Decree in parting from my Boy?
 "Some vult'rous Bird may pick out thefe bright Eyes;
"Thy tender Body bear thro' vaulted Skies!
"Like *PHAETON*, or ICARUS, o'erpower'd;
"Thy Cries regardlefs, by dread Fifh devour'd!
 "O Heav'ns! suppofe that fafe to Land it gains,
"Unlefs it haps amongft young Nymphs and Swains;
"What may I think of dreary Rocks, and Sands?
"Or Monfters, fierce, if falling in their Hands!
             "Nay,

---

* JONAH iii. 5, 6, &c.

"Nay, Paws of Wolves, or Tygers feeking Prey;
"Grim, and more horrid, than the raging Sea!
"That nothing fpare, unlefs it be a Wonder;
"And foon would rend this Offering afunder!
　"Or favage Wretches, who near Shores beguile;
"That grin for Murders, and at Shipwrecks fmile;
"How may fuch Villains fnatch thee; laugh, and fkip,
"Whilſt Life they take, and rob thy little Ship!
　"O whither muſt my pretty Lamb now go!
"See how it looks. —— Alas! it does not know.
"Burſt, Heart of Grief, fince true Affection's vain;
"So ſtrong the Impulfe, and fo great my Pain!
　"My Soul's diſtreſt —— Yet fomething bodes I may,
"If Fate proves kind, fee him another Day.
"Diſtraction fure doth feize on every Side.
"I wiſh I'd ne'er been born, or Young had dy'd.
　"It muſt, it muſt depart —— fome Spirit tells,
"That tunes my breezing Sighs like Paffing-Bells!
"Ye Pow'rs, unfeen! preferve the GIFT I fend.
"Waft him, freſh Gales, while my fond Pray'rs afcend.
　"Farewel, once more, my Child. — Unhappy me,
"With boundlefs Griefs! No Comforts can I fee.
"Adieu —— farewel!" This faid, then fwoon'd away!
"Her Face turn'd pale, and Body feem'd as Clay.

CHAP. II.

How the Bark, which contain'd the Infant, was laid upon the River, and borne to the Sea; from thence taken and saved by a KING, who put it to Nurse; and called him ISCARIOT, *because discover'd floating upon that Coast.*

WHILST thus fuccumb'd lov'd BERENICE thro'. Care,
　　Let's turn our Thoughts upon the Father dear.
Alas! his LAMENTATIONS were not fmall:
For, with his Son, he fear'd her FUNERAL!
　All future Harms, then, wifely to prevent;
No Way could eafe, but anfw'ring her Intent;

Since

Since nothing could thofe MARKS eradicate;
Thofe deep-prefs'd *Stygmas* of Life-lafting Fate.
 A trufty Servant quick he call'd; to whom,
The Plot made known; the fad determin'd Doom!
Bids, Lay the Veffel, fmall, in current Tide,
Mid'ft rapid Streams, on ebbing Waves to glide.
 'Twas foon obey'd, in his obfequious Arms;
As quick difcharg'd to the wide Ocean's Harms.
Soon did the floating JUDAS difappear;
And Winds, impetuous, drove him Heav'n knows where.
 To fkreen his Fate, and to prevent their own:
For 'twou'd be death to them had it been known;
Gave out, with rural Nurfe the Child did die;
And forg'd EPISTLES to conceal the Lie.
 More to difguife the TRUTH, in Mourning, wide;
She cloath'd herfelf, and ftalk'd in folemn Pride:
Both in long fable Garments to the Heel:
But where's fly ART, that can from Heav'n conceal?
 By this DEVICE none did miftruft at all;
But ftill themfelves lamented at his Fall!
And well they might conclude the Infant loft,
In merc'lefs Waves, or perifh'd on bleak Coaft.
 But let us now tell what's become of Him;
Who on inceffant moving Waves did fwim.
He is preferv'd by SUPERNAT'RAL POW'R,
That nothing, but Himfelf, can LIFE devour.
 Toft to and fro, exalted and caft down;
Ungriev'd, fecur'd, who was not born to drown:
Senfelefs that circling Dangers, dread! attend;
And innocent how HEAV'N becomes his Friend.
 No Food he craves, nor melting Tears demand
A Mother's Breaft, or Nurfe with helping Hand.
Extenfive GOODNESS him in Safety keeps;
Who, heav'd by changing aqueal Pillows, fleeps.
 From hardeft Rocks, that are moft high and fteep,
Proceed the largeft RIVERS, fmooth and deep:
Idoneous

Idoneous Places to mount *PHAROS* high;
Or tower'd Castles near fair azur'd Sky.

On fam'd *Iscariot's* Coast was such a Mount;
Bless'd with a SPRING; a useful, limpid Fount;
Clear as Saint WIN'FRED'S salutary Well; *
Still fresh in Virtue, that few can excell.

Near Dales, and Risings, with salubrious Air;
Where chirping Choiresters adorn'd the Sphere;
Nothing appear'd but HARMONY and Love,
Like what concentred in thick *IDA'S* Grove.

To this Retreat of old did PRINCES come;
Pleasant as that imperial Isle, near *ROME:* †
But far more holy, as from Lust unstain'd;
No Blemish that an *Asylum* was gain'd.

For here, TRADITION tells, a KING, in Fame,
(Pity more extant was not spread his Name!) ‖
In *SUMMER'S* sweet Recess did oft regale;
And took Delight to view Ships under Sail.

AURORA scarce had usher'd in the Morn;
And *Phœbus*, glitt'ring, with spread Rays, adorn:
What should appear unto the *Prorex*' Eye,
But the small Bark with Freight come tott'ring by!

Concluding, then, some Vessel cast away,
And this but Part of Goods upon the Sea;
He sent a Pilot quick with Aid to bring;
Which, soon secur'd, was laid before the KING.

But when the same was open'd, what Surprize
To view an Infant!——All lift up their Eyes!
The Cloth, well-oil'd; and tight with Pitch 'twas lin'd;
The Babe unhurt, from Water, or the Wind.

With Food likewise, that, should it reach the Land,
It might be fed by some kind Creature's Hand:

Upon

---

* *A famous salutary Spring in* Wales, *of which there is extant a religious* POEM, *inducing to Piety and Virtue.*

† *Noted for Retirement in* JUSTIN, SUETONIUS, &c.

‖ *Some have exhibited, that it was* VALERIUS, *of Consular Dignity.*

Upon its Breaſt a PARCHMENT did proclaim:
Wou'd me you know? Why, JUDAS *is my Name.* †
The KING, at this Adventure, was amaz'd;
And, wond'ring at the NAVIGATOR, gaz'd!
Whilſt he, inſtead of weeping at his Caſe,
With lift-up Eyes, ſmil'd in the Monarch's Face.
Thou ſhalt be call'd Iſcariot, (ſaid the KING)
Beſide thy own, *thou pretty,* little THING!
So all the World will know, that, when near loſt,
Thou wert from Death preſerv'd on this our Coaſt. ‡
Thus, as *PILUMNUS*, royally did ſave
PERSIUS, and Parent, from a wat'ry Grave:
So PITY mov'd him to preſerve the Creature;
But little thought he'd prove ſo ſtrange in Nature.
Go, ſeek a Nurſe, he ſaid. —— Quick ſhe appear'd;
A blooming, young ONE; worthy high Regard.
Here, take this Stranger *to your tender Care;*
And bring it up, for no Expence I'll ſpare.
'Twas done —— and wond'rous did the Child improve:
For royal BOUNTY much attracted LOVE.
Still more and more his Charms allur'd the Sight;
ALL, but the MARKS; and thoſe were veiled quite.
Thus having ſhown his Birth, and firſt Succeſs;
From infant Scenes to future Wickedneſs;
'Tis juſt, in Order, that I hence proceed,
In the next Place, to tell what *Judas* did.

CHAP. III.

How, ripening into Years, he became highly advanced: But in a Duel unfortunately kill'd the King's Son.

WHEN fit, the YOUTH to learned Schools was ſent,
With PARTS, ſurprizing! ſoon to Letters bent.
The *Hebrew* Knowledge; THINGS he prized beſt,
That form the SPEECH; of them became poſſeſt.

Soon

---

† *Or* JEHUDA. *By Counſel of one of the ancient Patriarchs, ſo call'd, young* Joseph *was ſold,* Gen. xxxvii. 26, 27. *Yet by Repentance of another Fault, and nobly offering to be Bondsman for* Benjamin. xliv. 16 to 34. *he came to regal Dignity. But of this Youngſter's Actions, King* DAVID *ſeems to indigitate,* Pſal. xli. 9. *and* lv. 12, 13, 14.

‡ *Or* ISHARIOT, *Diſtinguiſhed.* Mat. xxvi. 14. Mark xiv. 10, 11. Luke xxii. 3, 4, 5, 6.—21, 22.—47, 48.

Soon after fkill'd in *Latin*, and in *Greek*,
So as, with niceft ART, both Tongues could fpeak:
And *Genius*, moft occult, made him defcry
Inveftigation of *PHILOSOPHY*.
   For this the *Mathematicks* he explor'd;
And, what the wifeft Men could then afford;
What Skill, or Nature, at all Ages, can
The Courtier form, or the young Gentleman.
   Thus by a lib'ral Education train'd,
The Love of Princes, and of Nobles, gain'd.
The KING himfelf, thro' bright Perfections won,
Made him Companion with his only Son.
   Still, to proceed, as Wifdom did abound,
While call'd to Counfel for Advice profound;
Nothing could more his Happinefs compleat,
Since blefs'd by Priefts, and honour'd by the Great.
   Befides the Pofts, that Riches brought immenfe;
New Acts, frefh Deeds, that frequent did commence;
Might caufe a Youth in Pleafures to abound,
With more Content than to a Monarch crown'd.
   But, ah! how oft are fhort-liv'd Favours great!
One Minute's Chance foon changes happy'ft State.
A Thoughtlefs Action, cruel Wound, or Thruft,
May Life betray, and Honour *lay in Duft!*
   So 'twas with *Judas*, paffionate, and fierce;
Who knew the *Sword*, and what were *cart* and *tierce;*
How to recoil; or, when to fpring a *Lunge;*
Or, as *Equeftrian*, fatal Spear to plunge!
   One glitt'ring Day, he, with the King's fair Son,
Refolv'd on Paftime, left the Court, and Town;
And, drinking hard, in Mid'ft of Cups, no doubt,
When *Wine was in*, thefe hot-brain'd Youths *fell out*.
   With fhining Weapons, made of fineft Steel,
Such Wounds they gave required ART to heal.
O curs'd Encounter! Ruin to impart:
For *Judas* ftabb'd the young Prince to the Heart!
                                                   Who

Who, rallying, fpoke: "Stay, Spark! tho' late, attend.
"You've kill'd no Foe; but you have flain your Friend.
"Alas! your Woes more piercing are to me;
"Becaufe I can't prevent what I forefee.
"My Comfort is, retaining fome fmall Breath,
"I can forgive; rejoicing, at my Death,
"That Heav'n with-held my oft-victorious Arm,
"From doing You, my fweet Companion! Harm.
"Yet ftay, and do not, Cruel! hafty go!
"One —— laft Embrace —— for paft Affection fhow."
He foon comply'd with what the Prince requir'd;
Who, fainting, thro' the lofs of Blood, expir'd!

Imagine, READER, what the KING did bear,
When he fore Tydings, this fad *News*, did hear!
No tearlefs Eye in the fair Ifle was found,
Which gen'ral Grief had quickly fpread around.

Now *Judas*, Lord High Chancellor, in Stealth,
Flies from the Purfe, late State, and mighty Wealth;
Prefers the fhorteft Courfe that fafe reveals,
Tho' Death and Fury follow at his Heels.

In Ship embarking, like a Wretch forlorn,
To *Joppa* fail'd, the Place where he was born:
But as a Servant, had no other Way,
To find Relief, or make a conftant Stay.

Still deep Compunction feiz'd his troubled Breaft:
For, fure, the Guilty never can find Reft.
Nemefian Vengeance with its Stings impart,
Diftract the Brain, and captivate the Heart.

But ftill he had a Call deep to repent;
And often wifh'd he had been innocent.
In vain —— for as it were by Fate decreed,
He turn'd a Thief, and made his Father bleed.

CHAP. IV.

How employ'd in Service, and unlucky Parricide.

NOT long *ISCARIOT* liv'd without a Place:
For being tall, and of a comely GRACE;
With winning GAIT, he fcarce for fuch requir'd,
But he obtain'd what his fad Soul defir'd.

And

And here behold inconstant Fortune's Change!
One, rich possess'd, forc'd from high Domes to range!
He, who did lord o'er others, must submit
To 'bate his Pride, and veil his courtly Wit.

No KING to serve, no fav'ring PRINCE to show
What royal Youth to EDUCATION owe.
Do what he will, there's none relieve him can;
But he must yield to serve a Gentleman.

Nay, more to vex him, in a low Degree,
Of skipping Footman, poor, submitted he:
And even then, a Life most unsecure;
Because high Pride could not mean Things endure.

His Mistress, walking forth to take the Air,
Espy'd some FRUIT, most delicately fair!
'Twas in a GARDEN, where wide-spreading Trees
Adorn'd the Walls; regal'd with gentle Breeze.

She, longing much to taste the luscious Juice;
As right conceiving what they must produce:
Here, take this Money; go, said she, *and buy
Some of that* FRUIT, *so pleasant to mine Eye!*

But such the Nature of the greedy Elf,
He thought to keep the Pieces to himself:
Nor dreamt the Place was by his Parents own'd;
Contiguous Buildings, with adjacent Ground.

The Wall he climb'd; the Trees began to pull,
Until his Father struck him on the Skull.
Provok'd to Rage, succeeded Blow for Blow;
With Falls, contus'd, alternate, high and low.

At length the Earth was tinctur'd with their Blood!
Both Combatants amazing Valour show'd.
The One, a young and griping Thief to tame:
The Other, to keep clear from Gaol, and Shame.

And thus they fought, none seeing them to part,
'Till *Judas* stabb'd his Father to the Heart!
Behold, as tho' the slaughter'd Victim lies,
And separating Slumbers close his Eyes!

Go,

Go, Parricide!——Yet, whither wilt thou fly?
Or hide thy Crimes from an All-feeing Eye?
Depart——Like poor Itenerate he roves:
Quich, now, like Hart; and, foon, as torpor'd, moves.
  His Sins, dy'd Scarlet! yet more, diff'rent, he
Was to commit before *CHRIST'S* Tragedy.
His Life portended Horrors for to come,
Beyond my Pen to trace impending Doom.

CHAP. V.
How Judas, *returning after a Year's Time, married his Mother; who was fully convinced that he was her Son.*

WHEN circling Year its annual Courfe had run,
  Judas return'd where firft his Life begun.
In *JOPPA*, like a fubterraneous Stream,
Days heedlefs pafs'd, as tho' *Time* prov'd a Dream.
  Handfome, and ftraight; fo courtly too in Port,
The People judg'd him not of common Sort;
And were bright Riches helping to evince;
'Twas probable they'd thought difguifed Prince.
  But wanting Wealth, to favour him unknown,
Employ'd his Wit, to fettle in the Town;
Whofe beft Perfections, when the People knew,
Procur'd him Love, and gain'd him Bus'nefs too.
  His Father now above Twelve Months was dead:
Then courted he his Mother dear to wed.
She lik'd the chang'd-name Spark; foon prov'd his Bride;
But little thought by him her Hufband dy'd!
  Some Time they liv'd together in fweet Love,
That from her Breaft paft Sorrows did remove;
'Till that the dire predicting Signs appear'd;
And ftruck her Heart with what before fhe fear'd!
  For as one rofy Morn, from Bed of Down,
Thofe Marks, indelible, *SOL'S* Rays made known;
Parent and Spouse, deep-wounded with Surprize,
Salt, trickling Tears, came flowing from her Eyes!
                                        " Tell

"Tell me, *said she,* my Dearest, whence you came?
"Who were your Parents? Tell me each their Name:
"For when that *Cross,* and *Gibbet,* I do see;
"It calls to Mind my Child, and that you're He."
　　Said *Judas,* "Truly, LOVE, I cannot tell,
"Who gave me Being; if defunct, or well;
"Much less *Abode:* But this I true may say,
"They seem'd not such, who laid me on the Sea.
　　"A KING preserved me from being lost;
"Who 'spy'd me failing near his hilly Coast:
"And when deliver'd from the Ocean's Thrall,
"*Judas Iscariot* then he did me call.
　　"But I, grown up, the Prince, his Son, did kill;
"And, flying, chanc'd your Husband's Blood to spill.
"These Crimes thro' Passion: But another Sort
"Made you my Spouse, as't were thro' Fortune's Sport.
　　"Thus, twice absconding, wilful, thro' my Sins.
"What's to be done, when Sorrow fresh begins?
"For now you've found, what re'terates sad Grief,
"Your Son, your Spouse, a Murderer, and Thief!
　　"This is the Substance of my wand'ring Life.
"Weep not, my Dear, that you are now my Wife:
"Let me bear all, since You are far from Blame:
"For my connubial Love shall be the same."
　　At this the LADY, lifting up her Eyes!
"Ah, no! fond Youth! her melting Tongue replies.
"Since now we know that Fortune does her worst,
"Let's not provoke the Pow'rs to be accurst.
　　"There is one *JESUS,* near the Age of you;
"Saviour divine! who can great Wonders do.
"Whether or no MESSIAH, I can't tell;
"But, like, at present, none on Earth excell.
　　"For JOHN the Baptist, Hermit, did proclaim;
"And *well-pleas'd* Heav'n pronounc'd his spreading Fame.
"Whose SERMONS on the Mount will guide you plain,
"To shun the Gulph of Hell, and Heav'n obtain.
　　　　　　　　　　　　　　　　"Haste

"Haſte, haſte, my Son; to fair *JERUSALEM*.
"Steer by his Rules; of Prophets, ſure, the Helm.
"Amend your Life; be mindful of yourſelf:
"Turn to the LORD, and ſlight all pompous Wealth.
 "He ſpeaks, I hear, as never Mortal ſpake:
"His Perſon, tall, and lovely, wond'rous, take.
"So beautiful does ev'ry ACTION ſhine;
"All paſt Deſcription, from theſe Words of mine.
 "The heavy-laden He invites to Reſt.   MAT. *xi.* 28.
"Sufficient GOD to all that are oppreſt.   ISA. *lxvi.* 13.
"Gird up with Speed; ſeek him, who'll welcome thee.
"You'll find more Comfort than you can with me.
 "'Tis hard to Think, ALL is by Heav'n contriv'd;
"Whence Juſtice flows, and Mercies are deriv'd;
"Unleſs it proves, for moſt diſtinguiſh'd Good,
"SALVATION gain'd by ſhedding precious Blood.
 "Alas, my Dear, we evermore muſt part!
"At leaſt, withdraw a tender Comfort's Heart.
"We cannot, ſure, but muſt the Heav'ns obey;
"Tho' Nature yields, diviner LAWS gainſay.
 "And now my Child, ſee you with Speed repent;
"The Fault is equal, tho' both innocent:
"But let our future Lives this Guilt attone;
"And no more dwell, as tho' we had been One.
 "Yet take a Wife and Mother's Kiſs once more.
"Look not behind; but mind what is before."
Embracing then, like Lovers, when they ſever;
They bid Adieu, for ever, and for ever.

CHAP. VI.

How JUDAS ISCARIOT *became one of our* SAVIOUR'S *Apostles; first betray'd him: and then in a miserable Condition, departed from the mad or trifling Members of the* Sanhedrim, *and hang'd himself, whilst his Bowels gush'd out of his Belly!* ACTS i. 16. 18. 25.

OUR Bleſs'd REDEEMER, being on the Earth,
 Proclaim'd, by Wonders, the *MESSIAH'S* Worth.
Both Sick, and Lame, that unto him did come,
Relief he gave; reſtor'd the Deaf, and Dumb! °

Whoſe

° Iſa. xxxv. 6. lxi. 2.   MAT. xii. 13. 22.   xiv. 15 *to* 21.   xv. 30. 31. xx. 30 *to* 34.   JOH. ii. 3. *&c.*

Whose Miracles did cause the *Jews* to frown;
The *Heathens* mad, their Idols should fall down;
That Persecutions follow'd; Blood, and Fire;
When many Martyrs did for TRUTH expire! †
　Accursed *Jews!* how could ye thus despise
An Heav'nly Extract, Powerful, and Wise?
How ludicrous to Him, who Earth adorn'd?　MAT. *xii.* 34.
Ye Race of *Vipers*, worthy to be scorn'd.　　　*xxiii.* 33.
　Methinks the Sweetness of his God-like Sight;
That melting Tongue, which charm'd with soft Delight;
Should make so bless'd a PERSONAGE admir'd;
His Looks belov'd, and healing Truths requir'd.
　No Wonder *Judas*, three Times sore distrest,
Should long for *CHRIST* to salve his wounded Breast;
Who pass'd that Way: And then it was not long
Before connected with th' *Hosanna* Throng.
　For num'rous of the changing People came;
As Wind, inconstant, just as prov'd his Fame:
When, *Hypocrite!*—nor backward than the rest,
Apostate prov'd, tho' outward CHRIST confest.
　Thus seem'd to journey with our Saviour dear,
Like Proselyte, religious and sincere:
Zealous as *PETER* did he seem to be,
As if none loved *JESUS* more than He!
　As tho', like him, could draw the frightful Sword;
Smite any Champion that durst seize his Lord;
Was past Rebuke from *Canticleer's* Abuse;
Nor valu'd *Hell*, tho' all its *Train* broke loose.
　Or tho' from Heav'n he Mercy should obtain;
Tho' blackest Traitor, yet elude hot Pain.
But, marvellous, our Lord should wash his Feet;
And, yet accuse him while he sat at Meat!
　But here's the Matter: Greedy of base Gain;
No less than GOD'S sweet Lamb must the be slain!

　　　　　　　　　　　　　　　　　　For

---

† *See Master* FOX'S Acts and Monuments.

For Thirty Pieces his REDEEMER fold:
So mean the Price, such sorry Silver told!
  Abandon'd Wretch! What Madness seiz'd thy Soul?
What Fears, what Horrors, must your Thoughts controul?
Deaf to Regards, our High-Priest to forsake!
Could no Reluctance such Intention shake?
  No, no; 'tis done —— the Fiend has seiz'd his Heart.
What will not Bribes? From Heav'n to Hell pervert.
As by the Sequel, READER, will appear;
And ought to make us cleave to JESUS dear.

  Tho' great Afflictions our dear Lord receiv'd,
For *doing Good*, tormented fore, and griev'd;
Yet many Followers his Preaching gain'd;
And the Faith triumph'd as they liv'd, and reign'd.

  Now what are *Ethnic* Scoffs and Scorns to us?
Or worthless Style of haughty *Tacitus?*
Or yet that fulsome Emp'ror *Nero's* Ire,
Who laid on *Christians* setting *Rome* on Fire?

  Quite diff'rent did the Holy *JESU* prove;
Whose Life was Beauty, and his Doctrine *Love!*
So great, it can't be thought he would bereave
The World of Blessings, which he came to save.

  He heal'd the Sick, restor'd the Blind to Sight;
The Lame to walk; the Bended stand upright.
Nay, rais'd the Dead with his reviving Breath;
And prov'd a sure Dominion over Death.

  It happen'd that our Lord to *Joppa* came,
Where *Judas*, having heard before his Fame,
And by his Mother told what Things were done,
To be his Follower resolv'd upon.

  Nor was he long; but, leaving native Home,
To ease his wounded Soul, with him did roam.
But, ah! his Faith prov'd like a tatter'd Rag:
For his Devotion center'd in the Bag.

  So zealous too, at first, made CHRIST admire;
Rais'd him Apostle; answer'd his Desire:

And

And yet he knew, when all was finifh'd, then
He'd be betray'd into the Hands of Men.
 What fhall we write? Since the Decree was made,
The Son of God fhould be on Earth betray'd?
Who true did know, tho' *Judas* feem'd a Saint,
He was the forefeen Devil that he meant.   Joh. vi. 70, 71.
 For he was one that parted from the Lord;
Walk'd not with him; unb'lieving of the Word. *ver.* 66, &c.
Eating his Flefh, and *drinking* of his Blood,
Were Myfteries, by them not underftood.
 That Life eternal was here juftly meant;
Becaufe Life-giving FATHER had HIM fent:
And as he liv'd by him, fo thofe that eat   *Ver.* 54, &c.
Should even live, thro' that cœleft'al Meat.
 Thus Bread and Wine were fweetly made adjunct;
Not like to *Manna,* eat by Sires defunct,   *ver.* 58.
But everlafting Bread, that nought could fever
From Heav'n's Enjoyments, which fhou'd laft for ever.
 And this, of *Judas,* leads us to fome Knowledge;
Who made a Vacance in the facred College:
Which proves, when Souls forfake GOD'S Paths for Sin,
They may be *loft* by Dæmons ent'ring in.
 Well might fuch believe, who faw the Deaf, and Dumb,
And knew the Dead, releafed from the Tomb!
So *Jefus* did; and left Difciples Pow'r
To bind and loofe, to make his Church fecure.*

 When thefe were finifh'd, ftill he thought of this,
How *Judas* fhould betray Him with a Kifs!
An ancient Sign of undiffembled Love;
But here defac'd, as much as Hell could prove.
 READER, but ponder —— Treafon to a King,
'Tis not ftupendous fhould Deftruction bring:
And vile Deceit, in order to trepan,
Deferves Rebuke from either GOD, or MAN,
                But,

---

* MAT. xvi. 19.

But, now, proceeding to his ending Cares;
Who well can read, or write, without falt Tears?
Who, while at his laſt Supper, thus ſhould ſay,
That an Apoſtle ſhould his LORD *betray?*
    They were ſurpriz'd: Each, with exploring Eye,
Look'd ghaſtly round, and aſking, *Is it I?*
Should all forſake him; yet St. *PETER* ſaid,
Such Words, as if he ne'er ſhould be betray'd.
    Judas ſpoke, pertly, too: *And is it I?—*
You've ſaid it —— JESUS, meekly, did reply.
Quickly the Devil enter'd in his Heart;
Who from our Saviour, and them all, did part.
    Hence, Villain —— Traitor, thirſty of vile Pelf;
'Till Vice, triumphant, makes thee hang thyſelf!
Memorial ne'er forgot while Earth remains;
On high Record, as if *hung up in Chains!*
    Mean time our Saviour goes to weep, and pray,
The bitter Cup from him might paſs away!
In *Gethſemene's* Garden fair he ſtood;
Then kneel'd, and ſweat, 'till trickled Drops of Blood
    And, coming to his griev'd Diſciples, found
Them faſt aſleep upon the humid Ground;
But they, awaken'd at his dear Return;
Their Aſpects ſhow'd how deep their Souls did mourn.
    Peter, ſaid he, *what! had'ſt thou not the Pow'r*
For Me, thy Lord, to watch one ſingle Hour?
Then thrice intenſely cry'd, *As I am Thine;*
Thy Will be done, O Father, and not mine.
    And, now, departing, who ſhould ſtalk along,
But Traitor *Judas,* with an armed Throng?
Who, when approach'd him, *Maſter, hail!* ſaid he.
The previous Token of his Treachery!
    Do'ſt thou betray me with a Kiſs? CHRIST ſaid.
Then, 'ſtead of Dauntneſs, MAJESTY diſplay'd!
Aſk'd, *Whom they ſought?* with ſuch an awful Sound,
Some ſtarted back, and others fac'd the Ground.

Yet, like a LAMB, he did himfelf furrender;
Amid'ft the num'rous Train,—fcarce one Defender!
His Fortune chang'd, the fad Difciples fly;
Or hid themfelves in this Extremity.

He's fcourg'd, and mock'd; tho' like a King array'd;
A Sceptre, ludicrous, by him is fway'd:
A Crown of Thorns that pierc'd his tender Head;
He's from Judge *Pilate* to King *Herod* led.

When ftrong fecur'd, he's to Tribunal brought;
Falfe Witneffes, like *Jezabel's*, are fought: I. *Kings* xxi. 8 to 15.
Expos'd, and flouted, as the moft accurft;
As if fcar'd Hell confpir'd to do its worft.

But fee how Heav'n did force the Traitor back:
For Day and Night his Soul was on the Rack.
'Twas worfe than Death to think what he had done
Againft his deareft Friend, GOD'S only Son.

No fooner he the *Jews* Defigns did know;
What Punifhment the LORD fhould undergo;
But he reftor'd the Silver, when he faid,   MAT. xxvii.
That Blood moft innocent he had betray'd.   4, 5.

I've finn'd, cry'd he.—— *See thou to that*, faid they.
He threw the Money down, and went away.
Now Grief and Horror do torment his Mind;
Before him Juftice, and grim Death behind!

Accurfed Wretch! what Madnefs feiz'd thy Soul?
Could not before Repentance thee controul?
And what from ftern *Jew* Priefts could you expect,
But judge you vile, tho' pleas'd at your Neglect?

May this give Warning to informing Tribes;
To fhun with Scorn all falfe perverting Bribes:
For mind the Villains that falfe Witnefs bring,
They can't be good to GOD, the Realm, or *King*.

Heav'n's Arrows ftuck clofe to his wounded Side;
He grows uneafy; can't himfelf abide.
If CHRIST he believed not GOD'S Son to be;
Yet is affur'd the beft of MEN was He.

Two

Two sanguine Murders he before had done;
Saw Blood of Parent dear, and King's fair Son!
But now to think what JESUS should endure,
So deep prick'd Conscience, there could be no Cure.

Visions and Dreams torment him Day and Night!
Impending Vengeance drives away Delight.
Thus Self-condemn'd, as tho' the vilest Elf;
The Scriptures tell, He *went and hang'd himself.*

And *so he dy'd* —— whose low-stretch'd Body found,
The Bowels gush'd; and welt'ring on the Ground,
As tho' serpentine, cause my Pen to shake;
Internal wound — my trembling Heart to ake!

And here, my Judgment, as to future State,
Requires Rest — 'till I CHRIST'S Death relate:
He, who, in Mercy, thought it humbly meet,
Without Exception, kind to wash *his* Feet.

This shews he did not Punishment extend
'Yond *Hades* Bounds, but 'till *this* Life should end.
Here change the Scene to what CHRIST underwent;
What pungent reason *Judas* to repent.

While many People did our Saviour hem;
How solemn rode he to *Jerusalem!*   Mat xxi. 9.
No Acclamations wanting in his Praise;
Nor Palms, to grace the Roads or crowded Ways.

This pompous Noise was but presaging Cry,   Luk. xxiii.
To sudden Change our Lord to *Crucify!*   21 to 24.
Who water'd fresh the CITY with his Tears;
Drench'd in his Blood, like Prophets in past Years.

On *Olivet's* high Mount, prime Scene of Thrall,
He's seiz'd; and hurry'd to the *Judgment-Hall;*
JUDAS, the *friendless* Friend, in Triumph mov'd;
And diff'rent Voices various Traitors prov'd.

Far from *Hosanna* to meek *SION'S* King,
Another Tune, with Scorns and Mocks, they sing.
Instead of Branches strawed on the Road:
Their Hearts are turned from the LAMB of GOD.

Weep

Weep not for me, ye CITY'S *Daughters* fair,
But *for your felves, and for your Children* dear!
Thus cry'd dear *JESUS*, knowing of the Doom,
Thro' TITUS, that great Emperor of *Rome*.

And when with Furrows *Jews* had plow'd the Skin;
In purpled Robe they mock'd, with envious Grin;
Which, when the fame with precious Blood cemented,
'Twas quick torn off, and tender Flefh fore rented!

Then, previous to the deepeft Tragedy;
Bleeding, compell'd to bear the pond'rous Tree!
With which, to Mount of *Calvary* he's hail'd;
And foon on that exalted Crofs he's nail'd.

And what faid he? In this tormenting View, *
Father, forgive —— they know not what they do.
He's crucify'd between two wretched Thieves:
One, far from Sorrow; but the other believes.

Thus did the Proto-Martyr, *STEPHEN*, dye!
Fill'd with the Holy Ghoft! Who did he 'fpy,
But GOD and JESUS? *Lay not this to* them, Act. vii. 60.
From *Murd'rers* fprung, of *old Jerufalem*. ver. 52.

King *CHARLES* the Firft, how worthily difplay'd;
As Tranfcript, fair; becaufe, like Him, he pray'd.
Read but the *ICON* —— There the *Royal Mind*,
As well as *Perfon*, fet forth *true*, you'll find.

To weep, and pray (as for our daily Food)
For thofe who'd rather do us Harm, than Good;
Is fuch a Love, as, fure, will upward foar;
And meet that Splendour, where it fhin'd before.

Now view the Lamb, the holy Lamb, in Pains!
What precious Blood proceeded from his Veins!
Some of thofe Drops did pious *Jofeph* bring
To *Arviragus*, when (of *Glafton*) King. †

Thus to a Period brought, as firft propos'd,
The Birth of *Judas;* Life, and Death, difclos'd;

Let

---

* Luke xxiii. 34.
† *See my instructive History of* England, *pag.* 20, &c.

Let Inſtance, ſad, our Paſſions vile reſtrain;
No Fame pervert; or, to ſeduce, no Gain.
  What *profit* they who in *wing'd* Riches roll,
To *gain the World*, if *loſt* a precious *Soul?* ‡
Nor was Addition to that Queſtion ſtrange:
What can by Man *be given in Exchange?*
  Let what we ſeek be interceſſive L O V E;
Salvation's AUTHOR, from Heav'n's Throne above; ||
Who ſent the *HOLY SPIRIT* to inſpire,
That we, at length, may join the Heav'nly Choir. §

    With ſome Remarks I'll now conclude;
    I hope 'twill be for publick Good.

    Againſt *Raſh Judgment*.

Tho' *Judas* ſlaughter'd, when he ſcarce knew why,
Had he repented of each T R A G E D Y;
He might have dy'd, howe'er by Grief oppreſt,
With Glimpſe of Peace, or Sight of *promis'd* Reſt.
  No holy S C R I P T U R E of the Traitor tells,
That Hell reſounds, like *Dives*, with his Yells!
Or how, in Torments, he could ſee Heav'n fair;
And *Abr'ham's* Boſom, with poor *Laz'rus* there.
  So none may judge *his* Soul, if ſav'd, or loſt.
G O D only knows, who was concerned moſt.
It would be raſh, too hard to think upon
The regal P S A L M I S T, and King *S O L O M O N*.
  Of P O N T I U S P I L A T E we may frequent read,
And daily hear from Apoſtolick C R E E D:
See, in the *Acts*, he fain wou'd ſet him free:
But they preferr'd a *Robber* more than *He. Joh.* xviii. 40.
  Reluctant Chief! few Writers could upbraid.
'Twas not his W I L L *C H R I S T* ſhould be *Victim* made!
Or ſcarce a Fault, when ſuch coercive Crew
Forc'd him averſe to what he meant to do.
                                    For

---

‡ Mat. xvi. 26. || Hebr. xii. 2.
§ *See my History of the Great Eastern Window.*

For in no Judge or Jury Crime appears,
When the true Knave in falfeſt Manner ſwears;
Who might, for leſs than Two-pence, Life betray;
Or black defame, to ſpunge a needful Prey.

    The *Preſident*, ſome write, himſelf had drown'd;
And in a Lake of *Switzerland* was found; *
Whoſe pallid Ghoſt, judicial like, near Banks,
Was dreary ſeen, by People of all Ranks.

    But GOD'S dear Son, what Character has he,
Read *LENTULUS*, full ſatisfy'd you'll be.
And tho' *ISAIAH* high is in Eſteem,
The former differs, ſweet in Words, from him.

        Againſt *TREACHERY* and *MURDER*.

    How came off *Joab*, for his *treach'rous* Acts? II. *Sam*.
Did he not ſuffer for his bloody Facts?   iii. 27. xx. 9. 10.
And did not the Avenger, *SOLOMON*,   I. Kings
The *Curſer* puniſh, who leaſt thought thereon?   ii. 44, &c.

    What was the End of wicked *Jezabel?*
From Tower thrown, as if caſt into *Hell!*   II. Kings
And, partly, found, by *Jehu's* juſt Commands,   ix. 33. 35.
How look'd the Remnants of her late fair Hands!

        On righteous *Judgments* and *Puniſhments*.

Elijah's Fires, and *Eliſha's* Bears,   II. Kin. i. 10, 11, 12.
May warn the Sinner, if he reads, or hears. ii. 23, 24, 25.
And *Elymas*, exemplary, ſtruck blind,   Acts xiii. 8 to 11.
So *Alexander*, as his *Works*, conſign'd.   II. Tim. iv. 14.

    Let's leave all Things, like JOB, unto the Lord,   i. 21.
With *Will*, like *Eli*, humbly to accord;   I. Sam. iii. 18.
Or, as King *David*, 'ſtead of Vengeance due. II. xvi. 5 to 13.
Examples, bright, that Chriſtians may purſue.

    'Twas once my Fate to be incarcerate;
Not long, nor common; but as One of State;
And then I ſtole —— not worthleſs to impart:
It was not *Money* —— but a VIRGIN'S Heart!
                                           Sweet

---

    * See "The Legend of Mount Pilate," on p. 229 of the preſent volume. *(Editor)*.

Sweet Innocence, and Virtue, *LOVE* affuag'd.
My *ADELIZA* long was pre-engag'd:
Yet filver *Thames* can witnefs how I griev'd,
From fweet PARTHENIA'S Care too foon reliev'd.
I was the firft, the WORLD may plainly fee,
That wrote, and nam'd, my *Work* YORK Hiftory.
Approv'd, it fold: And printed Lines exprefs,
My *COMMENDATION*, by Learn'd *F.R.S.**
And as I am a PRINTER of *right* Strain,
With Emendations I will more explain;
If GOD but grants me Health; and that I fee
Some kind Subfcriptions for to ftrengthen me.
My *PICTURE* drawn, by Artift's fkilful Hand;
And BOTH accepted in this famous Land;
Bleft by *PHILANDER*, who perceiv'd my Cafe;
And, in meer Pity, kept me in my Place.
DEATH, moft inexorable! to tranflate,
From *Me!* my SPOUSE to fair St. *MARY* Gate:
Where, near King *Olave's* Church, fhe refts in Peace,†
Beyond *hard* Fate *to jockey from* that Place.
Whofe

---

* EBORAC. *Pref.* p. 8.

† "*P.M.S.* Near are depofited the Remains of Mrs. *ADELIZA*
"*GENT;* Once amiable for Beauty, VIRTUE, and Beneficence:
" Who died *April* 1, 1761. *Ætat.* 78."

    I Thought in the Arch-Angel's Ground,
      Near my first Husband dear,
   My CHARLEY GENT for to have found;
      But TOMMY brought me here!

   Who did, and wrought, what Spouse could do,
      To guard ME from Distress;
   And often told, what well he knew,
      My Way to Happiness!

   In Love, sure, scarce was sweeter Twain;
      More grac'd the nuptial Bed;
   Near fifty Years I knew my Swain;
      Near forty to him wed.

   May HE, whom VIRTUE e'er cou'd charm,
      Here come——and both arise,
   To meet, like Lovers, Arm-in-Arm,
      Our SAVIOUR, in the Skies.   A. G.

   Lamented Shade! accept this Tribute, due;
   Which, with my Tears, I consecrate to YOU!   T. G.
   READER, while sacred Monuments you see,
   Think of Bless'd Fate, and Immortality.

    Rev. ii. 10. Esto fidelis usque ad mortem, & dabo tibi coronam vitæ.

Whose Character will shine, tho' in her Grave;
Near lofty Trees, which gentle Zephirs wave;
And the dissolving Ruins, being nigh,
Make People think on *FATE*, as well as I.

Of four Great KINGS I've either seen, or heard;
For VALOUR, grac'd; for PIETY, rever'd;
Lov'd *England's* Friends; kept foreign Foes in Awe;
As fam'd, and glorious, as the Great *NASSAU*.

Four QUEEN's, the Glories of the *British* Crown,
Adorn'd with Beauty, Wisdom, and Renown;
Who, when distinguish'd *of* fam'd *ANGLIA*, fair;
Greater PERFECTIONS no where could appear.

And, here, to end—I'd, humbly, have it known,
While good King *George* the *Third* adorns the *Throne*,
I am alive—And trust in Heav'n to see
His Name, as Others, grace my HISTORY.

FINIS.

The Legend of Mount Pilate.

BY THE EDITOR. *See second stanza on p.* 226.

VARIOUS versions exist of this interesting legend. One relates that Pilate, convicted of peculation, was banished by the Emperor Tiberius to Gaul, and that, being tormented by pangs of conscience, he drowned himself in the gloomy mountain tarn, on Mons Fractus, or Fracmont (now Mount Pilate) near Lucerne, in Switzerland. Another story asserts, that after being re-called from Judea, he was made Governor of the town and district of Vienna, in Gaul (Vienna on the Rhone), and both the castle in which he dwelt, and the precipice down which he threw himself, are shewn to the credulous tourist at the present day.

The legend current in Switzerland, is as follows:—Pilate, re-called to Rome in consequence of his maladministration of the province of Judea, was brought before the Emperor Tiberius, who, to the surprise of everybody, received him with every mark of esteem and favour, and, instead of calling him to account, loaded him with presents and honours. This occurred several times, until the courtiers, rendered suspicious, began to whisper that Pilate must have about him some amulet or occult charm, by means of which he secured the emperor's favour. The ex-governor was at last seized and searched, and was found to wear, underneath his ordinary garments, the seamless coat of our Saviour. This relic was taken from him, and the consequence was, that the next time he appeared before Tiberius, he was immediately accused and condemned to death. After execution, his body was thrown into the Tiber; whereupon such dreadful storms ensued that the corpse was at length recovered from the river and sent to Vienne in Gaul, to be there thrown into the Rhone. Similar scenes were enacted there: after a succession of direful storms, the body was fished out of the Rhone and taken to Lausanne, in Helvetia, to be there sunk in the unfathomed depths of the lake. Upon the same dreadful natural phenomena still pursuing the accursed corpse of the governor, the inhabitants of Lausanne resolved to carry the body to a solitary mountain lake in the centre of Switzerland, amidst the uninhabited wilds of the Alpine region, south of Lucerne. This lake was the now well-known tarn on Fracmont, or Mount Pilate (now rendered accessible by a mountain railway).

Pilate's body at last found permanent rest in this new abode, but not without leaving it from time to time, and haunting the neighbourhood as a dreadful spectre. Sometimes he would be seen wading in the shallow part of the lake; at other times he would sit on some rocky fragment on the shore; at other times again he would be engaged in conflict with another dire spectre, that of King Herod, who was also banished into those wilds. But at all times he was the same evil spirit, who brought sudden storms and tempests upon the adjoining country, terrified the shepherds, dispersed their herds, drove their cattle over precipices, and wrought havoc of every description within the circle of his influence.

This state of affairs becoming at length intolerable, and as no other place or country could be found to receive the accursed body, the inhabitants sought the help of a powerful magician, a disciple of the far famed university of Salamanca, to whom they promised a large sum of money if he would lay the unquiet spirit and rid them of their troublesome neighbour. The magician entered upon the perilous undertaking. Ascending the horrible mountain, he found the spectre perched on a lofty summit, and immediately commenced his adjurations: to no effect, however, for Pilate kept his ground. The magician then ascended a peak opposite to that on which Pilate was seated, and used most dreadful formulas to exorcise his opponent; the struggle between the two now waxed so terrific, that the ground trampled upon by the combatants has remained bare of all vegetation ever since. Pilate's power of resistance at last failed him, and he so far submitted to the victorious magician, as to promise to keep quiet within his lake for the future, on condition that a serving spirit should be given to him, embodied under the form of a black mare, so that he might, riding upon it, revisit once a year the scenes of his terrestrial life in a manner befitting a Roman Knight. These terms were granted. Upon the appearance of the black mare on Fracmont, Pilate bestrode her, but full of wrath at his defeat, he spurred the animal on to such terrific leaps and bounds, that the impressions of the hoofs penetrated deep into the rocks near his lake (which impressions, of course, also remain to the present day).

Pilate has faithfully kept his bargain and his promise; only every Good Friday, the anniversary of the day when he condemned our Saviour, he is seen to hover disconsolately about the shores of his lake, dressed in his official habiliments as Roman proctor. But woe to the human being who beholds the spectre on those occasions (for he is certain to die before the year is out); and if stones are thrown into the lake, or insulting words are shouted near the spirit's abode, his anger breaks forth in violent hurricanes.

THE
Pattern of Piety:
OR,
Tryals of Patience.
BEING
The Moſt FAITHFUL
Spiritual Songs
Of the LIFE and DEATH of the once
Afflicted   J O B.

In Five Books.

SHEWING,
The abundant Riches of that Great and Good Man, in his Family, Goods, and Cattle: The latter of which were deſtroy'd; all about him reduc'd; and he himſelf, ſmitten with Boils, in the moſt deplorable Condition; In all which Poverty, and Miſeries, as he never charg'd GOD fooliſhly; ſo it pleaſed the Divine Being, not only to reſtore him again to his Health, but to give him a double Portion of his former Plenty and Proſperity.

Qui ſeminant in Lacrymis, in Exultatione metent, Ps. 126.

SCARBOROUGH:
Printed by THOMAS GENT, in the Year of our Bleſſed LORD, 1734.

To Mr. *J. F.*

WHEN *I began to tell you my Design,*
  In my obsequious Way, of JOB, *to print;*
And show, in Volume small, what he, divine!
  Endur'd in this vain World, while he was in't:
You was so good to lend Assistance kind,
To grace the Subject, and adorn my Mind.

Fine are those Lines; for me, alas! too deep,
  As much as what I had before too mean:
Those Fountain Streams too clear, the Mount too steep
  For me to drink of, or for me to gain:
Both climb to TRUTH: *yet diff'rent Ways perplext;*
Which made me keep the middle Path, the Text.

But too, too copious is the WHOLE *to trace;*
  And yet as much as this small Book will bear;
Withall, the best, and what suits ev'ry Case,
  In Human Life, I do exhibit here:
JOB'S *Sighs, Despair, and Griefs, so like our own,*
With Tears, and Pray'rs, and Hope (above all!) shown.

Heav'n knows, there's none on Earth from Troubles free,
  But often moans within this Vale of Tears!
Tho', it is true, none suffers such Degree,
  As in this Book our Noble Hero bears:
For which, as in this World he did abide,
So GOD *was pleas'd, he should be glorify'd.*

But, suff'ring Christians! seek not here below
  For just Rewards; first hence you must depart:
Christ's Kingdom was not here: Himself, you know,
  Was fill'd with Sorrows, and pierc'd to the Heart.
What Joy's on Earth, to HIS FAIR CHURCH *belongs,*
In Pray'rs divine, and sweet seraphick Songs.

There, there, my Friend, may you 'till Age enjoy
  The sweetest Raptures of a peaceful Life;
Free from such Cares, which do our Peace destroy,
  Resembling Heav'n, that's void of Grief, or Strife:
And when like JOB'S *full Shock of Corn, you sever,*
Be blest Above, for ever, and for ever!

THOMAS GENT.

The Pattern of Piety.

BOOK I. Job's *Afflictions*.

IN *Idumea's* Land, or *Uz* by Name,
Illuftrious *Job* there liv'd in Wealth and Fame;
Seven Sons he had, of comely Mein and Air,
And three fweet Daughters, much like Angels, fair.
   Seven thoufand Sheep adorn'd his verdant Plain,
Three thoufand Camels did his Grounds contain;
Five Hundred Affes (She) he had to breed,
And twice five hundred Oxen there did feed.
   Servants in Numbers were at his Command;
Some in the Houfe; others to till the Land:
His Chefts and Coffers ftately to behold;
Some fill'd with Garments, others, Store of Gold.
   As 'twas the Cuftom of the bounteous Eaft,
His beauteous Sons and Daughters held a Feaft:
Mean time, *Job* offer'd up to GOD his Pray'rs,
That Heav'n might blefs 'em: Such his pious Cares.
   There was a Day, on which the Sons of Light,
Came to prefent them to *JEHOVAH'S* Sight:
Satan prefum'd amongft the Throng to break;
But God perceived him, and to him did fpeak.
   Whence comeft thou? Said Satan, "To and fro,
"In Earth I've been, both up, and down below."
Haft thou, faid God, *my Servant,* Job, *beheld:*
An upright Man, by none to be excell'd?

                                                          "Yes,

"Yes, I obferv'd him, (Satan makes Reply)
"But don't at all admire his Piety:
"His Subftance thrives, and thou haft hedg'd him round,
"No Wonder then he fhould be righteous found.

But do, to try him, draw thy Bleffings Store,
And give him Grief, for Joy, he had before;
Sure, as I'm here, he'll brook not thy Difgrace,
But curfe thee, Lord, unto thy very Face.

Behold, faid God, all that he has is Thine:
With that, do what thy Temper does incline:
But to his Perfon ftretch not forth thy Hand.
Then Satan vanifh'd, as he had command.

Upon a Day, *Job's* eldeft Son did make
A Feaft for his lov'd Kindred to partake:
Mean while to *Job*, a Servant running in,
In Tears and Sorrow thus he does begin.

Sad Tydings! As th' Oxen plowing were,
And Affes feeding by them very near;
The *Sabeans* came, and took them quite away,
When they had flain thy Servants in the Fray!

They arm'd with Swords, nothing we had to quell
Thofe savage Robbers; fo like Victims fell!
I, only I, efcap'd to let thee know,
What melts my Soul, to caufe my Mafter's Woe.

Scarce had he fpoke, ('tis very feldom known
That one Affliction vifits us alone)
But comes another Meffenger, who faid,
Thy Sheep are perifh'd, and thy Servants dead.

The Fire of GOD from Heav'n has fallen down,
And quite confum'd them, faying me alone:
Me, the diftreffed Meffenger, to tell
Such News to you, whom I do love fo well.

A third comes running, thus beginneth he,
The fierce *Chaldeans*, form'd of Bodies three,
Fell on the Camels, and thy Servants flain,
To tell which News I only do remain.

A fourth

A fourth appears. Says he, Thy Children fair,
As they were feasting with their Brother dear,
The House was blown down by an Hurricane,
And all, (but I, who brings the News) were slain.

Then *Job* arose, and straight his Mantle rent,
Shaved his Head; and, as tho' GOD had lent,
Fell to the Ground, did worship, yet did mourn,
Naked came I, and naked must return.

The Lord hath given, from the very Womb;
He takes away, and brings us to our Doom.
Thus gives, and takes, as best it seemeth fit;
His Will be done; to Him I do submit.

BOOK II.

JOB *afflicted with painful Boyls.*

THE Sons of GOD did worship and adore
Upon a Day, as they had done before;
Satan then ventures to intrude agen,
Perceiv'd by GOD, tho' unperceiv'd by Men.

Well, faith the Lord, now, now you plainly fee
That righteous *Job* keeps his Integrity:
Confider'st thou, how he obeys my Laws?
Why is thy Malice thus, without a cause?

Satan replies, What wou'd Men give for Life?
But Skin for Skin: Put forth thy Hand in Strife:
Touch but his Bone and Flesh, to past Disgrace,
You then shall find he'll curse thee to thy Face.

The Lord then said, Go, tyrannize thee o'er
His Person, as thou didst his Goods before;
But spare his precious Life: Press not in vain
For what thou never, never shalt obtain.

So

So then went Satan from *Jehovah's* Sight,
And foon in Execution put his Spight:
With painful Boyls poor *Job* was fmitten down,
From Sole of Foot ev'n to his very Crown.

Thus bare and naked, he a Potfherd took,
To do the Office of the cryftal Brook:
That was, to fcrape, who could not wafh his Sores,
In Afhes laid, and open all his Pores.

To add Affliction, thus his Wife did cry,
Husband, exclaim; cry out; curfe God, and die:
Shall thy Integrity keep thee in Pain:
But *Job* reply'd, Thou foolifh Woman, vain.

Shall we receive Good at the Hand of God?
And finful Sinners, never feel his Rod?
Thus did *Job* fuffer, yet his Lips were pure,
He trufted ftill that God would grant a Cure.

Now ELIPHAZ, the noble Temanite,
Soon heard of his poor Kinfman's fearful Plight:
BILDAD, his valiant Friend, who reigned o'er
The Shuhites, knew the fame, which griev'd him fore.

ZOPHAR the Naamathite, who much did pry
In Nature's Womb, and deep Philofophy,
With ELIHU the Buzite, each would mourn
With *Job*, and give him Comfort in their Turn.

They came: But when on him they fix'd their Eyes,
They knew him not, yet much did fympathize:
No Words could utter, Cries did upward foar,
And Tears did flow, 'till they could flow no more.

Seven Days bright *Phœbus* gilt the radiant Eaft,
And pafs'd along, declining, to'ards the Weft:
As often *Cynthia's* pallid Face was fhown
To nightly Trav'llers, when the Day was gone:

Before the Tempeft, ftriving in their Mind,
Could thro' their Lips a doleful Paffage find,
'Till *Job*, unable longer to contain,
Broke forth, and thus with Ardour did complain.

BOOK

BOOK III. Job's *Lamentation.*

LET that Day perish, when that I was born;
  Also the Night, when said, that I, forlorn,
Was then conceiv'd. Let horrid Darkness move,
Nor GOD regard that Day from Heav'n above.
  Death's shady Stains and dismal Clouds then dwell,
That Night be Darkness: Let no Number tell,
That it is join'd unto the passing Year;
Nor Sun, or Moon, or Stars so bright appear:
  Because it shut not up my Mother's Womb,
But gave me Passage in this World to come.
Why dy'd not I? Why did the Knees prevent?
Or vainly suckl'd, to feel Discontent?
  Oh! had I perish'd; then, upon the Breast
Of balmy Death, I had enjoy'd sweet Rest,
With Kings and Counsellors, that Places build,
Or Princes Houses, with rich Metals fill'd.
  Or, like untimely Birth, I had not been;
As Infants dear, which never Light had seen:
But where the Wicked cease for to molest;
And where the weary Souls enjoy sweet Rest.
  The fetter'd Prisoners there find sweet Repose,
Hear no Oppressor's Voice, and fear no Foes:
The Small and Great seem but as one Degree:
For here the Servants are from Masters free.
  Why do the Beams of Life resplendent roll
To one in Grief? Or Breath giv'n to the Soul
In Bitterness, which longs for Grief, but comes not?
And digs for it as Treasures, yet it dooms not?
  What Joys, exceeding, do poor Mortals crave
From Death, when wishing for their peaceful Grave?
Why is Light giv'n to one, whose Way is hid,
And he so hedg'd, as GOD his Steps forbid?

                                            Before

Before I eat, alas! my Sighs appear:
My Tears run down my Cheeks like Waters clear:
Tho' Safety, Rest or Quiet I ne'er thought on;
Yet Trouble came, and all thefe Things has bro't on.

When *Job* had done, and thus his Mind reliev'd,
Said *Eliphaz*, Wilt thou, my Friend, be griev'd,
If to commune with thee we Freedom take?
To hear you thus, who can forbear to fpeak?

O thou Inftructor, Strengthner of Men's Hands,
Why fainteft thou, or confidently ftands,
As tho' thy Ways were juft? Whoe'er, I pray,
Was innocent, and brought to fad Decay?

Sure they who plow Iniquity, and fow
Vile wicked Acts, pray what from thence muft grow,
But that in Juftice, they fhould reap the fame:
God blafteth them, and yet is not to blame.

The Roarings, Voice and Teeth of Lions break:
The Old Ones perifh, and the Whelps forfake.
In fearful Vifions of the fleepy Night,
Methought appear'd, before my Eyes, a Spright!

And faid, "Shall Man be purer than his God,
"Who chargeth Angels? Shall Men fcape his Rod?
"They die:" And Wrath the foolifh Wretch doth flay.
Man's born to Trouble, as Sparks fly away.

If, therefore, *Job*, thou doft to GOD return,
And for thy Sins, as thy Afflictions, mourn:
Indulgent Heav'n, at laft, will pity thee,
And from thy wretched Torments fet thee free.

Were I like you, before his Feet I'd fall:
He fmites, but yet he heals us too withall:
In Famine feeds us, and in Battle guards us,
And from the Stabs of fpiteful Tongues awards us.

Tho' frightful Ruin circumjacent lies,
Peace fhall attend thee, Foes thou fhalt defpife:
And to the Grave defcend, like Shocks of Corn:
Thy Soul to Heaven by bleffed Angels borne.

To this, *Job* said, O were my Sorrows weigh'd,
And my Calamities in Balance laid,
They'd heavier prove than Sands upon the Shore:
God's Arrows wound me, drink my vital Gore.

And now I long from this vile World to part;
Come, gentle Death, for best of Friends thou art.
Return, Companions; too hard you conclude,
'Cause I'm afflicted, I was never good.

Is't not appointed that all Men should die?
My Flesh is cloath'd with Worms, and broke am I.
Swifter than Weavers Shuttle are my Days:
As Clouds consume, so Anguish me decays.

Lord, gracious Lord! Why do'st with me contend?
Shall my Complaints be bitter, without End?
Am I a Sea, or Whale, that I need Bounds?
My Couch, or Bed, can't ease my painful Wounds.

Thou terrify'st me with strange Sighs and Dreams,
My Soul can't bear, nor Life endure Extreams.
I hate, I lothe it! Why do'st love poor Man?
Yet ev'ry Moment try'st his Life: A Span!

O thou preserver! Why set'st me before
Thee as a Mark, too sinful to explore?
Rather, why do'st not pardon me my Crimes,
Who soon shall sleep, yet rise in After-Times?

Then answer'd *Bildad*, how long wilt thou speak?
Pervert God's Justice? Doth he Judgment break?
Tho' he thy Children for their Sins has slain,
If yet thou'dst pray, thy Prayers wou'd not be vain.

As bright *Aurora* might thy Age then shine:
Even Noon-Day should unto thee decline:
Secure in Hope, thou safe shall dig about thee,
And rest in Safety, tho' thy Foes might flout thee.

Nay, should make Suit: But, ah! the Wicked fail;
Escape not Snares, because their Sins prevail:
Endeav'ring not, like tott'ring Barks are lost,
And all their Hope's like giving up the Ghost.

Job

Job to his Friends did make this found Reply:
Wife as you feem, Knowledge with you fhall die.
Man, born of Woman, foon his Days are done,
Comes as a Flower, and is foon cut down.

Like to the Shadow, doth he flide away;
Or as the Waters failing from the Sea.
I know, like you, GOD'S juft, and never can
Do Wrong to me, or any mortal Man.

Yet fee no Caufe, why me *Jehovah* hath
Thus fingled out, to bear his burning Wrath;
Nor can I blame myfelf for any Crime,
Which you unjuftly urge Time after Time.

Says *Eliphaz*, provok'd, Thou cafts off Fear,
And what God loves, keeps back, thy fervent Pray'r.
Was thou the firft Man born? Nor firft fhall fade:
Or yet before the Hills and Mountains made?

What's Man that he fhould think himfelf fo clean?
Of Woman born, can GOD perceive no Stain?
He puts no Truft ev'n in the very Saints,
And Heav'n feems unclean, where his Mind's againft.

Sure then, more filthy finful Man appears,
And much more he who never Counfel hears.
Darknefs and Horror fhall his Soul furround,
And Defolation in his Tent be found.

Oh! miferable Comforters ye are,
Said *Job*, to me, who many fuch Things hear.
When I was rich, and did in Splendour fhine,
My Voice could found like yours, your Cafe as mine.

Had it been fo, I fhould not add to Grief:
My balmy Words had giv'n your Souls Relief:
But now to fpeak, or yet for to forbear,
'Tis all as one, I'm overcharg'd with Care.

So weary grown, that Friends feem defolate:
The Wicked fmite me, thofe who GOD do hate:
Heav'n, like a Giant, cleaves my very Reins:
My Prayer is pure, yet it no Favour gains.

But

But ſtill to God I ſhall make my Appeal:
Altho' my Breath's corrupt, thou wilt not fail
To lift our Hearts 'gainſt Tongues opprobrious grown,
Which may aſtoniſh, yet not caſt us down.

Yet, yet my Days are paſt: Death, ſeize my Heart.
Corruption, vile, thou ſure my Father art.
O Worm! my Mother; Siſter too you be:
Where's now my Hope? As for it, who ſhall ſee?

Then *Bildad* ſaid, When will you make an End?
Or why thus treat you ev'ry faithful Friend?
The Wicked's Light ſhall be extinguiſhed:
His Strength ſhall fail, and Terrors make him dread.

No Kindred ſhall remain to ſpread his Fame,
But his Remembrance periſh with his Name:
From Light to Darkneſs, chaſed from the World,
And to moſt doleſome diſmal Dwellings hurl'd.

Tho' I cry out, alas! I am not heard:
My Glory's gone! For me none has Regard!
As Enemy to Heav'n, GOD'S Troops ſurround me!
My Friend and Kinſmen fail, my Foes do wound me.

Thoſe, living with me, count me Stranger poor:
My Servant's ſilent, when I him implore:
Strange is my Breath to my once loving Wife;
Young Children ſlight me, wretched is my Life.

Pity me, Friends! See, ſee the Caſe I'm in!
Behold my Bone cleaves to my very Skin!
God's Hand has touch'd me: Like him, perſecute not.
Spare, ſpare Reproofs, and with you I'll diſpute not.

Oh! that my Words were written in a Book;
Or 'grav'd with Lead and Iron on a Rock:
With Iron Pen, that ſo the Letters never
Might be obſcure, but ſeen, and laſt for ever!

For ſure I know, that my Redeemer lives,
And that he ſhall (which to me Comfort gives)
Stand at the latter Day upon the Earth,
To judge all thoſe, that ever had a Birth.

           And

And tho' after my Skin, Worms shall destroy
This Tabernacle; yet, in Flesh, with Joy,
Shall I see God; mine Eyes thus pleasing doom'd,
Altho' my Reins within me are consum'd.

Zophar replies, Know'st thou not Truth sublime?
The Wicked triumphs but a little Time;
Flies as a Dream; and, as a Vision glides;
He's curs'd, because that Heav'n him not abides.

His Iniquities will be all reveal'd;
Terrors fall on him, not to be conceal'd:
Before God's Wrath his Goods shall ever fly,
And he himself left in Extremity.

Job said, Why then do wicked Men live great?
Appear in Pomp, grow old, and dwell in State?
Num'rous their Seed, their Houses safe from Fear,
And Cattle gend'ring ev'ry circling Year.

Their Children dance, with pretty taking Airs,
The Timbrel, Harp and Organ chant their Ears:
Thus spend the Day; tho' sometimes, in their Prime,
Death takes their Lives within a Moment's Time.

And hence I know their Judgment's manifest;
The Happy and Unhappy are at Rest:
That is, alike they in the Dust lie down,
And Worms shall cover them, when they are gone.

The Wicked is reserv'd to future Time,
When Wrath shall be inflicted for each Crime.
Then *Eliphaz* reply'd, Can Man, so poor,
Profit his God, and not himself much more?

Are thy good Deeds a Pleasure to his Sight?
Or, were they so, when didst thou him Delight?
From thy dear Brother thou a Pledge has took
For nought, and kept the Water of the Brook

From weary'd Trav'ller; yet more may be said,
Thou hast depriv'd the Hungry from their Bread;
Stript the poor Naked, sent the Widows empty,
And let the Orphans taste not of thy Plenty.

Therefore

Therefore both Snares and Fears do now abound:
Darknefs upon thee does thy Sight confound:
Yet GOD fees through thee: With Him be at Peace,
That fo you may, with Joy, behold his Face.

Job, tho' moſt innocent, yet hereat was mov'd:
He groans, and longs to fee the God he lov'd.
O that, fays he, I knew where him to find,
My Words fhould flow, to eafe my troubled Mind.

I know his Mercy's great: He'll not ufe Power;
But ſtrengthen me, and never bring me lower:
Forward I go to feek him: He's not there:
Backward return: Ah me, nor find him here!

Yet as my Foot within his Paths was held,
I've not declin'd; but rather been impell'd.
What he defires, he does: What is decreed
For me, performs: So wondrous is each Deed,

Each Word, that it is Food, and fweet Delight.
And yet I dread appearing in his Sight!
My Heart is foften'd, when on him I think,
Who faves me yet, tho' on Deſtruction's Brink.

Some remove Land-Mark, take away the Flocks,
The Orphan's Afs for Pledge, and Widow's Ox:
They force the piteous Naked to moiſt Caves,
Murder the Innocent, or make them Slaves.

Exalted thus, a while they do remain;
But Heav'n doth fee, and bring them down again;
Made impotent, as tho' at firſt, when born,
They are cut off like Tops of Ears of Corn.

Says *Bildad*, Fear and Might are with the Lord:
Unnumber'd are his Armies, whilſt his Word
Speaks Peace to lofty Places, and his Light
Extends to all: Yet nothing in his Sight

Is juſtify'd: Not even *Cynthia*, fair,
Or Stars are pure, tho' fpangling in the Air.
Thus each repeated Argument requir'd
Job's Anfwer, which in Grief was more infpir'd.

As

As God doth live, who long my Soul hath vex'd,
My Lips fhall fpeak no Ill, tho' fore perplex'd;
Nor, 'till my lateft Moment, when I die,
Will I remove my firm Integrity.

For, let the Wicked ftill againft me rage;
The Sword, at length, their Anger fhall affuage:
They multiply, tho' not content with Bread:
Dying, their Widows weep not when they're dead.

But oh! that joyful Day I could recall:
When Heav'n's Munificence, like to a Wall,
Adorn'd with Tow'rs, did me quite furround;
My Temples with a fhining Luftre crown'd!

When God was prefent ftill to give me Aid,
And pratling round me my dear Infants play'd;
Whilft mighty Hoards of Corn the grateful Soil
Return'd, repaying well the Peafant's Toil.

When every proper Fund did freely ftream:
Soft Oyl, and all Things ufeful we can name:
With all the Pleafures of a rural State:
Or, when that e'er I pafs'd (throughout the Gate)

Towards my Seat, prepared in the Street,
And there with moft profund Refpect did meet;
When young Men fled, and hid them from my Sight,
And rifing Elders ftraightway ftood upright:

When talking Princes from their Words reftrain'd,
And filent Tongues from nobles foon obtain'd;
When ev'ry Ear, that heard me, blefs'd the Sound:
With joyful Eyes, that witnefs'd for me round:

'Twas then I eas'd the needy Poor that cry'd,
Whofe Bleffings came upon me ev'ry Side:
The Widow's Hearts, to fing, I caufed them:
Righteoufnefs crown'd me, as a Diadem.

Eyes to the Blind; Feet to the Lame was I;
To Poor, a Father: I fearch'd Iniquity;
And brake the Wicked's Joys, his Teeth pull'd out.
Thus in good Deeds I fpent my Time about.

And,

And as a King before his Army sways,
All paid me Duty, and all spoke my Praise:
But, thro' Vicissitudes, I'm the Reverse,
And seem the Scorn of the whole Universe.

Youth of mean Parents now do me deride,
Who scarcely for themselves could e'er provide;
But, idle, begg'd their Bread, or liv'd on Roots:
These me abhor, and each one at me hoots.

Sometimes they fly; or near, then in Disgrace,
They spit their nasty Spittle in my Face:
Deride with Songs, their Children push my Feet;
And thus Afflictions ever do I meet.

My Bones are pierc'd; my Sinews take no Rest:
As Dust and Ashes, I'm by all confest.
Lord, I have cry'd; but me thou heardest not;
And if I stand, alas! thou me regardest not.

Cruel Opposer! causing me to ride
Ev'n on the Wind, dissolv'st me every Side!
I know thou'lt bring me at the last to Death;
Tho', when I please, you'll never take my Breath.

My sympathizing Soul would oft unite
With poor Afflicted Brethren in my Sight.
I, who did weep, as well as help the Poor,
Am thus rewarded, now at Sorrow's Door!

My Harp is turn'd to Mourning; Organ, Tears;
'Stead of the Sun, a gloomy Cloud appears.
If ever I in Vanity have walk'd,
Or, in Deceit, my Feet more vainly stalk'd:

Me, weigh'd in Balance, let th' Almighty try,
And see my faithful true Integrity.
Or, if my Steps, or Heart, have turned wrong,
Then let my Offspring ne'er continue long.

Or any Blot has made me incompleat,
Then let me sow, and let another eat;
If e'er the Bridal Bed I have defil'd,
The fame I should deserve, or worse beguil'd.

If I my Servant's Cause did ne'er defend,
When they, with Justice, might with me contend;
Then may God slight me when my Tongue bewrays
The truest Answers to his pow'rful Ways.

 The Poor in Heav'n, have him for Advocate:
God made them in the Womb, as well as Great.
If I've witheld from them what they defir'd,
Or, fail'd the Widows Eyes when they requir'd:

 Or, eat my Morsel by my self alone,
Denying Orphans, pittying not their Moan;
Seen the Poor perish, for the Want of Cloaths;
Nor warm'd them with the Fleece, but, like to Foes,
Made Use of Weapons, with my Hand upheav'd,
When at my Gate I might have them reliev'd;
Then let my Arm fall from my Shoulder Blade;
Broken, a Victim to God's Vengeance made!

 If Gold, refined, ever was my Hope;
And gaining Riches prov'd my only Scope;
If e'er the Sun or Moon I did adore
Beyond that God, who made them, and much more:

 If I rejoiced at the Fall of those,
Who've been deceitful Friends, or worst of Foes:
If Strangers found not Hospitality,
And weary Trav'llers welcome not to me:

 If I my Sins have cover'd in my Breast;
Or, like old *Adam*, glory'd unconfest:
Let God for all these Things now punish me,
As best agreeth to his Majesty.

 Would he but please my righteous Cause to hear,
And my Contention with my Foes severe;
Upon my Shoulders, I should take the Task,
To answer justly every Thing they ask.

 Like as a Prince, I'd ask them every Thing:
Demand their Witness? Every Proof wou'd bring
Of all my Steps, not doubting but to clear,
And make my Reputation bright appear.

For

For if the Land has e'er of me complain'd,
Or Furrows yet unpaid, which I've obtain'd,
Eaten the Fruits, or took the Owners Life,
Vile Act! to plunge their Families in Strife:
  Let pricking Thistles grow, instead of Wheat;
Cockle, instead of Barley, be my Meat.
At which *Job* ended; silent were the rest
Who spoke; then thus *El'hu* himself exprest.

BOOK IV.

BEHOLD I'm young, and ye are very old.
  Tho' Days should speak, Heav'n gives a Spirit bold
By Inspiration: Let me *Job* address,
And, 'stead of God, with Argument express.
  Amaz'd they were, and silent did become;
So *Elihu* did his Discourse resume.
Now, hear me, *Job*, My Words, which I impart,
Shall righteous prove, and wound thee to the Heart.
  Stand up, and reason with me, if you can:
Tho' in GOD'S Room, alas! I'm but a Man:
Let not his Terrors make thy Soul afraid;
His heavy Hand, shall not on thee be laid.
  Surely, says he, *You've spoken in mine Ears*,
Saying, *I'm clean, no Sin in me appears;*
And yet he finds Occasion against me;
My Feet imprisons as an Enemy.
  In this, O *Job*, behold thou art not just;
Why strivest thou, that art but sinful Dust?
Sure he is greater far than *wretched Man;*
Speaks once or twice, 'fore *he* perceive it can.
  Lo in a Dream, or Vision of the Night,
When Sleep obscures, and shades us from the Light;
Or else in Slumbers opens he our Ears,
And seals Instruction, which the Righteous hears.

He

He brings him low, ev'n to the Gates of Death;
Again reſtores him, and reſumes his Breath:
But is not bound to give Men Reaſons, why
He lets them live, or cauſes them to die.

By various Ways, or by Afflictions great,
Or Miniſtry, while his bleſt Angels wait:
He to Repentance doth the World incite,
To bring their Souls to everlaſting Light.

If thou canſt ſay againſt it, ſpeak I pray:
If not, hear further what I have to ſay:
GOD cannot act Iniquity to none;
And what Man ſuffers is from Man alone.

Yet oft on him th' Almighty ſets his Heart.
Who to a King can ſay, *Thou wicked art?*
Much leſs to him, from whom all Bleſſings ſprings,
And is a King above all King of Kings!

Or ſhould his Hands ſome ſinful Acts requite,
He lays on Man no more than what is right:
In Love he'd have you 'gainſt vile Sin to arm;
And when he's for you, none can do you Harm.

Our Good, alas! or Evil, can't extend
Or make Him to us either Foe or Friend:
But as his Pleaſure truly is divine,
He both regards, to make the better ſhine.

Obſerve me, *Job;* his ſecret Judgments lie
Far, far beyond the reach of human Eye:
Look to the Clouds, perceive the fruitful Rain,
Which quickly comes, and ſoon is ſtopt again.

One while it bleſſes, then doth overflow,
And drown the Products of the Earth below.
He viſits Kings, eſtabliſh'd in their Throne;
And, by juſt Diſcipline, he brings them down.

If they obey him, GOD doth crown each Day:
If not, their Splendour, with their Lives, decay:
Beware his Wrath, who, if you Him provoke,
Can take your Health, or Life, but with a Stroke.

No Wealth, or Glory, can anticipate
His conq'ring Arm, when he intends thy Fate:
Men may behold his Works, which far appear,
And all his wondr'ous Doings muſt revere.

The ſpreading Clouds, can any underſtand?
Or Tabernacle's Noiſe? He, with his Hand,
Spreads Light o'er all; covers the watry Pit;
And, with his Clouds, again obſcures the Light.

The Heav'ns, intire, 'tis He directs them all:
His Lightning ſtrikes the univerſal Ball:
Thunder ſucceeds! Amazing is his Voice!
Sometimes we tremble, other Times rejoice.

Thus Rain or Hail, He ſends for Reaſons good;
Seals up Men's Hands; whoſe Work is underſtood:
The Beaſts retire unto their Dens and Caves:
The Whirlwind, coming from the South, out-braves.

Cold from the North; From Breath of GOD Froſt's given:
Waters reſtrain'd by Wall 'twixt them and Heav'n:
The thick Cloud wearies, and the bright One ſcatters,
And for Correction, or for Mercy, waters.

Stupendous Counſels! ever turning round,
Muſt ſure the Wiſdom of poor Man confound:
The beauteous Rainbow, very frequent ſeen,
And Nature, ſmiling, with a verdant Green.

How Clouds are balanc'd: Why thy Garments warm,
When with the South Wind He the Earth do's charm.
Haſt thou with Him ſpread forth the limpid Sky,
As in a Glaſs, apparent to the Eye?

Oh! who can ſearch the wond'rous Works of God?
Or find Him out, in His Moſt High Abode!
Whoſe Power, Juſtice, Judgment excellent
Afflict not one, but yield to all Content.

Men love and fear Him: Thoſe he doth deſpiſe,
That righteous ſeem in their moſt ſinful Eyes:
Therefore, O *Job*! 'tis Time now to give o'er;
Let Tears and Pray'rs prevail, diſpute no more.

BOOK

BOOK V.

THUS fpoke the Youth, when foon a Whirlwind rofe,
The LORD did anfwer, and himfelf difclofe:
What Man is this, who, with blind Reafon durſt
Vie with his GOD, as tho' in Wifdom firſt?
　Come tell me, now, how this moſt beauteous Frame
Of all Things from the Womb of Nothing came?
When Earth's Foundation was with Wonder laid,
And faſten'd; where was you when all were made?
　Who gave forth Meafures, ſtretch'd the utmoſt Line,
And fix'd the Corner Stone by Power divine?
When all the Morning Stars did fweetly fing,
And Sons of GOD made Hallelujahs ring.
　Who ſhut the Sea in Bounds, or within Doors?
Limits the Tide by ſteep or pleafant Shores?
Gave it a fix'd Degree, fo far to come?
So far, no farther, dare its Waves prefume.
　Can'ſt thou command *Aurora* to arife?
And gild, with Crimfon Beams, the bluſhing Skies?
Or yet demand the Sun for to relate
The Crimes committed by the Poor, or Great?
　Proclaim thy Power, or withdraw its Beams,
From thofe who run into the worſt Extreams?
Or haſt thou entred in the Ocean's Springs?
Or Depth of Sea, where's Riches fit for Kings?
　The Breadth of Earth declare: Where dwelleth Light,
Or Darknefs? Can you tell the Paths of Night?
Or fee the Treafures of the milk-white Snow,
Or heavier Hail that vifits us below,
　For Battle kept? How parted is the Light,
Scattering the Eaſtern Winds? Or difunite
The Grounds for Waters diff'rently to flow?
Or yet a Way for Lightning quick to go?

Where

Where no Man is to caufe it there to rain?
To make the parched Ground not thirſt in vain?
To help the tender Herb forthwith to fpring?
The Rains and Dew to yield their Offering?
 When came the Froſt, or Ice, that every Brook
Seems in a Glafs, or does thro' Diamond look?
Can'ſt bind the Influences o' th' * *Pleiades*,
Or loofen † *Orion's* Bands for Winter's Eafe?
 Canſt thou bring ‡ *Mazzaroth* in Seafon fair?
Or guide § *Arcturus*, make his Sons appear?
Do'ſt thou the Ordinances of Heaven know?
Or fet Dominion in the Earth below?
 Canſt lift thy Voice up to the very Clouds?
That Waters ſhould defcend by their Abodes?
Or Lightnings fend to tell how they impart?
Or fay, who Wifdom fends into the Heart?
 Who number can the Clouds? Or, Floods yet ſtay?
How Clods do cleave? Or hunt for Lion's Prey?
And when fo done, bring to their Whelps and feed?
Or help young Ravens in their Time of Need?
 Or eafe the tim'rous Hind in Travel great,
And from her Pain refume her former State:
The Months canſt number? Tell when forth to bring
How young ones grow, and how like Corn they fpring?
 Can'ſt lofe the Afs, or bind the Unicorn?
Who both the Horfe, alfo his Rider, fcorn?
Or give the latter Strength? And, what's a Wonder,
Afford him Strength, or cloath his Neck with Thunder?
 Can'ſt him affright with vain and idle Fear,
And make him fportive like a Graſhopper?
No:

---

* PLEIADES, *the 7 Stars, arifing when the Sun is in* Taurus: *That is, in the Flowery Spring.*

† ORION, *a Cælestial Sign, (consisting of 33 Stars, or as other write 16) that introduceth Winter.*

‡ MAZZAROTH, *the Twelve Signs.*

§ ARCTURUS, *the North Star, with Attendants.*

No: The Horse tears with active Feet the Ground,
And stoutly prances at the Warlike Sound.

Mocks at all Fear, and in the Vally paws;
Laughs at the Trumpets; swallows with his Jaws
The yielding Ground; and, without dreadful Fears,
Meets Death or Conquest 'midst the glitt'ring Spears.

Or doth the Hawk, by Wisdom of thy Mouth,
Stretch forth her tow'ring Wings towards the South?
Or yet the Eagle upward soar to build
At thy Command, and there her young ones yield:

Whilst from the Rock or Crag she spys her Prey,
Which, seized soon, she quickly bears away;
With bloody Dainties feeds her youthful Guests,
Each quickly on the welcome Victuals feasts.

How long, O Man, wilt thou thy God reprove!
Instructs thou me, who pities thee in Love?
Lord, I am vile, said Job, *Pity, therefore;*
Once, twice, I've spoken, but I'll say no more.

Then from the Whirlwind did the Lord reply,
Wilt thou deny my Challenge? Or that I
Can have no Love for Human Race I've made;
When of the same they many Instance had?

Hast thou an Arm of Length, or Force like mine?
So great a Voice? Then let thy Power shine
To bring the Proud, ev'n to the very Pit,
And tread the Wicked down beneath your Feet.

Do so, and I'll confess, that thy right Hand
Shall save and make thee famous in the Land:
See * *Behemoth*, who eats Grass like an Ox,
And peaceful dwells amongst the tender Flocks.

None of them fears him, none that he doth fear,
Moves like a lofty stately Cædar fair:
Strong are his Joints, with Ribs like Iron-Bars,
His Bones like Brass, firm, fitting for the Wars.

His

---

* *'Tis thought to be an Elephant.*

His Strength is in his Loyns; and lo his Tail
Doth like a great and lofty Tree prevail:
GOD'S Handy Work; and he, that made him, can
By his ſharp Sword fall quickly down again.

Thro' Snares he pierces, thro' the Willows looks,
And drinks the Waters of the purling Brooks;
The Mountains feed him; and fair *Jordan's* Stream
To ſwallow up, truſts he can do the ſame.

But ſee another Object of my Power,
And if thou canſt ſubject, and make him lower;
The Great Leviathan amidſt the Deep,
Of Fiſhes King, who Sov'reignty doth keep.

Canſt thou, with Angle, draw him to the Shore?
Or, with a Cord, thou letteſt down, explore,
And ſeize his Tongue? Or, with a piercing Thorn,
Bore thro' his Jaw, like Captive moſt forlorn?

Soft Words or Supplications will he make?
Or wilt thou him for ever Servant take?
Bind him for Maids! Play with him as a Bird?
Or, conq'ring him with Spears, become his Lord?

Alas, ſuch Hopes are vain: For ev'n his Sight
Is fierce enough poor Mortals to affright!
If none dare ſtand againſt him, thro' their Fear,
Who then ſo bold before me dare appear?

Who has oblig'd me, that I ſhould repay?
The Earth is mine; o'er it I bear a ſway.
I'll not conceal his Parts, Proportion, Power.
His Garments who can ſee? What Foe devour?

With double Bridle who durſt to him come?
Open his Mouth, which ſeems an horrid Tomb!
His Teeth ſet round, as Iron Spikes, about;
And his proud Scales, like Seals, together ſhut:

So cloſe they are, no Air can interpoſe:
His Neeſings cauſe a Light; his Eyes, like thoſe
Ev'n of the Morning: From his Mouth aſpire
Strange burning Lamps, and Sparks of dreadful Fire.

Out

Out of his Noſtrils thickeſt Smoke proceeds
Like that from Caldron; his ſtrong Breath it breeds
A Flame, which from his gaping Mouth pours out,
Stiff is his Neck, with Joy he ſprings about.

Flakes of his Fleſh are joined as 'twere in one,
They can't be mov'd; his Heart as firm as Stone
Raiſes himſelf, the Mighty are afraid:
He values not the Sword that's on him laid.

The Spear, nor Dart; nor Habergeon prevails;
Iron, ſeems Straw; as rotten Wood, Braſs fails:
Arrows and Stones do ſeem to him a Bubble:
The Spear he laughs at, Weapons counts as Stubble.

The Sea, as boiling Caldron makes to foam,
Or Ointment Pot; in ſhining Paths doth roam:
The Deep ſeems hoary: Like him's none beſide,
Beholding high Things; yet King over Pride.

Then *JOB*, ſubmiſſive, anſwer'd, Mighty Lord,
Thou can'ſt, I know, do all Things at thy Word:
No Thought ſo ſecret, but you may diſcloſe;
No Aƈtion paſſes, but th' Almighty knows.

I've often heard of Thee, by Hearing's Senſe;
But now my Eyes ſee plain thy Providence.
Wherefore, abhorring of my ſelf, repent,
I ever thought, that I was innocent.

The Lord, appeas'd with *JOB*, began to ſpeak
To *Eliphaz*, that he ſhould Off'ring make.
Saith he, My Wrath is kindled much at thee,
And thy two Friends, who ſpoke to *Job* of me.

Therefore, now, take ſeven Bullocks, and ſeven Rams,
And offer them in ſacred hallow'd Flames:
JOB'S Prayers, for you, in Mercy will I take,
And ceaſe to puniſh for my Servant's Sake.

He's not thus dealt with me, ſo much to wrong,
As each of you, by an opprobrious Tongue:
Howe'er his Sacrifice ſhall me allay,
To waſh your Sins, which led you quite aſtray.

So

So *Eliphaz* arofe; to *Zophar* went,
And *Bildad*, then to *Job* moſt innocent;
Offer'd the Victims they commanded were.
The Lord was pleas'd, the good Man was his Care.

Then the Almighty touch'd the Hearts of all,
Both Friends and Kindred, whether great or ſmall;
They came, and with him in his Houfe eat Bread,
Bemoan'd paſt Evils, and him comforted.

Befides, to raife him, 'tis by Scripture told,
That each gave him an Ear-Ring of bright Gold,
Befides a piece of Money; and his Strength
And Beauty, came upon him at the Length.

So that the End of this good Man was bleſt;
More than at firſt, his Riches were increaſt.
Sheep fourteen thoufand feed upon his Plains,
Six thoufand Camels his bleſt Land contains.

Befides two thoufand Oxen; Affes Store;
She-Ones a thoufand; no doubt He-Ones more.
Seven Sons he had, and charming Daughters three,
For Wit and Beauty bleſt in high Degree.

All thefe provided for, it plain appears,
Job after liv'd an hundred forty Years.
His Sons, and Sons' Sons faw, ev'n to four
Fair Generations, who could wiſh for more?

At length b'ing old, and very full of Days,
From Earth to Heav'n God did his Servant raife:
There, ſtill a greater Happinefs to gain,
With God and Angels evermore to reign.

FINIS.

RUINS OF FOUNTAINS ABBEY.

PIETY Diſplay'd:

IN THE

HOLY LIFE and DEATH

Of the Antient and Celebrated

St. ROBERT,

HERMIT, at *Knaresborough.*

SHEWING,

How he relinquiſh'd the Hopes of an Inheritance, as having been the Heir of his Father, who was twice Chief Magiſtrate of YORK; and lived abſtemiouſly upon Herbs, Roots, &c., on the narrow Banks of the River *Nid:* Near which, in the Rocks, are to be ſeen his moſt ſolitary Cave, and wonderful Chapel, at this very Day.

Collected from Antient and Authentick Records. By T. GENT.

Videre vitam beatam donum eſt Altiſſimi.
To ſee a Life that's pure and bleſt,
Is, ſure, the Gift of Heav'n confeſt.

Quidquid Cœli ambitu continetur inferius ab anima humana eſt, quæ faƈta eſt, ut ſummum bonum ſuperius poſſideret, cujus poſſeſſione beata fieret. AUGUST. Sol. Cap. 20.

The Second EDITION, *with* Additions, *adorn'd with* Cuts.

YORK: Printed by THOMAS GENT, near *Stone Gate.*

CHAP. I.

Of St. ROBERT'S *Birth, and Holy Education.*

ABOUT the Year of our Bleſſed LORD, 1159, this Saint was born, in the antient City of *York,* when ROGER, furnam'd *The GOOD,* who built the famous Choir of the Cathedral, was Archbiſhop of the See, whilſt SAVARIC preſided as 4th Abbot of the Monaſtery, dedicated to the Bleſſed Virgin; ſome Ruins of which remain near to the pleaſant Banks of the River at this very Day. The Child's Father is, by ſome, ſaid to have been call'd ROBERT *de Cockcliff;* by others, *Took Floure,* or *Tocklefs Flower:* He was Chief Magiſtrate, or Mayor, *Anno Chriſti* 1195; alſo a 2d time, in the ſame Reign, when King *Richard* the Firſt ſway'd the Sceptre. His Spouſe, SMIMERA, or SEMENIA, the Mother of St. ROBERT, was reputably deſcended. No virtuous or learned Education was in the leaſt wanting to their Son; who imbib'd it as freely as the parched Earth could ſuck in deſcending Showers: Even in Infancy, Heaven had inſpir'd his Soul with ſublime Apprehenſions of the Sacred BEING! He would often ſecretly retire to Prayer, with a ſweet, juvenile Ardency; which made him to be honour'd by the Elders, while he was but young: And as he grew in Years, their Wonder increas'd at his Extenſive Knowledge, and Divine Penetration.

In more antient Times, there was, at *Streanſhall,* a famous Monaſtry, founded by St. HILDA, Daughter to Duke HERERIC. Here it was, that King Oswy, of *Northumberland,* (according to his Vow, for obtaining a Victory over PENDA the *Mercian* Prince) gave his young Daughter EANFLED to be conſecrated in perpetual Virginity; where, in Proceſs of Time, this pious Lady, the good King, her Father, her Grandfather EDWIN,

with

Chap. I.   *St.* ROBERT'S *Manner of Holy Living.*   259

with feveral of the Nobility, were bury'd ; a Place honour'd as being an Academy to 5 Archbifhops of *York;* and which was afterwards deftroy'd by *Hunguar* and *Hubba,* cruel *Danes,* who had obliged TITUS the Abbot to fly to *Glaftenbury* with the Relicks of its moft excellent Foundrefs : Upon thefe deplorable Ruins, *William de Percy,* who accompany'd the Conqueror, and one of his Pofterity in the Reign of HENRY *the Firft,* rebuilt another Abbey, confecrated to St. PETER and St. HILDA. (*a*)

The Monaftery, in the Time of St. *Robert's* Youth, having been in a flourifhing Condition, was thought by his indulgent Parents to be the moft proper Place for holy Improvement. Here he continu'd for about 5 or 6 Years, in the fable Habit of a *Benedictine;* and, thro' his conftant Study, with unaffected Piety, became very confpicuous: The fuperiour Clergy, feeing fo happy a Conjunction, juftly concluded, *That fo unfpotted a Life was purely the Gift of Heaven;* and therefore he was foon defervedly ordain'd a Subdeacon. After which, he had Liberty to vifit his Father and Mother.

Leaving *York* a while, to fee his younger Brother, who was at the New Monaftery of *Ciftercians;* fo charm'd was he with the Manner of their Devotion, Innocency, and Behaviour, that (with fome difficulty obtaining Permiffion of the Abbot of *Whitby)* he became one of them, and remained there about 4 Years; being equally admired, as a moft fhining Pattern of Goodnefs: When, taking a kind Farewell, the *Convent* (*b*) gave him their unanimous Benediction; and fo, returning to *York,* was received by his Parents with great Joy.

CHAP.

(*a*) The Ruins of it, at *Whitby,* are yet to be feen ; without any Infcriptions therein, except the following, in *Saxon* Characters, cut on a Pillar in the N. Crofs Ifle. JOHANNES *de* Brumton, *quondam famulus Domino* DE-LA-PHE, *has columnas erexit in metum & honorem beatæ Mariæ.* i.e. JOHN of *Brumton,* formerly Servant to Lord *De-la-phe,* erected thefe Columns to the reverential Efteem of the Bleffed Virgin MARY.

(*b*) Each of thefe Religious Perfons wore a white Habit: The whole Order were called the *Bernardine* Monks, of *Fountain's* Abby,

about

CHAP. II.

How S. Robert privately left his Parents.

BEING at home a while, and confidering the fhort State of this Life,- with the Immortality of the next; he rightly judged, That the Lands and Riches (to which he was the indubitable heir) tho' they might indeed exalt Man, yet would infallibly ruin the Saint. And therefore he was refolved to forfake the Delights of the one, for the Defires of the other; in Imitation of *Paul, Hilarion, Bafil,* and other devout Perfons. But, thro' Fear of Prevention, not thinking proper to acquaint his tender Parents, he fecretly travell'd to (*c*) *Knaresborough;* where he found, amongft the Cliffs, a fort

---

about 3 Miles S. W. of *Rippon :* Some of whom, encourag'd by Archbifhop THURSTAN, had departed from St. *Mary's* Monaftery, *YORK*, about the Year, 1311 ; but with fo poor an Endowment at firft, that their Lodging was beneath the Shade of an Elm-Tree, with the Want of all neceffary Provifions. Five Years after, the new Monaftery was begun to be built, thro' the Piety of RANULPHUS *de Merlay;* Hugh, Dean of *York, &c.* To which, King RICHARD I., Earl ALLAN, Archbifhop HENRY, HUGH *de Bolebeck,* WILLIAM *de Casule,* AALIZI *de Gant,* BERTRAM and WILLIAM *de Haget,* RICHARD *de Hedune,* ROGER *de Lacey,* RALPH Lord of *Middleham,* ROGER *de Mowbray, (who gave 9 Lordships, and whose Effigy, as tho' armed in a Coat of Mail, is still preserv'd):* ALICE *de Rumeli,* ROBERT *de Sarz,* and SWANE *de Tornetun,* were Benefactors: It was, at the Diffolution, rated at 1073*l.* A great Part of the Walls and Steeple, are yet remaining, as partly defcrib'd in the Cut on p. 256. In a Nitch, North of the latter, is a beautiful Image of the Virgin MARY, with another of the Bleffed Infant in her Arms : And round, on every Side, is faid to be this moft devout Sentence : *Soli DEO Omnipotenti sit Gloria per Sacula Sæculorum. Amen.*

(*c*) A Town in the Weft-Riding of *Yorkshire,* in *Claro* Hundred, remarkable upon thefe Occafions, *viz.* 1. The *Sweet* Spaw, or *Vitrioline* Well, very palatable, found out (near *Harrowgate*) by Mr. SLINGSBY, about the Year 1620; which is adorn'd with a Bafon and Spout, Steps on each Side, the running Streams clear like Cryftal, and decently covered on the Top with arched Stone. 2. The *Sulphur* Well, in like Manner

Chap II.   *Turns Hermit at* Knaresborough.   261

fort of an Hermit, who appear'd mightily pleas'd with fuch an holy Companion. This mutual Bleffing was foon diffolv'd: For, alas! that feeming fanctify'd Perfon, thro' the Devil's Inftigation, returning to the World, left St. ROBERT to a more filent Solitude. His Cell was at firft a dreary Cavity in the low Part of a prominent Rock: Down to this gloomy Recefs is yet perceivable a Defcent, (once much more rude) which the Saint had wrought into eafier Steps, or Gradations. About the Mouth of this Cave, he pick'd up Roots and Herbs: The Streams of the River, which ran not far from it, afforded him Drink: And in this abftracted Manner was his Body but poorly fubfifted; whilft his Soul became richly fed by Prayer and Contemplation.

One Time, walking to the Houfe of a rich Matron, not far diftant, and befeeching Alms, fhe gave him St. *Hilda's* Chapel, (fome Ruins of which remain in the Parifh of *Spofforth*, antiently the Seat of the *Percies*) with as much Ground, near it, as he was able to cultivate: But the little Provifions, which by hard labour were produced, having been ftolen away, he went to *Spofforth* aforefaid, where People daily affembled

to

Manner ornamented: The Waters of which, tho' unfavoury, and loathfome both to the Tafte, and Smell; yet prove an infallible Remedy to promote the Cure of *Spleen, Gout, Scurvy, Dropsy*, and *other* Diftempers. 3. The Well of St. MONGAH, or KENTIGERN, from the Name of a Bifhop in *Scotland*. And, 4, *Dropping*, or *Petrifying* Spring, defcending from an high Rock, (oppofite the Caftle) the Streams of which have turn'd the Ground beneath it into the like Subftance, but fpungy, and porous, that extend for fome Yards into the River; over which, are handfome Stone Bridges: One is called the HIGH Bridge: The Other MARCH Bridge; probably from the Extent of the Abbey-Lands; MARCH, or MARC, in the *Teutonick* Language, (of which our's is but a Branch) fignifying a Limit, *&c.* This laft *Petrifying* Well is lefs for Utility, than Curiofity: Which may yet lead the Mind profitably to admire the wonderful Works of GOD, in the expanfive View of His Creation; that, while He affords us the Means of Health for our decaying Bodies, with no lefs comfortable Imaginations, He furnifhes our immortal Souls, which his beloved SON hath redeemed.

to hear his moving Eloquence, with his harmonious Elocution. Endeavouring to ſhun Praiſe, by ſecretly preparing for Departure; the Monks of *Adley*, by a Meſſenger, invited him to their Monaſtery. Here, entering into the Fraternity, he was admired by the antient Gentlemen, for his chearful Submiſſion to their regular Diſcipline: His white, thin Garment, ſerv'd rather to veil, than nouriſh his mortify'd Body: The Bread, he eat, was 4 Parts of Barley-Meal, ſtirr'd about, to give it ſome Subſtance. But theſe, and other Auſterities, being unpleaſant to the younger Sort, who envied his ſublime Virtues; the peaceful Saint return'd to the Chapel of St. HILDA. His joyful Patroneſs, PHILADELPHIA, not only repoſſeſs'd him in the Land about it; but order'd the building of a Barn for his Corn, with other Neceſſaries. At certain Times of the Day, he would labour very hard; moſt Part of the Night too, he ſpent in Prayer; and, when he did ſleep, it was even upon the bare Ground. He kept 4 Servants: Two he employ'd in Tillage; a third for various Occaſions; and a 4th to collect the Alms of charitable People, for the Support of holy Perſons taken into his Community.

Whilſt our Saint was performing Works of Devotion, his Mother SEMENIA was taken with a violent Fit of Sickneſs: So raging was the Diſtemper, that ſhe attempted to riſe often from her Bed; and, like other dying Perſons, as Death approach'd the nearer, with an Imagination of certain Judgment, ſhe was both comforted, and afflicted, thro' different Apprehenſions, as tho' made ſenſible by good, or bad Angels, according to her former Virtues, or Vices. At laſt, having been releas'd from the Priſon of Mortality, ſhe was ſumptuouſly bury'd, in the Priory of Holy Trinity, in *Mickle-Gate*, *York*, which *Ralph Paganel*, a Nobleman, had retriev'd from Ruin, by Conſent of King *William* I. Herein *Walter*, one of the Family, was intomb'd; and others of them, in Proceſs of Time, had the Honour to be interr'd in the Cathedral; particularly *James Flower*, Armour Bearer to *John* Lord *Scroope*, who deceaſed about the Year 1453.

One

One Day it happen'd, that St. ROBERT, tir'd with Mortification, thought to bury his Cares a while, on the verdant Grafs, by a fhort Repofe: But his filent Slumber was foon difturbed thro' the feeming Appearance of his tender Mother SEMENIA aforefaid, pale, confus'd, trembling, and weeping, about the third Day after fhe was laid in her Grave. He thought he heard her fay, *My dear Son, I have now pafs'd the fable Waters of Death, and am no more in this World: Wherein, tho' I feemed to lead a pious Life; yet now I find I am to fuffer fevere Punifhments for Ufury, and feveral private Sins, unlefs relieved by the Efficacy of your Prayers!* At which, being much troubled, he not only made a Promife to implore the Almighty for her, but took Care to perform it : and, after that, fhe re-appear'd, with a chearful, fhining Countenance; when, giving him hearty Thanks, fhe glided up on high, finging Praifes melodioufly to the King of Kings.

CHAP. III.
How St. ROBERT was perfecuted, and preferv'd.

WILLIAM ESTOTEVILL, Lord of the Forreft, paffing by the Cell, demanded of his Servants, Who lived there? They anfwered, ROBERT, an Holy Hermit. *No,* faid he, *rather a Receiver of Thieves:* And, in a Rage, made them deftroy it. Then St. ROBERT, bearing this proud Infult with the moft Chriftian Patience, had Recourfe to the Cliffs, near *Knaresborough;* contriving a new but fmall Receptacle, (not far from the Chapel dedicated to St. *Gyles)* made with Boughs of Hedges, and Trees. But the Enemy of Mankind, envious at his increafing Virtue, influenced (*d*) ESTOTEVILL to attempt his Overthrow.

That

(*d*) He was alfo Lord of the Caftle, (a Tower of which contains an Iron Cheft, wherein the Forreft Laws, &c., are yet preferv'd; and near it appear the Ruins of ftrong and hollow Walls, fubterraneous Paffages, large Gates, and lofty Turrets) built for the moft part on a Rock, (near the River *Nid*) faid to have been erected by a Relation of
MONOCULUS

That Lord, with his Attendants, riding by the Saint's Cell, took Notice of fome Smoke that afcended from it; and demanding, Who dwelt there? was anfwered, ROBERT, *the Hermit.* Is it him, *(faid he)* that I expell'd my Forreft? 'Tis the

---

MONOCULUS, Lord of *Knaresborough*, called SERLO *de Burgh*, Uncle by the Father's Side to EUSTACE VESCY, who fprung from IVO VESCY, an Attendant of King WILLIAM I. EUSTACE, a Defcendant, Son of JOHN, is celebrated by the firft Monks of *Fountain's* Abby; becaufe, in their extream Want, when they had given their laft Loaf away to a poor Stranger, that Nobleman, hearing of their Diftrefs, pioufly fent them a Cart-Load of Provifions from his Caftle; which, after his Deceafe, became the Seat of the ESTOTEVILLS, who were of a *Norman* Extraction. In the Reign of King STEPHEN, ROBERT ESTOTEVILL (or *de* STOUTEVILLE) bravely affifted, with the Barons of the Realm, in the Overthrow of DAVID, King of *Scotland*, at *Northallerton*, Anno 1138: And one of his Pofterity, perhaps his Son, called by his Name, was High-Sheriff of *Yorkshire*, in the Year 1174, when King HENRY II. ruled the Land; And another, alfo named ROBERT, (all of 'em defcended from ROBERT GRANDEBŒUF, a Baron of *Normandy*) by King JOHN'S Permiffion, built *Cottingham* Caftle, about three Miles from the Place, where *Hull* was erected. Some of his Family were ftyl'd Earls of this County, the largeft in *England*. Nor were thefe Great Men, or other honourable Perfons thro' their Proximity of Blood, lefs famous for Religion and Charity: For ROBERT ESTOTEVILL, Abbot of *Kirksted*, in *Lincolnshire*, was a very devout Perfon: Another ROBERT, if not the fame, with a Kinfman call'd GOSFRID, proved great Benefactors to St. *Mary's* Abbey, YORK; giving (to the fupport of that once noble Structure, &c.) fome of their Lands at *Buttercram, Cukewald, Edelingthorp, Harton, Hovingham, Kirby, Langton, Straingham, Wreth* Ifland, and the Fifheries: A third ROBERT, if not one of the two former, along with a Relation, named EUSTACE ESTOTEVILL, were alfo beneficent to St. *Leonard's* Hofpital (to which King *Athelstane* had been a Benefactor) in the faid City, by poffeffing the Mafter and Brethren with Eftates at *Kawthorne, Little Aton*, &c. — *Kirby-Moreside*, in the faid County, and *Liddel-Castle, Cumberland*, were in the Poffeffion of the ESTOTEVILLS, with a Barony adjoining; which afterwards came to the WAKES, a noted Family: From thofe ESTOTEVILLS defcended the faid WILLIAM. In fucceeding Times, King HENRY III. gave this Caftle, Honour, &c., to HUGH *de Burgh;* EDWARD II. to PIERS GAVESTON; and EDWARD III. to his 4th Son, JOHN, Duke of *Gaunt*, afterwards of *Lancaster;* to which the Town belongs, and is an Appendage of the Crown.

the very fame, Sir; reply'd his Servants. Whereat he fwore, by the Eyes of GOD, the next Day, to pull it to the Ground, and drive the Holy Man from that Retirement for ever.

But, when the Curtains of Heaven were drawn, about the Middle of the Night, while ESTOTEVILL was in a deep Sleep, there appeared a Vifion of Three Men, fearful to behold! Two bearing a burning Engine of feeming Iron, befet with hot and fierce Teeth; a Third, of a Gigantick Stature, carrying Two Iron Clubs in his Hands, came furioufly towards his Bed, faying, *Cruel Prince, and Inftrument of the Devil, arife quickly, and make Choice of one of thefe to defend thyfelf, for the Injuries thou intendeft to do againft the Man of God, for whom I am fent hither to fight thee.* Hereupon ESTOTEVILL, with Remorfe of Confcience, feem'd to cry to Heaven for Mercy, with Proteftation of Amendment: Whereat the frightful Vifion vanifhed; and that Lord, coming to himfelf, prefently conftrued this was a juft Revelation from God for the Violence done and intended againft St. ROBERT: Therefore, the next Day, he gave him all the Land between his Cell and *Grimball* Bridge (or Cragg) Stone, for perpetual Arms. Tho' fome Writers mention it *Grimbald;* yet, I think, more truly *Grimoald:* Not only becaufe it was the Name, and might be in Memory, of a moft pious King of *Lombardy*, who erected the Church of St. *Ambrofe* at *Paphia*, in the 7th Century; but alfo that it is a German Word, fignifying *Power over Anger.* The Stone is now loft: Which, perhaps, was then fet up by Lord ESTOTEVILL, both as a Confirmation of his pious Donation, and as a preventive Mark againft the wicked Effects of an ireful Paffion levell'd at the Servants of GOD: So far from which was ESTOTEVILL now converted, and becaufe the Ground he had given fhould not lie untill'd, that he prefented St. ROBERT with two Oxen, two Horfes, and two Cows, for his better Support.

CHAP.

CHAP. IV.

Some remarkable Accidents concerning St. ROBERT.

NOT long after, he took into his Company one Ivo (or INO) employing him as an Overfeer of the Poor, and a Diftributer of their Alms: But this very Man, at a certain Time, being overcome by the Devil, fled from the happy Saint; and, in his Flight, chancing to fall, and break his Leg, St. ROBERT, by Divine Revelation, quickly knew of his Affliction. Making hafte therefore to his Affiftance, he moft feverely reprehended him; but Ivo acknowledging his Fault, and defiring Pardon, the Holy Man, forthwith bleffing his Leg, and laying his Hand on the Part imbrued with Blood, reftored him to his former Condition, and brought him back to his Cell.

So great was the Saint's Care of the Poor, that, for their better Relief, he defired his Patron, ESTOTEVILL, to beftow another Cow upon him, which was granted; but withal, (thro' the Means of an ill natur'd Servant) fuch a fierce Creature, that it was even terrible to approach. However, the Man of God, making hafte to the Forreft, foon perceiv'd her; and, putting one Hand over her Neck, fhe went home with him as meek as poffible. The wicked Servant, before-mention'd, told Lord ESTOTEVILL of the Action; faying withal, That he would devife a Way, how to get the Cow from the good Man: And tho' his Mafter difproved of the Motion; yet the envious Wretch, feigning to be in a lame and poor Condition, begg'd the Saint's Affiftance, not only for himfelf, but his Wife and Children; who were, as he pretended, miferably opprefs'd with. Hunger and Want. Compaffion foon wrought upon the Holy Hermit: *As GOD,* faid *he, has given to me what fhould feed the Wants of me and mine ; fo a Part of His Bleffings fhall be return'd to Him again, in fupplying the Neceffities of you, and your's. There is my beft Cow, to nourifh you all with her Milk: Take her, if what you tell me be*
Truth

Truth indeed; but if not, the same Afflictions, you pretend to suffer, will certainly be the just Reward of such sinful Hypocrisy. And thus it prov'd: For when this Deceiver thought to depart with the Cow, and had unloos'd the String, by which his Leg and Ham were ty'd together, he found them more closely united, by a vindictive and supernatural Power. Let not a Christian doubt of this, since *Cicero*, tho' an Heathen, writes, *Nihil est quod Deus efficere non possit, & quidem sine labore ullo.* As much as to say, *There is nothing, however so great and surprizing, but what God Almighty can accomplish, either as a Punishment of a wicked Sinner, or the Reward of the just Person; and truly with the greatest Ease, or without any Labour.* This the Wretch felt with a Witness; and thereupon cry'd out, *O Holy St.* ROBERT, *pardon the Injury I intended against you; and beseech the Divine Being, in Behalf of me, his unworthy, but repenting Servant.* The indulgent Father mercifully comply'd with his Request; when, having restor'd him to his former Ability, he returned to his beloved Cell, and was received with Joy.

A Company of Deer, from the Forrest, haunting his Ground, spoiled his Corn, and did him much Harm: Whereupon, making Complaint to the Lord ESTOTEVILL, received this Answer: *Good* ROBERT, *I give thee free Leave to impound, and detain them, 'till you obtain ample Satisfaction.* Then went the Holy Man into the Field; and, with a Rod, drove those swift Creatures out of the Corn; afterwards secur'd them with as much Ease as if they had been tender Lambs; and so shut them up in his Barn: Which done, he went to his Patron, acquainting him therewith; who, being surpriz'd at the strange Event, freely gave them to the Saint, to use either in the Plow, or for any other Service of rural Affairs. ROBERT, humbly thanking the beneficent Lord, returned home; and, taking the Deer out of the Barn, put them under the Yoke, and made them to plow his Ground like Oxen, to the Amazement of all Beholders. To commemorate which, St. ROBERT is depicted, in a Window belonging to the North Isle of *Knaresborough* Church, as tho' he was plowing with the Deer.

CHAP.

CHAP. V.

How St. ROBERT *form'd a Chapel in a Rock.*

AND now the Saint began to work at his New Chapel, within a folid and high Rock; which, in Procefs of Time, he accomplifh'd; making convenient Steps, to the nearer Banks of the *Nid:* A River famous, becaufe that near its Streams a noted Synod was held, in the Reign of King OSRED, *A.D.* 708, when St. *WILFRID,* Abbot of *Rippon,* and Archbifhop of *York,* was obliged to be content with the See of *Hexham,* in *Northumberland,* made fuch by THEODORE, Archbifhop of *Canterbury;* tho' fome affert, that (before he died, which was in the Year of CHRIST 711, and buried in *Rippon* Monaftery) he became fully poffeffed of his former Dignity. The Stones, dug out of the Rock, feem laid as the Foundation for a pleafant Paffage from St. ROBERT's Chapel, about 46 Yards on the fubfiding Banks, now to be feen (as defcrib'd in the cut of the Title-Page) 'till it ends at a little Gate; from which to the Water is between 4 and 5 Yards more: And, on the Oratory's Out-Side, was carved the Image of an armed Man, no doubt in Memory of the defending Vifion, with which the Lord ESTOTEVILL was formerly terrify'd. With like Reafon, tho' the Chapel now bears his own Name, he dedicated it to St. GYLES, a noble *Athenian,* once Abbot, Monk, and Hermit in *France,* inftead of his Oratory, (confecrated to that Saint) when his Houfe was made with Boughs, interwoven with Thorns. Within are Seats, on each Side, either to kneel before, or reft upon: The Length of this Chapel is 3 Yards and $\frac{1}{2}$, its Breadth 3 Yards, and 2 Yards and $\frac{1}{2}$ high, up to a curious arched Canopy, plainly difcernable from the Light of a Window, adorn'd with Tracery; which alfo difcovers an Altar, partly carv'd like real Pillars. At the right Hand are Venerable Faces, that are believ'd were defign'd to reprefent the HOLY TRINITY: All of the Rock;

Rock; and yet a further Space or Nitch is feen behind the Altar, very probable, either for the Image of the Bleffed Virgin MARY, or a Reprefentation of our dear Redeemer's bitter Crucifixion! Before which, according to antient Cuftom, he would often proftrate himfelf; offering up his Prayers, to CHRIST in Heaven, with fuch affectionate Devotion, as if, under that mournful Similitude, he had really beheld him bleeding, and dying on the Crofs. *Eft mea fpes Chriftus folus, qui de Cruce pendet.*

King JOHN, in his Travels, fometimes courfing along the Country, to divert the melancholy Thoughts occafion'd by the Troubles of his Reign, came at length to *Knaresborough*, attended by his Courtiers, both of the Laity, and Clergy. As they once fat at Dinner, his Chaplain confirm'd the Renown of St. *Robert's* Sanctity; for which, indeed, his Majefty, who had often heard thereof, intended to vifit him. Accordingly, he came, with few Attendants, to the Saint's poor Cell; where St. ROBERT entertain'd him, and his Retinue, in the moft courteous Manner, with extraordinary Piety, and becoming Gravity. In fhort, the Monarch was fo charm'd with his Converfation, that, commiferating his Poverty, he granted him 40 Acres of wafte Ground, (with the Appurtenances of another Place) near adjoining to what he had before; and which was as much as he could now conveniently till with one Plough, or Team.

The Lord BRYAN, coming one Day to obtain his Benediction, defired withal to know, What Succefs he should have in a Journey and Voyage he was to take on the King's Service, and how the Event would prove? *Very profperoufly*, anfwered the Saint; *but, my Lord, you will never return again.* And this was fulfill'd by Death.

Not long after the faid Lord's Departure, he foretold, That, when his own Diffolution fhould happen, the Monks of *Fountain's* Abby would make an Attempt to take his Body from them by Force: *But*, (faid he, to Thofe of his Houfe) *I befeech*

befeech you to refift them; and, if there be Occafion, do not fail to call fecular Power to your Affiftance: For, in fome Part of the Place, belonging to That, where I fhall give up my lateft Breath; there, indeed, would I have my Body remain, in Peace, I hope, 'till a Bleffed Refurrection fhall recall it from the Duft. Accordingly, his Defire, of being buried at *Knaresborough*, (which Town he loved exceedingly) was effected, as mentioned in the following Chapter.

CHAP. VI.

Of the lamented Death of St. ROBERT; *his decent Burial; and of the Monaftery, founded to his Memory, for Religious Perfons, call'd* Robertines.

THE Holy Man, perceiving himfelf to draw near his End, and being prepared to dye, with a humble and pious Heart, defired, that the Bleffed Sacrament might be brought unto him, as the beft *Viaticum* for his Heavenly Journey. At which Time, the Monks of *Fountain's* Abby, hearing of the Saint's approaching Death, made Hafte to come unto him: Not only to yield their Affiftance, in his lateft Agonies, by their fervent Prayers; but alfo brought with them a *Ciftercian* Habit, to Inveft his Body for Interment. To whom the dying Saint, with great Humility, faid, *I thank you for your Care of my departing Soul, but as for the perifhing Body, my ordinary Garments are really fufficient; neither, indeed, do I defire any other.* As he lay very near the point of Death, Ivo, with the reft of the Servants, and others, came weeping before him, defiring his laft Bleffing: Which he willingly gave them, in the moft reverend Manner; and, in that, with other pathetick Exercifes, pioufly yielded up the Ghoft, about the Year of Salvation, 1216; in which his Royal Benefactor, King JOHN, departed this mortal Life, in a Caftle, at *Newark-upon-Trent;* and his Son, HENRY III., then but a Child, reigned in his Stead.

The

Chap. VI. *The Saint's Remains honourably intomb'd.*

The Saint's Body was, with due Reverence, made ready for the Grave: And fome of the Monks of *Fountain's* Abby, (who no doubt had waited 'till the Time of his Diffolution) left the Habit they had officioufly brought, that his Corps might be more decently wrapt up therein: Moreover, they endeavour'd to carry away the Body by Force, in order to inter it in their own Monaftery; which they certainly would have accomplifhed, had not a Company of armed Men, that belong'd to the Caftle, refifted them; and fo they were obliged to return home exceeding forrowful for fo great a Lofs.

To honour the Funeral Obfequies of St. ROBERT, (who is defervedly celebrated, on the 7th of *June*, in the Old *Englifh* Kalendar, where he is ftyl'd both Abbot of *Knaresborough*, and Confeffor) there came great Numbers of People, High and Low, Rich and Poor, who devoutly kiffed his holy Corps, in the Icy Arms of Death, as he lay in the Coffin, before its laft Enclofure: And then he was carry'd, with mournful Solemnity, to the Chapel of the *Holy Crofs*, where his Body was laid in a New (*e*) Tomb prepared for the Reception of it. This was the pious End of that Holy MAN, when he was about 57 Years of Age; paying that common Debt which is

due

(*e*) The upper Stone of which now lies (in the Church at *Knaresborough*, North of the Altar) over the Body of Sir HENRY SLINGSBY, who was beheaded, *Anno Dom.* 1658. The Inscription runs partly thus: *Sancti* ROBERTI, *huc Saxum advectum est, sub eodemque nunc jacet* HENRICUS SLINGSBY, *&c.* For *William de Slingsby*, (one of the Ancestors of this loyal Family) marrying the Daughter and Heiress of *Thomas de Screven;* had with her the Place, call'd *Screven*, (near *Knaresborough*) with other Possessions; in Consequence of this Union, he became Heir to *Thomas de Walkingham*, whose only Daughter the said *Screven* had been formerly espoused to. And it's but of late, that one Sir *Henry Slingsby* built a fair Habitation at a Place call'd *Red House*, which is another Seat of the Family. King *EDWARD* I. made Rangers of some of them, because of their great Fidelity: "Whose Ancestors, the Posterity of GAMELLUS, " once Keeper of the Forrest, *as an Historian confirms*, took the Name " of SCREVEN, from their antient Seat, or Habitation."

In

due to Nature, by returning to native Duſt: And then his happy, immortal Soul, difunited from its Earthly Manſion, and hovering on the Wings of Bleſſed Angels, was, no doubt, carry'd up into Heaven, where it mingled with the glorious Company of Martyrs, Confeſſors, and other Saints, to praiſe, in Seraphic Hymns, the Ever Holy, and Adorable TRINITY, to all Eternity.

Bleſſed therefore is the Memory of St. ROBERT; who was divinely inſpir'd, and *greatly* happy, even whilſt he exiſted in a trouble-

---

In old *English* Characters, at the West End of *Knaresborough* Church, are these pious Lines, carved, on a single Stone

JESU CHRIST, who dy'd upon the Rood! Grant us Grace, our End be good,

In the Church, on the North Side of the Altar, are these Epitaphs, beside those exhibited in the History of York, *Page* 249, &c.

DEO, Omnipotenti, Magno. Gulielmus Slingesbeius, eques auratus, ex inclyta Slingesbeiorum familia, in agro Eboracensi oriundus; Francisci, optimi viri, et Mariæ, unicæ sororis Thomæ & Henrici Percy, comitum Northumbriæ, feminæ honoratissimæ, et pientissimæ, filius; Knaresburgi, 29 Jan. Anno 1562 natus: In armis, aula, et magistratu, sub quatuor Regibus sic claravit; ut in bello, exercitus Elizabethæ, quo oppidum, classis, insulaq; Cadiz, felicissime, intercepta sunt, munitionum publicarum commissarius generalis, anno 1596: In aula, sub serenissimo Jacobo Rege, Annæ Reginæ illustrissimæ, ad mensam cibicida honorarius, 1603: In magistratu, ab eodem Jacobo Rege, Scotiam versus, progrediente, Middlesexiæ comitatus, primorum locum tenentium: unus sub magno sigillo Angliæ constitutus, 1617: qui, etiam, negotia adeunda, in singulis commissionibus, pro ejusdem comitatus regimine, sub Divo Carolo etiam cum laude transegit.

Vado; sed nec me tædet vivere, nec timeo mori. August, 1634. [Thus Englished:]

To the Great Omnipotent GOD. WILLIAM SLINGESBY, *Knight, (descended from the illustrious Family of the* SLINGESBIES, *in* Yorkshire; *Son of* HENRY, *one of the best of Men, and* MARY, *one of the most pious and honourable of Women, the Sister of* THOMAS *and* HENRY PERCY, *Earls of* Northumberland) *was born at* Knaresborough, *the 29th of* January, 1562. *He so distinguish'd himself, under four crowned Heads, thro' his Valour, courtly Behaviour, and prudential Discharge of the Trust reposed in him; that, as to the first, he was elected Commissary-General to the Forces of the renowned Queen* ELIZABETH; *by whom, a Town, Fleet, and the Island* Cadiz, *were taken by surprize, in the Year* 1596. *In Court, whilst his Serene Majesty King* JAMES *the First, along with the most illustrious Queen* ANNE, *sat upon the* British *Throne, Anno* 1603, *he was honour'd in being made Carver at their Table: And, whilst in his Office, during the same King's progress to* Scotland, *was appointed by his Majesty to hold one of the most honourable Places in the County of* Middlesex. *So great a Favourite he became, that, in* 1617, *he was constituted, under the great Seal of England:*

Who,

troublesome World: Which agrees with what the *Roman* Orator truly asserts: *Nemo magnus fine aliquo afflatu divino unquam fuit;* that none but the Person, whose Soul is warm'd with such Cœlestial Respiration, can be truly dignify'd. But we must go still farther: For tho' this Good Man was reposed in the silent Grave; yet MATTHEW PARIS, a *Benedictine* Monk of St. *Alban's,* makes the Trumpet of Glory still louder, by writing thus: *Claruit fama Sancti* ROBERTI *Heremitæ apud* Knaresburg; *cujus Tumba Oleum medicinale fertur abundanter emisisse:* That is, *The Fame of St.* ROBERT, *Hermit at* Knaresborough, *shone very conspicuous; from whose Sepulchre a medicinal Oyl plentifully issued forth;* which, as we are further assured, occasion'd many wonderful Cures. Thus did his Merit seem to former Ages. And tho' the healing Unguent has ceased long since to shed its oily Streams; yet the sweet Odour of his Sanctity is still refreshing to our desiring Spirits, notwithstanding so many Centuries past, and ever will be whilst *the Remembrance of the Just shall be blessed.* And so much was he esteem'd by RICHARD PLANTAGENET, the young King's Brother, (who was then Earl of *Cornwall,* and in Process of Time became King of the *Romans*) that two Years after, A.D. 1218, he erected a Monastery for Religious Persons, who were called *Robertines,* from the Name of the holy Saint, as tho' he indeed had been the original Founder. The Estate, that St. *Robert's* kind Patroness had given him; the Lands, with the Appurtenances of *Swinesco,* presented by King JOHN, as also

Halikelde-

Who, also, pass'd thro' other Preferments, with great Applause, in their respective Commissions, for the Government of the aforesaid County, in that Monarch's Reign, as likewise in that of the Pious King CHARLES *the First.*

I depart; but neither am I weary of Life, or afraid to die. August, 1634.

Three other Inscriptions are as follow:

Hic jacet Henr. Slingesbie filius & hæres Francisci & Mariæ, mense a pride anno XLIV. Eliz. R. milit. qui oblit Decem. die 17. Anno Dom. 1634. Ætat. suæ 74 annos, et 10 menses. Sed omnia vanitas.

Here lies the Body of Dorothy Slingesby, late Wife of Sir Thomas Slingesby, of Scriven, Bart. Daughter and Coheir of George Cradock of Careswell Castle, in Staffordshire, Esq. She died the 24th Jan. 1673. by whom he had 3 Sons: Henry, Thomas, and George; and 3 Daughters, Dorothy, Elizabeth, and Barbara.

Perfectum fuit hoc opus p. Hen. Slyngesb. 24. Junii 1602. Unitrino Deo consecratum Anno Ætat. suæ 42, et 5 Mens. Anno Eliz. R, 44. Mors vitam aufert, & affert.

Halikeldefyke Wood, that lay North of the River; all thefe were conferr'd upon this Society, ftyled *De Redemptione Captivorum*, alias *Sanctæ Trinitatis*. The Church, Convent, and other contiguous Buildings, were, it's fuppos'd, pull'd down at the Diffolution, in the Reign of King HENRY VIIIth; but a Gate thereof is ftill remaining. The *Cœmiterium*, or Place of Interment, is yet difcernable; where a reverend Perfon lies buried: Over whom is a large Grave-Stone, about a Foot in Thicknefs; the Length and Breadth is form'd proportionable to the Stature and Bulk of a well-siz'd Man. Upon which, towards the Head, is carved a *Crofs-Moline*, like the *Little One*, here reprefented, on the *Side of the Great*. The Form of the longer Part of the *Latter* is pourtray'd towards the Feet. In the Middle of it, from the Breaft downwards, are thefe Letters, (but in *Saxon* Characters) *HIC JACET* J. BEMER: That is, *Here lieth* JOHN BEMER: Before the firft Article (*HIC*) are thefe Letters, *I.O.Y.*, &c. as fuppos'd, being almoft worn away: But, after the venerable Name of *J. Bemer*, are thefe: *B. B. O. V.*, which, perhaps, might be for *Baccalaurius Beatæ Ordinis Viginis:* So that, probably, it was a Gentleman of another Order, related to fome Perfon belonging to This, of the *Moft Holy Trinity*. Which Society, befides what I have mention'd, became poffefs'd of Lands, Privileges, &c., upon Failure of Black Canons of the Holy Sepulchre; who were placed in the Suburbs of *Warwick*, by HENRY, Earl of that *City*, founded upon a Rock; and render'd famous, thro' the moft renowned G U Y, once in the fame Station, in the Reign of King *Athelftane*. The Land, belonging to this Convent at *Knaresborough*, was fold to the Earl of *Shrewsbury*, in the Reign of EDWARD the VIth. The *Robertine* Members of that antient Society were frequently employ'd to travel, collect Money, and intercede for the Redemption of Chriftian Captives; the third Part of their Revenues being apply'd for that Purpofe: To which venerable Convent, the Princely Founder's Brother, King HENRY

the

Chap. VI. *A Pious Conclusion to the* WHOLE.

the Third, in the 12th Year of his Reign, (and his moſt unfortunate Grandſon, EDWARD the Second, in the 5th of his) confirm'd, with ſome Additions, there ſeveral Benefactions (which, thro' charitable Piety, at Sundry Times, had zealouſly been given them) by their Royal Sanction.

About a Year after the Death of St. *Robert*, WALTER GREY, Archbiſhop of *York*, departed this Life; whoſe Monument (hereunder partly imitated) remains yet in the Cathedral.

To conclude: May what has been written, and the Places which are yet to be ſeen, call to our Minds the Vanity all tranſitory Enjoyments whatſoever: And, whilſt we ſeriouſly ponder upon theſe Things, may we be incited to beſeech ALMIGHTY GOD, That the Members of CHRIST'S Holy Catholick Church, now militant on Earth (particularly that pure Part of it eſtabliſhed in this Kingdom) may, hereafter, through the Merits of our dear REDEEMER, reign triumphantly with HIM in Heaven.

THE END.

On Holy Wells.

(Extracted by Permission, from Messrs. Chambers's " Book of Days.")

JULY 1, 1652, the eccentric John Taylor, commonly called the Water Poet, from his having been a Waterman on the Thames, paid a visit to St. Winifred's Well, at Holywell, in Flintshire. This was a place held in no small veneration even in Taylor's days; but in Catholic times, it filled great space indeed.

There is something at once so beautiful and so bountiful in a spring of pure water, that no wonder it should become an object of some regard among a simple people. We all feel the force of Horace's abrupt and enthusiastic address, " O Fons Blandusiæ, splendidior vitro,' and do not wonder that he should resolve upon sacrificing a kid to it. In the middle ages, when a Christian tinge was given to everything, the discovery of a spring in a romantic situation, or remarkable for the brightness, purity, or taste of its water, was forthwith followed by its dedication to some Saint; and once placed among the category of holy wells, its waters were endued, by popular faith, with powers more or less miraculous. Shrewd Thomas Powell, writing in 1631, says: 'Let them find out some strange water, some unheard-of spring; it is an easy matter to discolour or alter the taste of it in some measure, it makes no matter how little. Report strange cures that it hath done; beget a superstitious opinion of it. Good-fellowship shall uphold it, and the neighbouring towns shall all swear for it.' So early as 963, the Saxon king Edgar thought it necessary to forbid the 'worshipping of fountains,' and the canons of Anselm (1102) lay it down as a rule, that no one is to attribute reverence or sanctity to a fountain *without the bishop's authority.* Canons, however powerful to foster superstition, were powerless to control it; ignorance invested springs with sanctity without the aid of the church, and every county could boast of its holy well.

The most famous holy well in the three kingdoms is undoubtedly that dedicated to St. Winifred (Holywell, Flintshire),

St. Winifred's Well, Flintshire.

at whose shrine Giraldus Cambrensis offered his devotions in the twelfth century, when he says she seemed 'still to retain her miraculous powers.

The spring rises from a bed of shingle at the foot of a steep hill, the water rushing out with great impetuosity, and flowing into and over the main basin in a smaller one in front. The well is enclosed by a building in the perpendicular Gothic style (dating from the beginning of Henry VII.), which 'forms a crypt under a small chapel contiguous to the parish church, and on a level with it, the entrance to the well being by a descent of about twenty steps from the street. The well itself is a star-shaped basin, ten feet in diameter, canopied by a most graceful stellar vault, and originally enclosed by stone traceried screens filling up the spaces between the supports. Round the basin is an ambulatory similarly vaulted.'* The sculptural ornaments consisted of grotesque animals, and the armorial-bearings of various benefactors of the shrine; among them being Catharine of Aragon, Margaret, mother of Henry VII., and different members of the Stanley family, the founders both of the crypt and the chapel above it. Formerly, the former contained statues of the Virgin Mary and St. Winifred. The first was removed in 1635; the fate of Winifred's effigy, to which a Countess of Warwick (1439) bequeathed her russet velvet gown, is unknown. On the stones at the bottom of the well grow the *Bissus iolethus*, and a species of red *Jungermania* moss, known in the vulgar tongue as Winifred's hair and blood. In the seventeenth century, St. Winifred could boast thousands of votaries. James II. paid a visit to the shrine in 1688, and received the shift worn by his great-grandmother at her execution, for his pains. Pennant found the roof of the vault hung with the crutches of grateful cripples. He says, 'the resort of pilgrims of late years to these Fontanalia has considerably decreased; the greatest number are from Lancashire. In the summer, still a few are to be seen in the water, in deep devotion up to their chins for hours, sending up their prayers, or performing a number of evolutions round the polygonal well; or threading the arches between it and the well a prescribed number of times.' An attempt to revive the public faith in the Flintshire saint was made in 1805, when a pamphlet was published, detailing how one Winefred White, of Wolverhampton, experienced the benefit of the virtue of the spring.

---

* *Archæological Journal*, iii. 148.

The cure is certified by a resident of Holywell, named Elizabeth Jones, in the following terms: 'I hereby declare that, about three months ago, I saw a young woman calling herself Winefred White, walking with great difficulty on a crutch; and that on the following morning, the said Winefred White came to me running, and without any appearance of lameness, having, as she told me, been immediately cured after once bathing in St. Winefred's Well.' It was of no avail; a dead belief was not to be brought again to life even by Elizabeth Jones of Holywell.

St. Madern's Well, Cornwall, was another popular resort for those who sought to be relieved from aches and pains. Bishop Hall, in his *Mystery of Godliness*, bears testimony to the reality of a cure wrought upon a cripple by its waters. He says he 'took strict and impartial examination' of the evidence, and 'found neither art nor collusion—the cure done, the author an invisible God.' In the seventeenth century, however, the well seems to have lost its reputation. St. Madern was always propitiated by offerings of pins and pebbles. This custom prevailed in many other places beside; Mr. Haslam assures us, that pins may be collected by the handful near most Cornish wells. At St. Kilda, none dared approach with empty hands, or without making some offering to the genius of the place, either in the shape of shells, pins, needles, pebbles, coins, or rags. A well near Newcastle obtained the name of Ragwell, from the quantity of rags left upon the adjacent bushes as thank-offerings. St. Tegla, of Denbighshire, required greater sacrifices from her votaries. To obtain her good offices, it was necessary to bathe in the well, walk round it three times, repeating the Lord's Prayer at each circuit, and leave fourpence at the shrine. A cock, or hen (according to the patient's sex) was then placed in a basket, and carried round the well, into the churchyard, and round the church, The patient then entered the church, and ensconced him or herself under the communion-table, with a Bible for a pillow, and so remained till daybreak. If the fowl, kept all this while imprisoned, died, the disease was supposed to have been transferred to it, and, as a matter of course, the believer in St. Tegla was made whole.

TABLE OF CONTENTS.

EDITOR'S INTRODUCTION	7
LIFE OF THOMAS GENT *(by the Editor)*	10
LIFE OF S. WINEFRED. GENT'S PREFACE, &c.	25
,, ,, BOOK I.	35
,, ,, BOOK II.	61
,, ,, BOOK III.	85
,, ,, BOOK IV.	105
,, ,, BOOK V.	131
,, ,, EPITOME AND INDEX	153
GENT'S ADVERTISEMENTS	171
HISTORY OF CHRIST AND THE APOSTLES	177
JUDAS ISCARIOT	201
THE LEGEND OF MOUNT PILATE *(by the Editor)*	229
THE LIFE OF AFFLICTED JOB	231
ST. ROBERT OF KNARESBOROUGH	257
ON HOLY WELLS *(by R Chambers)*	276

www.ingramcontent.com/pod-product-compliance
Lightning Source LLC
Chambersburg PA
CBHW031937230426
43672CB00010B/1957